ELAINE LOMBARDI

G.I.F.T.S. A Voyage Home to Yourself

The Keys to Unlocking Your True Light and Purpose

MEL BOOKS

First published by MEL BOOKS 2026

First edition

ISBN: 979-8-9940940-0-6

Cover art by the talented team at getcovers.com. The designer captured the perfect spirit of this book.

This book was professionally typeset on Reedsy.
Find out more at reedsy.com

Contents

Dedication   v
A G.I.F.T.S. Companion Book   vi

I   SEASON'S CALL

1   The Parking Lot   3
2   The Dock   11
3   Ahoy, Captain!   18

II   GRATITUDE SHORES

4   The Trail   25
5   The Climb   33
6   Moonlight Walk   43

III   INTUITIVE ISLAND

7   The Canyon   51
8   The Dive   59
9   The Cave   67
10   The Lighthouse   75

IV   CONNECTION COVE

11   Changing Tides   85
12   The Meadow   89

13 Community Square   98
14 The Forest   106
15 Heritage Heights   114
16 The Arbor   131

V TREASURE ISLAND

17 The Storm   139
18 The Arrival   147
19 The Question   160
20 The Studios   170
21 Process of Elimination   184
22 Rooted In Purpose   199
23 Fair Winds and Following Seas   224

VI SELF-CARE SPRINGS

24 New Horizons   233
25 Filling Your Own Cup   246

VII HOMEWARD

26 The Crossing   267
27 First Steps   276
28 The Library   282
29 The Gathering   287
30 This is Home   298

EPILOGUE: FULL CIRCLE   312
About the Author   323

Dedication

For my incredible daughter Kristina,
mother of five, teacher, nurturer, warrior.
In the midst of homeschooling, activities, laundry,
and loving so many, may you never forget to
save space for yourself.
I am so proud of the mother you are
and in awe of the woman you've always been.
Graceful, resilient, fiercely loving, and absolutely remarkable.
You've always been gutsy, and with age you've grown wise,
courageous, tender-hearted, and extraordinary in every way.
Watching you live and love with such faith and devotion
fills my heart beyond measure. I love you so much.
You are a true gift to this world.

A G.I.F.T.S. Companion Book

G.I.F.T.S. A Journey Home to Yourself: The Keys to Unlocking Your True Light and Purpose is a companion book within the G.I.F.T.S. family. It brings the G.I.F.T.S. Method to life through personal stories, reflections, and nautical themes that illuminate what the five key areas can look like in everyday experience.

For the full step-by-step framework and practical system, read my signature core manual titled **The G.I.F.T.S. Method: The Five Keys System to Lasting Change.**

To my reader,
Always remember, your gifts are within you. Let them shine!
Elaine Lombardi

I

SEASON'S CALL

*"Challenges are gifts that force us to search for
a new center of gravity."*
— Oprah Winfrey

1

The Parking Lot

The phone call came on a quiet Tuesday afternoon.

You sit in your car with the engine off, the grocery list soft in your hand. The same list as every week: milk, bread, chicken breasts, salad ingredients. Food for two now instead of four. You still catch yourself reaching for the sugary cereal your son loves before remembering he left for college three months ago.

You thought you were prepared. After twenty-five years of mothering, you should've seen this day coming. You'd even felt ready for it. *I can't wait to have more time,* you thought. And you'd meant it. Except now you have more time, and you don't know what to do with it.

The house that was too small for years suddenly feels enormous. The kitchen where you packed thousands of lunches sits clean and quiet. The calendar on your fridge used to be crowded with practices, games, and appointments. Now it holds your husband's work schedule and a note that his truck needs an oil change. That's it. Nothing that's yours.

He's the same person he's always been. Kind, steady, and a good man. But somewhere in the years spent focused on parenting, you stopped being partners and became project managers running a household. Now the project is complete, and you're not sure what role you're supposed to play.

Your phone sits on the passenger seat. You should call your mother back. She left a voicemail yesterday. You should text your daughter. She's busy with the baby and her own family. You should do something. But you can't seem to find the energy for any of it.

You look around the parking lot. Other women move through their routines, loading groceries, scrolling through their phones, caught up in the rhythm of their lives. Some wear professional clothes, probably on lunch breaks from important jobs. Others have toddlers in car seats, still in the thick of what's behind you now. All of them seem to know who they are and what they're doing.

You're fifty-two years old. You have no idea who you are.

You've been Mom with a capital M. Your entire identity was wrapped in that role. And you were good at it. Room mom. Team mom. The one who hosted the birthday parties, drove the carpool, and stayed up late helping with science projects that were always 'due tomorrow'.

You started little businesses over the years, trying to bring in extra money, trying to create something that was yours. But they never got off the ground the way you imagined. You only seemed to take pride in being a good mom, being present, being the mother you'd wanted your own mother to be.

But now they don't need you. Your daughter has her own life, three states away. Your son is at college, his phone calls brief and distracted. They're doing exactly what you raised them to do: becoming independent, leaving.

And you're left with the same questions you've had for years, only now they're louder: How do I build something that's mine? How do I become visible in a world that only sees me as someone's mother? How do I show up to a game where everyone knows the rules except me?

The few friends you have don't really understand. They're busy with their own things. You've never been good at the friendship part anyway. You've always felt a little out of place in groups, even when standing among familiar people.

You glance at your reflection in the rear view mirror. When did you get so old? The gray you keep meaning to cover. The lines around your eyes that appeared while you weren't looking. You're not young anymore. You're not starting fresh. You're a middle-aged woman who spent twenty-five years being the best mother she could be. You have no career, no professional identity, and no idea what you're qualified to do besides mother. And nobody's hiring for that position.

The comparison spiral starts before you can stop it. That woman at the grocery store last week. The one who looked so confident, so certain of her purpose. You remember how she laughed into her phone, her tone light but focused, talking about a project, a meeting, a deadline. She looked like someone who mattered.

You had stood there with your cart of food for two and felt small.

I'm just a mom, you had thought, the words slipping in like an old habit. The shame of that thought still burns. It lingers quietly, the way certain memories stay lodged in your chest.

Your children are incredible humans. You are proud of them. Grateful for them. The years you spent raising them weren't nothing. They were everything. Yet somehow, you still feel invisible. As though all that devotion left you without a reflection of your own.

You look down at the grocery list again. The same items you've been buying for twenty-five years. The same routine. The same life. But now it feels like you're going through motions without purpose. Cooking dinner for two. Cleaning a house that stays clean. Managing a household that barely needs managing. It's what you know how to do.

But underneath the routine, there's always been this other thing. This wanting. This sense that you were meant to create something, build something, be something beyond the roles you play.

Last week, you found yourself crying in the frozen food aisle. Standing there with a cart containing one bag of vegetables, tears slipping down your face, overwhelmed by the weight of wanting something you can't name. A boy stocking shelves asked if you were okay, and you said allergies. But the truth is, you have no idea if you're okay. You don't even know what okay would feel like anymore.

You tried talking to your husband about it. This frustration. This feeling of being stuck. But he didn't get it. "You can do whatever you want now," he said. "Start that business. Take a class." As if the problem were simply boredom and not something deeper, like an unraveling of identity you can't name.

He still has his work. His routine. His place in the world. He's still the same person he was before kids. But you became someone else entirely when you became Mom. You folded every other part of yourself away to make room for nurturing everyone else. And it was important. Your children are proof of that. But now they don't need nurturing, and you can't remember what you folded away. You can't remember who you were before. You don't know if she even exists anymore.

Your phone rings. An unknown number. You almost don't answer, thinking it's another spam call or another reminder about your car's extended warranty. But something, maybe boredom, loneliness, and the need to hear another voice, makes you swipe to accept.

"Hello?"

"Hi there!" The woman's voice is warm and bright. "You entered our drawing at the Wellness and Life Purpose Expo last month. The Life-Changing Adventure specifically for women in transition?"

You pause, trying to remember. The expo had been a desperate Saturday when your husband was golfing, and the silence of the house felt unbearable. You wandered through aisles of vendors selling crystals, essential oils, and coaching programs promising transformation. You entered drawings just to have someone look you in the eye.

"Yes," you say slowly. "I think I remember."

"Wonderful. You won our five-island transformational journey. Congratulations!"

You almost laugh. Another promise. Another program. You've tried things like this before. Signed up for online courses. Started them. Never finished. The excitement always lasted about two weeks before the fear crept in. *Who do you think you are? You have nothing valuable to offer. Nobody cares what you think. You're not qualified.* The old voice always found its way back.

"What exactly is this?" you ask, cautious but curious.

"It's a journey," she says, her tone softening. "For women who spent years being wonderful mothers but never learned how to be visible beyond that."

You fall silent. Her words find their way to that private place inside you, the one you never talk about.

"Women who compare themselves to others and feel small," she continues. "Who start things but stop because they don't believe they have anything worth sharing. Women who are more than 'just a mom,' but have forgotten how to be anything else."

Your throat tightens. "How did you know?"

"Because I was once you," she says. "Fifty-two, empty nest, no idea who I was without my kids. I thought my life was over. I was wrong. It was just beginning."

Your heart beats faster. "What if I'm not brave enough?"

"Then you're exactly who this journey is for," she answers gently. "Bravery isn't the requirement. Honesty is. Being tired enough to stop pretending you're fine. And the willingness to admit you can't keep living like this. Are you there yet?"

You stare at the grocery list on your lap, the words blurring as you think about the past few months. The same aisles. The same routines. The same ache. You glance at your hands on the steering wheel, remembering all the years they held little hands, clapped at recitals, wiped tears. Now they're just… still.

You look out across the parking lot. The same one you've parked in for years, week after week, between the life you had and the life you don't know how to start.

You think of last night's dinner, the scrape of forks in silence, with the house seeming to hold its breath. This morning's coffee, alone. Tonight's plan, no different.

The woman's voice is still soft in your ear. "You can't see it yet, but there's more waiting for you on the other side of surviving all this. Sometimes, all it takes is saying yes."

You hesitate. "When does it start?"

"Saturday morning, nine o'clock," she replies. "Harbor Point Marina, Dock 7. Look for the *Golden Harmony*."

The name sounds like something out of a dream. "That soon?" you ask.

"That soon," she says, and you can hear the smile in her voice.

You sit in the quiet after she hangs up. The silence feels heavier than before, filled with something you can't quite name.

What did you just agree to? *You've always been the dreamer, the one who feels everything too much, but it's all trapped inside you. You don't do things like this.*

You replay her words in your mind, the way her voice slipped past your defenses. "One more thing," she'd said. "Bring your willingness to believe you are more than you've let yourself be."

You hadn't even realized you'd said yes until it was too late.

"Yes, I'll be there," you'd whispered, barely audible. And then she hung up before you could change your mind.

You stare at the phone in your hand, half-expecting it to ring again, for someone to tell you it was all a mistake. But it doesn't. The world outside carries on. Shopping carts rattle across the pavement. Car doors slam. The wind pushes a napkin past the windshield. Everything looks the same, but somehow it isn't.

You sit there for a long, suspended moment. Standing on the edge of something, holding your breath, waiting for what comes next

You don't know what this trip is or what you're stepping into. You only know you said yes, and it feels like the first real thing you've done for yourself in years.

Finally, you start the car. The engine hums beneath your hands. You pull out of the parking lot and drive toward home, but something inside you is still back there, in that space between endings and beginnings. You drive past the same streets, the same shops and corners, noticing things you've never really seen before. The golden light on a row of mailboxes. The shape of the clouds drifting by like thoughts caught in the windshield. The sound of your own breathing in the quiet.

You stop at the light, glance at the grocery list you placed on the passenger seat, and realize you never actually went inside. You turn around and head back, almost laughing at yourself.

You shop without thinking, reaching for the usual items, the old rhythm returning: milk, bread, chicken, salad. Ordinary things, but they feel different now. They belong to an old life that you're about to outgrow. Two versions of yourself, the one who came here and the one who's leaving.

At home, everything looks the same. The kitchen counters are clean. The clock ticks in its steady rhythm. The mail sits in a neat pile at the edge of the counter. Your husband's shoes are where he always leaves them. You set the groceries on the counter and stand there for a moment, just listening to the silence.

He comes into the kitchen, glances at the bags. "You get everything?"

"I did," you say.

Glancing at his watch, he asks, "Everything okay? You were gone a while."

"I got sidetracked," you tell him. It's true, though not the way he thinks.

He nods, distracted, flipping through the mail. "You all right?"

You pause, a small smile tugging at your mouth. "I think so," you say. "Actually… I think I'm going on a trip this weekend."

He looks up, one eyebrow lifting. "A trip?"

"Something I won," you answer, unsure how to explain it. "A retreat. Just for a few days."

He nods again, already looking back at the stack of envelopes. "That sounds nice."

You wait for him to ask for details. He doesn't. He picks up the mail instead. The sound of it opening fills the quiet space between you.

You start putting the groceries away, one by one. The same motions you've done a thousand times before. And you stand there for a long moment with your hands resting on the counter, the cool surface steady beneath your palms. You can feel your heart still fluttering from the call.

You can't tell if it's hope or fear that's settled in your chest. Maybe both.

That night, you lie awake beside him. He sleeps soundly, the way he always does. You stare at the ceiling, wide awake, replaying the sound of the woman's voice, the calm certainty in her tone. You think about the way she reached into the stillness and touched something inside you you'd almost forgotten was there.

You picture the marina, the dock, the boat waiting there. You can almost hear the water lapping against it. You can't explain why, but the thought of it makes you breathe a little deeper. Feel a little calmer.

You have no idea what waits for you on those islands, but you know you're going. You said yes… to something, to yourself. And for now, that's enough

2

The Dock

Saturday comes in with a soft gray drizzle, the kind that blurs the edges of things and makes the world feel suspended.

You almost don't go. Instead, you make coffee, scroll through emails, looking for reasons to stay put. Each small excuse whispers, *Stay comfortable.*

You count the usual worries swirling just beneath the surface: *what if it's a scam, what if it's foolish, what if nothing changes and you end up disappointed again.*

A free adventure retreat still feels unreal, something you barely remember signing up for. It makes you question your judgment.

But something tugs deeper than doubt. The quiet ache that's been following you for months, urging you to move before life becomes one long drift through the same routines.

You don't have language for it, but you know it's time.

You pack a small bag. You're not sure what belongs on a trip like this. A few changes of clothes. The unfinished book you keep meaning to finish. A water bottle. It feels like packing for something unknown and preparing for a life you haven't met yet.

The drive to the marina carries you through parts of town you hardly ever see. Strip malls and coffee shops blur past as Saturday slowly wakes. Lawns hum with mowers. Dogs tug at leashes. People move with quiet certainty through the same patterns that used to feel like enough.

With every mile closer to the water, your stomach tightens. The closer you get, the louder the voice of doubt becomes.

This could be nothing. You could turn around.

But your hands stay on the wheel.

Harbor Point Marina comes into view at the end of a narrow road lined with weathered buildings and peeling paint. The smell hits first. Salt air, diesel, and something faintly metallic. Possibility, maybe.

You park and sit for a moment, watching the water shift under the gray sky.

The marina is quieter than you expected. A few people move around their boats. A small world of competence and purpose. Some wear faded t-shirts and old sun hats, others look like they stepped straight out of a sailing magazine. Everyone seems to belong here, to know what they're doing. You, on the other hand, feel like an observer at someone else's story.

Dock 7 stretches ahead, slick from the morning mist, lined with boats of every kind.

Some bear the marks of years with peeling paint, frayed ropes, and tired hulls. Others gleam, fresh and confident, like new beginnings.

You walk slowly, reading their names painted in faded or polished script: *Sea Dreams. Wanderlust. Second Chance. Liberation.* Each one feels like a promise, a hope, or perhaps an escape from whatever was holding someone's story back on land, waiting to be claimed.

And there, at the end of the pier, waits the *Golden Harmony.* She isn't the largest sailboat, but something about her makes you stop. Her deep blue hull with gold trim seems to hold the light differently, like she's quietly aware of her worth. Her name curves across the stern in graceful gold script. Hand-painted, deliberate.

She doesn't look like a tourist vessel. She looks like someone's trusted companion. There's dignity in her silence, a kind of earned wisdom from storms weathered and journeys finished.

You stand there taking her in when footsteps sound behind you.

"You came."

You turn to see a woman approaching with the steady grace of someone who belongs near water. She looks to be in her early sixties, with long brown hair caught by the wind, a wide-brimmed hat held in place by a colorful scarf. Her clothes are practical. A checkered shirt, white shorts, worn deck shoes that speak of work, not leisure.

But it's her brown eyes that hold you. Bright, warm, lined with the kind of joy that only comes from surviving yourself and liking who you became. There's no pity in them. Only recognition.

"You must be Elaine," you say, shifting your bag on your shoulder.

"Guilty." She extends a hand, strong, calloused, steady. "And you look like someone ready for something new."

Her words land with uncomfortable precision. "I guess that's one way to put it."

"There are many ways," she says, her gaze holding yours. "Sometimes it looks like being stuck. Sometimes it feels like moving but going nowhere. Sometimes it's realizing you've built a good life but lost yourself inside it."

Each sentence touches something you thought you'd buried. You nod, unable to find words.

"Well," she says, turning toward the *Golden Harmony*, "then you've found the right place. I've been sailing this beauty for twenty years, helping women remember who they are when life stops defining them."

You look at the vessel. "Why the *Golden Harmony*?" you ask.

Elaine's expression softens. "Because that's what I seek in every journey. The golden harmony between who we are and who we're meant to be. Between the roles we play and the truth underneath. Between giving to others and honoring ourselves. This sailboat helps women find that balance. She's carried hundreds of women from fragmentation to wholeness. And now she's here for you."

The words settle over you like a promise. "Back to themselves?"

"Exactly. To who they were before they started shrinking to fit everyone else's needs."

She rests a hand on the rail, fingers tracing the grain like she's greeting an old friend. "The moment you answered that call, I knew. You're ready for something different. The only question is whether you'll let yourself have it."

You glance toward the boat. "Before I do, can you tell me what I'm getting myself into? Five days is a long time to commit to something I don't understand."

Elaine nods approvingly. "Fair question." She gestures to a nearby bench. "It takes a little longer than you might expect, but every island is worth it."

"I'm not sure yet," you admit. "How much longer? I only packed a few things."

"Come, let's sit over there."

You sit. The air hums with quiet expectancy.

"I'm sorry if that wasn't clear earlier. This journey has five islands. The whole voyage usually takes ten to fourteen days, not just five. Each island has a lesson. Some you might remember, some you'll discover for the first time. You'll discover things about yourself pertaining to…" She ticks them off on her fingers, "Gratitude. Intuition. Connection. Purpose. Self-care. The things that make life feel full instead of empty. The things often times your culture never taught you were essential."

"And you've been doing this for twenty years?"

"Yes," she says, grinning, "I'm Seventy-three now," watching for your reaction.

Your eyebrows shoot up.

She smiles at your obvious surprise. "I know," she says, laughing softly. "I'm more myself than I've ever been." She gestures at the boat, at the water, at herself. "This is what's possible when you stop fighting yourself and start living from truth, your body thanks you for the care you give it."

Her tone shifts, warm but grounded. "The islands will challenge you. Not the kind that breaks you. The kind that wakes you."

You listen, unsure whether to feel skeptical or intrigued.

"And at the end?"

"At the end," she says, "you won't find gold or jewels. You'll find what you misplaced. Your own gifts."

"Gifts?"

"The parts of you that got buried under doing and giving and worrying."

You take that in quietly. "What if I fail?"

Elaine looks at you with patience born of experience. "Then you'll learn something valuable about courage. But here's what I know after doing this for twenty years. Women like us don't fail. Raising humans. Managing households. Keeping everyone else functioning. You just forgot to notice how strong that made you."

Her words reach a tender place within.

"So yes," she says, standing. "Five islands. A ten to fourteen-day voyage for the time you need to remember who you are beneath the noise. Are you up for the challenge?"

You draw a slow, deep breath. "I'm ready."

"Then let's get you aboard."

You follow her up a short ramp. Your heart quickens with every step. The instant your foot touches the deck, you feel a loosening in your chest, like a string pulled too tight finally easing.

The *Golden Harmony* is more spacious than it looked from the dock. Everything gleams with quiet order. Thick ropes coil neatly near the mast. Through an open door, you catch a glimpse of the main cabin. Warm teak wood. Blue-cushioned benches that promise comfort after long days at sea. Brass lanterns. Everything speaks of care and intention from someone who takes pride in maintaining something both beautiful and functional.

"How does she feel?" Elaine asks, watching you take it all in.

"Solid," you say, surprised. "Like she's earned it."

Elaine smiles. "She has. She's a teacher as much as a vessel. Out here, away from everything that tells you who to be, you start hearing your own voice again."

You trail your hand along the railing, the grain smooth and sun-warmed. "So I'll learn to sail?"

"Among other things." She opens a built-in storage bench and lifts out an old scroll bound with braided twine, beside it a polished brass compass on a leather cord.

"This," she says, "is why you're here."

You step closer. "What is it?"

"Your treasure map and compass," she replies.

She unrolls the parchment, revealing a map, intricately inked and softly colored, edges curling from age. Five islands shimmer faintly in the gray light: *Gratitude Shores, Intuition Isle, Connection Cove, Treasure Island,* and *Self-Care Springs.* Tiny golden chests are drawn on each one.

"Treasure chests?"

"Each island holds a golden key," she says, "to unlock a gift you already carry."

You touch the compass. Its needle doesn't point north. The practical part of you wants to question it. But deeper down, something stirs. Curiosity, maybe belief.

"I don't understand," you admit. "If these treasures are mine, why do I have to find them?"

Elaine's voice softens. "Because life made you forget where to look. These islands and the gifts they hold are reminders. They're not lessons you learn but truths you uncover."

A soft wind rocks the *Golden Harmony,* the ropes humming their quiet song.

"Why me?" you whisper.

"Because you were still listening," she says simply. "You were brave enough to ask for more."

You look at her, searching for pretense, and find none.

"What would I have to do?"

"Visit each island. Find each key. Open each chest. Be honest with yourself. Let go of what no longer fits."

She places the compass in your hand. The metal is cool, the weight sure.

"Keep this close," she says. "It'll remind you where you're headed, even when you forget."

You slip the leather cord over your neck. The compass settles against your chest, pulsing faintly with warmth.

"How long do we spend at each island?"

"That depends on you," Elaine answers. "Every woman's rhythm is different."

The horizon brightens slightly, gray clouds parting just enough to reveal a hint of blue. For the first time in a long while, you feel the pull of possibility.

"What happens first?" you ask quietly.

Elaine nods toward the ropes. "First, we cast off. Then, when you're ready, you take the helm."

"I don't know anything about sailing."

"You'll learn. But this isn't about sailing. It's about remembering you can steer."

You look down at the compass. Its needle steadies.

Elaine's voice is gentle now. "Are you ready to leave the dock?"

You turn once more toward your car and the quiet ache of what was. And then back toward the open sea.

"Yes," you nod. "I'm ready."

3

Ahoy, Captain!

Elaine's smile radiates, lighting up the marina with warm confidence. "Then let's get this beautiful lady moving. First rule of captaining your own life. Nothing moves until you let it."

She moves with practiced efficiency toward the thick white ropes securing the *Golden Harmony.*

"See these dock lines? They keep us safe, but they also keep us from going anywhere new."

You watch her untie the lines, her movements sure and graceful. Each rope that slips free feels like a quiet permission. Another tether to your old life, releasing into the water.

"Can you get that one at the back?" she calls, pointing to the stern line.

You move carefully along the deck, surprised by how natural it feels to move with the boat's gentle sway. The rope is thicker than you expected, heavy with salt. As you work to untie the cleat hitch, following Elaine's quick demonstration, a flutter of anxiety stirs alongside a pulse of excitement.

"What if I mess this up?"

"Then you learn," Elaine replies easily. "That's what journeys are for. The worst that happens is we bump the dock. The *Golden Harmony* can handle it, and so can you."

The line comes free, and you feel the ship respond. She drifts slightly away, no longer tethered. Her movement seems subtle, but thrilling, as though the air itself shifted.

"How does that feel?" Elaine asks, coiling the last line.

"Scary," you admit. "But also... free."

"Exactly. Fear and freedom start the same way. Your body doesn't know the difference. Only your mind decides which story to tell."

She turns toward the mast. "Ready to catch some wind?"

The next few minutes unfold like a memory you didn't know you were missing. Elaine raises the mainsail with effortless strength. It snaps open with a sound like thunder, and the *Golden Harmony* surges forward, slicing through the gray water.

The transformation is instant. One moment, you're drifting; the next, you're moving with purpose. The sound of water rushing past the hull, the hum of wind through the rigging, the tilt of the deck beneath your feet. Each sensation blends into something electric and alive.

"Come here," Elaine calls from the helm, her hands steady on the worn wooden wheel. "Time to learn what it feels like to steer your own course."

You steady yourself with the rigging as you approach, the compass swinging softly from its leather cord against your chest. Up close, the wheel is beautiful. Smooth, aged wood polished by years of journeys.

"Put your hands here," Elaine says, guiding yours to the grips. "Feel that?"

The moment your palms touch the wheel, something hums through you. The *Golden Harmony* speaks in subtle language — each shift of current, each gust of wind, transmitted through the wood. It feels like holding the heartbeat of something strong and willing.

"This is incredible," you whisper.

"It gets better. Look at your compass. What does it tell you?"

You lift it from your chest. The needle points straight toward the horizon — a small dot of land barely visible through the mist.

"That's *Gratitude Shores*," Elaine says. "Your first destination."

She steps aside, her confidence calm and contagious. "Now, steer us there."

"Me?"

"You. Feel the wheel. Let the boat talk. Your job is to listen and guide."

She places her hands briefly over yours, showing a tiny movement. The ship responds immediately, graceful as breath.

"That small?"

"That small," she says, smiling. "Big corrections cause trouble. Small ones keep you on course."

You follow her lead, making minute adjustments as the wind nudges the sail. Each time you correct, the boat answers, smoother than before.

"There," Elaine says, pride in her tone. "You're doing it. That's all sailing is. Paying attention and adjusting."

"I did it," you say, hardly believing it.

"You're doing it," she corrects gently. "How does it feel?"

You breathe, really noticing: the rhythm of the waves, the pull of the wheel, the faint salt sting in the air. "It feels like… something I haven't done in twenty-five years."

"Like what?"

"Something new. Something that's just for me."

"What does it feel like?" she asks again, her voice stronger this time, encouraging you to let your excitement breathe.

"Alive." The word lands expressively between you.

Elaine lets you hold it for a moment before saying, "Remember that feeling. That's what you're here to reclaim. Not just for now, but for good."

You hold your course, loosening your grip as your confidence grows. The wheel steadies under your hands.

Noticing how you're handling the wheel, Elaine comments. "Control isn't about holding tighter. It's about trusting your touch."

You nod. Understanding.

The harbor opens into wide water. The wind strengthens; the *Golden Harmony* begins to rise and dip with the swells.

"This is different," you say, trying to keep your balance.

"Open water always is," Elaine replies. "No walls, no comfort. This is where you meet yourself."

A stronger wave hits. The ship lurches, and instinctively you tighten your grip.

"Breathe," she says calmly. "The boat knows what to do. You just stay present."

You force a breath and feel your body start to match the rhythm of the water. Not resisting, but moving with it.

Minutes pass. The island draws closer, its outline faint behind a curtain of gray fog.

Elaine points. "That's your passage. Everyone faces one before reaching *Gratitude Shores*."

Your stomach drops. The fog looks dense and endless.

"What if I get lost?"

"That's why you have the compass," she says quietly. "It stays true even when sight fails. Trust that more than what you see."

The *Golden Harmony* glides forward until the fog envelops you completely. The air chills; sound dulls. Elaine becomes a blur at the edge of your vision.

You can barely see the bow. Panic tightens your chest.

"I can't see!"

"I know," Elaine's voice answers, calm and near. "But not seeing isn't being lost. Check your compass."

You look down. The needle still points ahead, unwavering.

"It still points forward."

"Then that's your way. One breath at a time."

But the silence presses in. Every sound feels dangerous, every shadow a threat. Your own thoughts turn against you. *You'll fail. You'll mess it up. You always give up.*

Your jaw sets. "I don't have to listen to this."

"What was that?" Elaine calls back.

"I said I don't have to listen to this." Louder now. "These are old stories. They're not true anymore."

The words feel like a flare cutting through the gray. Something in you steadies. You grip the wheel, not from fear but resolve. The compass glows faintly in the dim light.

You breathe and keep steering.

The fog begins to thin. A faint warmth touches your face. Then sunlight.

Hesitant at first, then brilliant as it breaks through.

Suddenly, you're through it.

Behind you, the fog drifts apart like smoke. Ahead lies *Gratitude Shores*. Vivid, luminous, impossibly beautiful. Turquoise water. Sand shows specks of glitter. The air smells of salt and blooming jasmine.

You laugh softly, realizing you're crying. Relief, not sorrow.

Elaine stands beside you, her pride quiet but unmistakable. "You did it. You steered through the heavy and found your way to light. That's gratitude. Not pretending the fog wasn't there, but choosing to keep moving until you see clearly again."

You nod, voice catching. "I did it."

"You did. Well done, Captain."

The word *Captain* lands warm and right. For the first time in years, it feels like a title you've earned.

The *Golden Harmony* glides toward the island, sunlight sparkling across the water.

"How does it feel?" Elaine asks.

You look toward the bright shore, then down at the compass against your heart. "Like I'm stronger than I thought I was."

Elaine smiles. "Like you're exactly where you're supposed to be."

"Yes," you whisper. "Exactly like that."

II

GRATITUDE SHORES

"Gratitude unlocks the fullness of life.
It turns what we have into enough, and more."
— Melody Beattie

4

The Trail

Like the grace of a bird returning to its nest, you've never approached anything quite like this. The water beneath the hull is so clear it feels like floating on glass. Brilliant yellow and blue fish flash between coral formations, unbothered by the ship's quiet glide.

"We'll drop anchor here," Elaine says, pointing toward a sunlit patch near the curve of the beach. "Deep enough to hold. We'll wade ashore."

Together you lower the heavy anchor, feeling it sink and catch with a satisfying pull. When the chain stills, silence blooms. No city hum, no traffic. Just waves licking the hull and palm fronds whispering in the warm breeze.

"Look at this place," you breathe.

Gratitude Shores arcs in a perfect crescent, the sand itself flecked with gold that truly shimmers, not imagined sparkle but sunlight caught and held. Beyond the beach, palms sway, and narrow paths twist into the lush green heart of the island.

You lift the Mariner's Compass from around your neck. It guided you through fog to this shore; its weight now feels less like need, more like proof.

"I'll put this with the map," you say. "I won't need it on land."

"Ready?" Elaine lowers a rope ladder into the turquoise shallows.

You follow, and the instant your feet touch the water, warmth rises around your ankles like welcome. Each step forward feels like rinsing off something old. By the time you reach the beach, you're smiling without knowing why. The sand is soft, almost velvety, and when you glance back at the *Golden Harmony* floating in sunlight, pride flares. Real, quiet pride.

"I actually did it," you murmur. "I steered through fog."

"You did more than that," Elaine replies, wringing seawater from her shirt. "You trusted yourself when everything around you said turn back. That's no small thing."

She leads you toward a stone-lined trail rising between palms. Every detail here seems designed to make you slow down and feel, rather than hurry.

"This island teaches something that sounds simple but changes everything," Elaine says as you walk. "It helps you see what's here instead of what's missing."

You think of your life: the quiet house, the vanished career, the years that feel invisible. "That sounds impossible. How do I appreciate what isn't there?"

"That's the trick," Elaine answers gently. "You've spent years measuring absence. Gratitude begins when you notice presence."

The path widens into a clearing where several trails meet. A wooden post marks one broad lane:

GRATITUDE TRAIL — 2.5 miles.

"Ready?" she asks.

You nod, though you're not sure for what.

After ten minutes of gradual climbing, the trail opens onto a bluff that overlooks the island. A weathered mile marker pole reads:

THE OVERLOOK Mile 0.5

From here, the entire island unfolds. The beach, the palm trees, distant hills, and the glimmer of the *Golden Harmony* rocking in her cove.

"What do you see?" Elaine asks.

Your mind goes straight to what's missing. No houses. No roads. No people. "It's beautiful, but it feels empty. Undeveloped."

"Now tell me what *is* here."

You hesitate. "Water. Trees. Birds. The sound of waves. Clean air. Space. Beauty."

"Keep going."

You look again. "Warmth. Safety. Possibility." The word surprises you.

"Do you hear the difference?" Elaine smiles. "Same view, new lens."

You let her words settle. *The landscape doesn't change. Only your way of seeing does.*

"Let's rest before the next stretch," she says, and you both stand quietly at the overlook, listening to surf and wind until the rhythm finds its way inside you.

From the overlook, you take one last sweeping glance across the island. The beach gleams below, and far on the northern curve of the shore, you spot it. A slender white lighthouse rising from the rocks, sunlight flashing off its glass like a held breath of light. You can't explain why, but the sight steadies you. Something in its stillness feels like a promise.

The trail narrows again, dipping into dense green. Leaves filter the sunlight into patches that move across your skin. The scent changes too, with less salt, more earth, and something faintly sweet. A carved wooden sign waits ahead:

CORNERSTONE Mile 0.8

"Stop here," Elaine says. "Close your eyes."

You hesitate, then obey.

At first, all you notice is the quiet. Then gradually, layers of sound emerge: birds, the rustle of palm fronds, your own breath. You feel warmth on your face, breeze on your skin, your heart steady in your chest.

"Your body," Elaine says softly. "It's carried you through everything. Pregnancies, sleepless nights, disappointments, the invisible labor no one claps for. And even when you ignored it, even when you judged it, it kept showing up."

Something breaks open inside you. Not with drama, but with recognition. *You've spent decades critiquing this body, not once thanking it for staying.*

"I'm sorry," you whisper, the words surprising you.

"That's where gratitude begins," Elaine says. "With what's right in front of you. The ordinary miracles you've stopped seeing."

You open your eyes. The grove looks changed, though you know it's not. *You're the one seeing differently.*

The path winds deeper into shade, the air cooler now.

"Tell me something," Elaine says as you walk. "Where did you learn that wanting more was dangerous?"

The question startles you. "I don't know what you mean."

"You talk about your life like desire is a risk. Like hoping leads to hurt. Where did that begin?"

You search your memory and come up blank. It feels ancient, like something you absorbed before you had words. "It's just always been there," you say.

Elaine nods. "Most people inherit that belief. But what if it's not truth? What if it's just a story someone else handed you? And you've been living inside it ever since?"

You walk in silence, the idea echoing. *What if it isn't truth?*

You realize how many of your choices have been shaped by fear of disappointment, not the desire for joy.

Ahead, you hear it before you see it. The rush of falling water.

The trail opens into light.

A small waterfall spills over smooth stone into a clear pool. Mist rises in soft ribbons, catching sunlight into small rainbows. A marker nearby reads:

THE WATERFALL Mile 1.5

"Sit," Elaine says, motioning toward a sun-warmed rock. You sit beside her, both silent for a while, the water's rhythm filling the space between breaths.

"Tell me about a disappointment you still carry," she says at last. "Something that convinced you life doesn't work out."

The question cuts deeper than expected. "There was something I wanted badly," you admit. "I worked for it, believed in it, thought it would change everything. It didn't happen. It fell apart, and it felt like proof that hard work doesn't matter. That I don't matter."

Elaine listens without interruption, her gaze steady. "And since then?"

"I stopped getting excited. Stopped hoping. If things work out, great, but I don't expect them to anymore."

Elaine nods toward the waterfall. "Look at the water. What do you notice?"

You watch as it cascades over stone. "It's… beautiful. Constant. It doesn't stop."

"What happens when it hits the rocks?"

"It just goes around them."

"Exactly. The rocks don't end the flow; they shape it."

You study the water longer. The mist rises, glowing with refracted light. The music of the fall changes with every curve, yet it never stops moving.

"When that thing you wanted didn't work out," Elaine says, "what came next?"

"Other things. Opportunities I didn't plan for. People I wouldn't have met otherwise."

"And?"

"And I never saw them as gifts," you say slowly. "I thought they were consolation prizes. But maybe they were the point."

The words leave your mouth, and something releases. The old disappointment dissolves into the air like mist.

You look back at the water. It feels like it's showing you something simple and profound all at once. *Life doesn't stop at obstacles. It re-routes. Keeps flowing.*

"Oh," you whisper, breath catching. "I get it."

Elaine smiles softly. "That sound you just made… that's gratitude finding its way back in."

The trail continues beyond the waterfall, winding through palms heavy with coconuts. Some trees have dropped their fruit, and the ground is scattered with shells in every stage. Some cracked, others dried, fresh, and still sealed.

A wooden mile marker leans against a tree trunk:

COCONUT GROVE Mile 1.9

Elaine bends to pick up a coconut split clean in half. The white meat glistens in the sunlight as she hands it to you.

"What do you see?"

"A coconut," you say automatically.

"What else?"

You study it more closely. The tough outer husk. The hard shell. The sweet core hidden within. "It had to grow in layers," you say slowly. "The inside needed protection while it formed."

Elaine nods. "Twenty-five years of mothering. What did that time build in you?"

The question stops you. *You've thought of those years as something that ended, not something that built.* You turn the coconut in your hands, the weight of it grounding.

"I learned how to manage chaos. To problem-solve, to keep going when everything was falling apart. How to stretch what we had and still make it enough."

She nods for you to continue.

"How to teach, to see potential in others. To be patient. To show up when it's hard. To create something out of nothing."

Your throat tightens. "I thought I had nothing to show for those years, but I built all this. They're not just mom skills. They're *life* skills."

"They are," Elaine says softly. "You've just been measuring them by the wrong standard. The world doesn't pay for love or endurance or intuition… but that doesn't make them worth less."

You hold the coconut differently now. Not as debris, but as evidence. Proof of growth hidden inside ordinary labor.

Elaine picks up another coconut, green and whole. "Now you get to decide what you'll grow next… with everything those years taught you."

You set yours down carefully and stand. "They weren't wasted," you say. "They built me."

"They did," Elaine agrees. "And you're ready to build forward."

The path descends, light filtering through palms until the ocean comes back into view. The air smells of salt again. You hear waves before you see them, and then the trail opens onto a rocky stretch where tide pools reflect like small mirrors.

A weathered post leans against the stone:

THE TIDE POOL Mile 2.5

Elaine leads you to the largest pool, its water so clear you can see small shells and fish glinting about at the bottom.

"Look," she says simply.

You crouch beside it. Your reflection wavers on the surface. Not perfectly clear, but enough to see the woman you've been avoiding. The habit returns immediately: to catalog flaws, to find what's wrong.

"What do you see?" Elaine asks.

"Everything that needs fixing," you say before you can stop yourself.

"I know," she says gently. "That's the old pattern. But what if you looked with kindness instead? The way you'd look at anyone else you love."

You take a breath and try. Not the ideal version. Just you, here, now. Windswept hair, flushed face, eyes that have seen joy and grief and kept going.

"What do you see now?"

"Someone who's still here," you say quietly. "Someone who's survived. Someone who loved deeply and kept showing up."

"That's gratitude," Elaine says. "Not perfection. Presence."

As you keep looking, light flickers across the pool. Something glints below. You lean closer and catch your breath. A golden key rests on the white sand at the bottom.

"It's here," you whisper.

"It's always been here," Elaine says. "You just couldn't see it until you were ready."

You wade into the shallow water, reach down, and close your fingers around the key. It's warm, solid, heavier than it looks. You turn it in your palm, and engraved along the bow in elegant script, you read: *Gratitude*

The Key of Gratitude. Not given, not granted. Discovered.

"I found it," you announce, holding it up.

"You earned it," Elaine corrects gently. "By seeing what was already true."

You stand there a moment, feeling sunlight dry your skin, the key's weight in your hand anchoring something new inside you.

"What now?" you ask.

"Now," she says, "we walk to the lighthouse."

The coastal trail is smoother here, lined with low shrubs that smell faintly of citrus. The sun hangs low, gilding everything in honey-colored light. You hold the key as you walk, feeling its warmth pulse faintly against your palm.

The lighthouse rises from the rocks ahead, taller than it seemed from the overlook. Its white stone catches the light differently with every step. Sometimes soft, sometimes radiant.

"What's it made of?" you ask, running your fingers along the surface.

"Limestone," Elaine says. "Weathered and shaped by time, like all strong things."

The doorway is open, inviting you in. The air inside is cool and still, carrying a faint scent of salt and stone. A wooden bench curves along the wall, and on a shelf sits a leather-bound book. You open it to find page after page of names. Women who walked before you, each with a small note: *Found what I needed. See clearly now. Thank you.*

Elaine steps beside you. "You can sign it when you come back down," she says. "After you understand what waits above."

You close the book gently. The spiral staircase winds upward, disappearing into light. You tuck the **Key of Gratitude** into your pocket. It feels warm, sure, alive.

Elaine places her hand on the railing. "Ready?"

You nod. "Yes."

And together, you begin to climb.

5

The Climb

You follow Elaine up the spiral staircase, the sound of your footsteps echoing off the stone. The air cools as you climb, carrying faint traces of salt and the soft mechanical rhythm of waves against rock. The **Key of Gratitude** rests in your pocket, warm against your leg. A reminder that you've already begun to see differently.

The staircase curves upward, light spilling through small arched windows. When you reach the first landing, the space opens into a circular room. Windows face three directions: inland, toward the trail you walked, and outward, toward the wide horizon.

You step inside and pause, catching your breath. Through one window, you see the beach below, the *Golden Harmony* anchored safely offshore. Through another, the winding trail where you walked earlier, the waterfall's white cascade, the coconuts scattered under palms.

Elaine moves beside you. "Look how far you've come today."

You look, but your mind doesn't settle on distance. Instead, it fills with memories. Flashes of effort that went unfinished. The half-written stories. The courses you started and never completed. The ideas that began bright and fizzled out before they became real.

"I can see all the times I quit," you say quietly. "All the proof that I don't follow through."

Elaine doesn't contradict you. She just asks, "What were you reaching for in each of those moments?"

You think back. "Purpose. Something of my own."

"And what did you learn from trying?"

"That I didn't actually care about the thing itself," you admit. "I just wanted to matter. To feel like my life meant something beyond what I did for others."

Elaine nods. "So that attempt showed you what wasn't truly yours. That's not failure… that's discovery."

You move closer to the inland window, tracing the view back over the island. "The course I didn't finish. I thought it proved I wasn't disciplined enough."

"What did it really show you?"

"That I learn differently. That I need space to explore, not follow instructions word for word."

"So it taught you how *you* learn," Elaine says. "That's useful information."

The words begin to settle in. Each unfinished attempt, each "failure," didn't end something. It revealed something. Patterns. Preferences. *Pieces of who I am.*

You turn toward the ocean window. The light has shifted. It's late afternoon now. The sky, gold and wide. The horizon stretches endlessly, sunlight rippling like liquid metal.

"I wasn't a quitter," you say, almost to yourself. "I was learning what doesn't fit."

Elaine's smile is small, quiet. "Exactly. Every effort shaped you. The difference is, now you see it that way."

You stand at the window a moment longer, the ocean's shimmer reflecting faintly on the walls. The air feels lighter. Inside you, something that once tightened with shame now softens. You realize you've been carrying evidence of growth and calling it proof of failure.

Elaine gestures toward the stairs. "Shall we?"

You nod, still looking at the horizon one last time. "Yes. Let's keep going."

The next level feels different even before you step inside. The air shifts. It's warmer, quieter. You sense what's waiting before you know what it is.

This room opens on all four sides, windows framing every direction. Light pours in from the sea and through the palms inland. You move toward the ocean side, drawn to the view that seems endless. Water meeting the sky. The horizon stretching without a seam.

And then, without warning, your chest tightens. You don't see the ocean anymore. You see your children. Not as they are now, but as a mosaic of memories.

Toddler fingers clutching yours.

Laughter in back seats.

Teenagers slamming doors.

Suitcases packed.

Goodbyes at college.

The words escape before you can stop them. "I gave them everything. And they left anyway."

Elaine doesn't interrupt. She joins you at the window, standing close but not touching. "They grew up," she says softly. "That was the goal, wasn't it?"

You nod, but your throat aches. "I know that's what I was supposed to want. But it still feels like I poured twenty-five years into something that vanished. They don't need me anymore."

Elaine tilts her head, her eyes kind but steady. "Need changes shape. They don't need you to pack lunches or check homework. But does that mean they don't need you at all?"

You hesitate, remembering small moments. Your daughter's text when the baby was sick.

Your son's call from college, asking how to fix a ruined load of laundry.

The recipe questions.

The tiny check-ins that don't sound like dependence but still sound like love.

"They still need me," you say quietly. "Just differently."

"So why do you treat their independence as your failure?"

The question lands deep. You stare at the waves, your reflection faint in the glass. "Because if they don't need me the way they used to, I don't know who I am."

There it is… the truth that's been sitting in your chest like a stone.

"You defined yourself by being needed," Elaine says. Not judgment, just recognition.

"Yes."

"And now," she says, "you have the chance to define yourself by something else. Maybe not by who needs you, but by what calls to you. By what makes you feel alive."

You turn from the ocean and face the inland window. From here you can see the path you walked earlier. The waterfall sparkling faintly in the distance, the curve of the coconut grove, the trail that carried you here.

"They're thriving," you whisper. "They're good, capable people. Exactly what I hoped they'd become."

"Because of you," Elaine says simply.

You nod slowly. "The twenty-five years weren't wasted. They were my work. And I did it well."

Silence settles between you, soft but full.

You look back at the ocean. The surface gleams gold now, reflecting late-day light. In the glass, your reflection appears. Not the idealized version from years ago, but the one standing here: flushed from the climb, eyes bright with awareness.

You meet your own gaze. "Someone who's still here," you say softly. "Someone who raised love that now stands on its own. Someone whose story isn't finished yet."

Elaine doesn't move, but you sense her smile. "That realization," she says, "is a kind of freedom. You can love them fully and still belong to yourself."

You exhale slowly, and something loosens. That quiet guilt of being a mother who dares to want more.

The sound of the ocean deepens outside. The light shifts again, turning amber.

Elaine gestures toward the stairs. "Ready?"

You glance once more at the horizon. It feels endless, but instead of loneliness, it looks like… *possibility.*

"Yes," you say. "Let's keep climbing."

The next level feels smaller, more private. You notice the faint scent of limestone, tinged with salt. Two windows face opposite directions: one toward the west, where the sun is lowering in molten gold; the other toward the east, where shadows lengthen over the island below.

You stop between them, one hand on the cool stone wall. You know what's coming before Elaine even speaks.

"This room," she says quietly, "is about partnership. About truth."

You move to the western window. The light spills across your hands as you rest them on the sill. Outside, the ocean blazes gold, calm and endless. But what fills your mind isn't the sea. It's the ordinary moments of your marriage: the quiet dinners, the shared routines, the spaces that grew between you like unspoken miles.

You see yourself making dinner while he scrolls through the news on his phone.

You see the two of you on the couch, watching television, but not really together.

You see the version of yourself who once felt seen, and the one who slowly faded behind schedules and silence.

"He doesn't see me anymore," you say, the words catching in your throat.

Elaine moves toward the eastern window but doesn't look at you yet. "Does he know you want to be seen?"

The question makes you flinch. "He should. I shouldn't have to say it."

"'Should,'" Elaine repeats softly. "That word often hides a truth we're afraid to face. What if he simply doesn't know because you never told him?"

You want to argue. To list all the sighs and silences, the subtle clues you thought were obvious. But deep down, you know she's right. You've been waiting to be understood without speaking. Hoping he'd notice without being told.

"I don't know how to say it," you admit, staring out at the waves. "It feels needy. He works hard. He provides. I should just be grateful."

Elaine steps closer. "Grateful, yes. But not silent. Partnership isn't about guessing games. It's about allowing yourself to be known."

The words sting, not because they're harsh, but because they're true.

You turn toward the east-facing window, the one that looks back toward the day's beginning. The trail, the beach, the place where everything started. The light there is softer, silvering the horizon.

"What if I tell him," you say, "and nothing changes? What if he doesn't want to?"

Elaine's voice gentles. "And what if he does? What if he's been waiting too? Just as unsure how to reach you?"

You imagine it. Sitting down across from him at the kitchen table, no distractions, no sarcasm to hide behind. Saying what you've never said aloud. *I miss us. I miss feeling like we're in this together.* The thought terrifies you, but under the fear, something else flickers. *Hope.*

You rest your forehead against the cool stone. "It might be fixable," you whisper. "If I'm brave enough to be honest instead of waiting for him to guess."

Elaine nods. "That's all anyone can do. Speak the truth with love. The rest is choice. His and yours."

You lift your head and look at her. She's standing in the fading light, her expression soft but sure. "You've spent years holding everything together by staying quiet," she says. "Maybe the healing begins by speaking."

The room glows now with a mix of gold and rose light. The sun lowers toward the horizon, and for a brief, perfect moment, the eastern and western windows mirror each other. Beginning and ending reflecting the same sky.

You move to the center of the room, between them. "I thought gratitude meant accepting what is," you say.

Elaine shakes her head gently. "Gratitude also means honoring what's worth fighting for. Seeing clearly enough to love truthfully."

You take a long breath, the words sinking deep. *Gratitude isn't passive. It isn't quiet endurance. It's presence. Choosing to stay awake to love, even when it's hard.*

You look once more through both windows. Sunrise and sunset, beginning and continuation. You feel both at once.

Elaine smiles faintly, sensing the shift in you. "Ready for the final climb?"

You nod, voice steady now. "Yes. I think I am."

The final stairs wind upward in a tight spiral. The iron railing is cool beneath your hand, and with each step, light grows stronger. Not harsh, but golden, pulsing softly through narrow windows. By the time you reach the top, the air feels charged, as though the island itself is holding its breath.

The Lantern Room opens before you in a sweep of glass and brightness. Windows encircle the space, offering a full view of everything. The ocean glowing with the last fire of sunset, the beach a pale ribbon below, the trails you've walked curling through shadow and light.

You step inside, and for a moment, you forget to breathe. The great lamp in the center, brass and glass, beautiful in its simplicity, catches the last light of the day and bends it into brilliance. The whole room seems alive with motion, color, and reflection. You are standing inside the light itself.

Elaine joins you quietly. "This is the Lantern Room," she says. "It gathers light and sends it out, so others can find their way."

The truth of that sinks in slowly. You've spent years dimming your own light to make others comfortable. Here, the brightness doesn't shrink. It expands, filling every inch of the space until it touches you.

At the lamp's base sits a small chest. Wooden, weathered, beautiful in its plainness. A lock catches the light, faintly in the soft glow.

Your pulse quickens. "This is it," you whisper.

Elaine nods. "The treasure you've been moving toward."

You draw the **Key of Gratitude** from your pocket. It feels warm, as if it recognizes where it belongs. The lock opens easily, like it's been waiting for you.

Inside, cushioned in soft fabric, are the gifts. You lift the first one. A pair of simple glasses with clear lenses.

"What are these for?" you ask, running your thumb along the frame.

"Gratitude glasses," Elaine replies. "They help you see what's real. Present. Not what's missing or broken. You've always had this ability, but these remind you to use it."

You put them on. The frames settle perfectly on the bridge of your nose. The world sharpens instantly, but not in detail, in *presence*.

You notice everything at once. The rhythm of waves far below, the breath in your chest, the steady beat of your heart, the whisper of wind moving through palm leaves. The world hasn't changed. *You have.*

You take them off carefully, smiling.

The next object is a small journal, bound in soft leather. You open it. Blank pages, creamy and waiting.

"You used to write, didn't you?" Elaine asks. "Words that helped you see what mattered?"

"Yes," you say softly. "I stopped when life got too full," you remember. "There wasn't space for me anymore."

"There is now," she says. "This isn't for recording. It's for rediscovering… your voice, your thoughts, your becoming."

You close the journal, feeling its weight. Small but grounding.

The final object rests at the bottom. A mirror with a simple silver frame. You hesitate before lifting it. When you do, you're surprised.

The reflection that greets you doesn't sting with criticism or regret. You see wind-tangled hair, sun-touched skin, eyes that have seen deeply today. A face that belongs wholly to you.

Elaine's voice is soft. "This one's for the hardest practice. Seeing yourself with compassion. The same grace you give everyone else."

Your throat tightens. "That's still hard for me."

"It will be," she says. "But you've started. That's enough."

You lower the mirror back into the chest and rest your hand on all three items. The glasses, the journal, the mirror. They feel ordinary, but you know they're not. They're reminders of how to live mindfully grateful.

Elaine's eyes meet yours. "These gifts aren't meant to stay here. You carry them forward. When you remember gratitude, you light the way for others."

You close the lid gently, the **Key of Gratitude** still warm in your hand, as if to say, 'carry me with you'.

You catch a glimpse of the sun slipping beneath the horizon. The lamp catches that last beam and magnifies it, sending light in wide, sweeping arcs across the sea. You realize then that you are not standing in the light. You are part of it.

Elaine's voice is barely a whisper now. "That's what gratitude does. It turns reflection into illumination. You are the light," Elaine says simply. "You've become the light you were looking for. And now you get to carry it with you."

The Descent

You descend the lighthouse together. You keep one hand on the railing, the other brushing the wall. It feels cool, real, and grounding. The spiral staircase winds down through each level you climbed. Past the room where you saw your marriage with new eyes. Past the windows where you reframed your mothering. Past the view where you realized you weren't a quitter, just someone still figuring it out. The echo of your footsteps mixes with the soft hum of wind through the tower, a rhythm like integration, the return from revelation to embodiment.

When you reach the lower level, the air is different, touched by salt and light. You pause in the doorway, remembering…

Through the doorway, you see that dusk has deepened into violet. The first stars shine through the thinning light, and a full moon rises, slow and sure over the water. It's bright enough to cast shadows, the kind of light that makes everything feel softer, more forgiving.

Suddenly, you recall the visitor's book. You cross the quiet room again and lift the leather-bound book from its shelf. The pages smell faintly of salt and age. You flip to the most recent entries of names, dates, and a few short notes written in different hands. *"I see clearly now." "Thank you." "Found my way."*

Elaine stands silently nearby as you pick up the pen she offers.

You hesitate only a moment before writing your name. The letters look smaller than you expect, a little uncertain, but real. Proof that you were here. That you climbed. That you found what you came for.

You pause, pen hovering over the page. What can possibly capture all of this? The fog, the trail, the waterfall, the light. Finally, you write just three words.

I see possibility.

You close the book and rest your hand on its worn leather cover. The gesture feels like both an ending and a beginning.

"Ready?" Elaine asks from the doorway.

You nod, tucking a loose strand of hair behind your ear. "Ready."

You step out into the night, carrying your quiet light within you.

6

Moonlight Walk

You glance up one last time toward the lantern above, watching its beam sweep the sea. A reminder. A rhythm. A promise you'll remember when you forget.

Outside, the sky meets the edge of day, folding softly into night. The air is cooler now with the scent of flowers that open only after dark. The sound of the waves is gentler than during the day, more like breathing than motion.

"We'll walk back by moonlight," Elaine says softly.

The idea feels perfect, quiet, unhurried, exactly what this moment calls for.

You begin the walk along the coastal path, the treasure chest cradled carefully in your arms. The sand still holds a trace of the day's warmth, and the moonlight silvers every ripple and curve. The sound of your footsteps blends with the hush of waves rolling onto shore.

"I haven't walked in the dark like this in years," you say after a while. "Not since the kids were little and we'd take them to look at Christmas lights."

"What stopped you?" Elaine asks.

You think for a moment. "I don't know. Maybe I stopped doing things without a reason. Everything had to have a purpose, an errand, a task, something that needed to get done. Just walking for the sake of walking felt… indulgent."

"And now?"

"Now it feels like exactly what I need."

Elaine smiles but doesn't reply. The quiet between you feels easy. You fall into the rhythm of the waves, the breath of the island around you.

The path looks different at night. The same stones, the same palms, but transformed. Softer, more mysterious. The world has slowed to a whisper. You hear sounds you missed before. The night birds calling from the trees, the gentle hiss of sand shifting under your feet, the distant hum of insects hidden in the dark.

Everything feels closer.

"Everything sounds louder in the dark," you say.

"Or maybe," Elaine answers, "you're just listening more carefully."

Her words settle over you like the warm air itself. You realize she's right. Gratitude, too, is a kind of listening, not just to the good things, but to what life is quietly saying underneath the noise.

When you reach the waterfall, you stop automatically. In the moonlight, the cascade looks like silver threads tumbling through shadow. The sound is softer now, more like music than motion.

"This is where it clicked for me," you say, watching the water shimmer in the dim light. "When I finally understood that disappointment wasn't proof that life doesn't work out. It was redirection."

Elaine looks toward the water, nodding. "Do you believe that?"

"Yes," you answer, and the word feels steady. "It's not just an idea anymore. It's something I know."

You watch the water for a while longer before turning back toward the trail.

The path leads you through the coconut grove, the palms now only shapes against the deepening sky. You can barely see the fallen coconuts scattered beneath the trees, but you remember them. All those layers protecting what grows within.

"I have skills," you say quietly, the realization resurfacing. "Real skills. I'd forgotten that."

"You'll forget again," Elaine says gently. "And you'll remember again. That's why you have reminders," she says, glancing at your treasure chest. "To help you come back to what's true."

You walk on, her words weaving into your thoughts.

A soft breeze moves through the trees, carrying the scent of salt and the sweet night-blooming flowers near the shore. You close your eyes as you walk, trusting your feet to find the path. Your body feels tired, but not drained. Strong, in a way you haven't felt in years.

You whisper, "Thank you."

You're not sure who you're speaking to: your body, Elaine, the island, or maybe something larger that's been guiding you all along. But it feels right to say it out loud.

When you open your eyes again, the trees thin, and you find yourself at the overlook.

From here, you can see nearly everything. The curve of the beach gleams under moonlight. Farther out, the *Golden Harmony* floats in the harbor, a single golden light glowing softly in the cabin window. And beyond it, across the dark expanse of water, the lighthouse beam sweeps in steady rhythm, a long, slow arc of light crossing the waves.

You stop, watching it move.

"It's still going," you say, your voice low. "Even after we left."

Elaine folds her arms loosely, following your gaze. "That's what light does. It keeps going."

For a long moment, neither of you speak. The silence feels sacred. You're aware of your breath, of the pulse in your wrists, of the faint weight of the key in your pocket.

You think about what this day has given you. Not just lessons, but perspective. Gratitude isn't a list of blessings, you realize. It's the way light keeps reaching even when night falls.

Finally, you say, "I walked more than these two and a half miles today." The words come out not as pride, but as recognition. "I haven't done anything like that in twenty-five years. I forgot I could."

"The first island is always about remembering," Elaine says. "Remembering that you're capable. That you already have what you need. Gratitude isn't about adding more. It's about noticing what's already here."

You look at the lighthouse again, the beam steady and sure. "It's beautiful," you whisper.

"It's you," Elaine says simply.

You turn to her, uncertain what she means, and she smiles. "The light you saw up there? You were standing in it. It moved through you. That's what gratitude does. It reminds you that you've always been part of the light."

Something loosens in your chest. The kind of relief that's quiet but absolute. You feel it in your throat, in the corners of your eyes, in the steady rhythm of your heartbeat.

"Then maybe," you say softly, "I can learn to keep shining too."

Elaine nods, her expression full of quiet pride. "You already are."

You both stand there a moment longer, the ocean breathing beneath the moonlight, the lighthouse beam sweeping over the water and back again, endless as gratitude itself.

When you finally move, it's slow and deliberate, as if your body knows you're leaving something sacred behind. The trail winds down toward the beach, the sand cool beneath your feet now, holding faint traces of your earlier footprints. You pause where the path meets the shore, looking back once more toward the lighthouse. Its light arcs across the water, steady and sure, not asking to be seen, just shining because that's what it was made to do.

You exhale softly. "It keeps going," you say again.

Elaine follows your gaze. "And so will you."

The tide laps at your ankles as into the water, its warmth surprising after the cool night air. You lift the chest slightly, holding it close, careful and reverent. Each step feels like a baptism, washing away the last remnants of hesitation, leaving only the quiet confidence of someone who knows she's changed.

The *Golden Harmony* rocks gently in the harbor, her single light glowing like a lantern waiting to welcome you home. Elaine climbs the ladder first, then turns to take the chest from your hands before you follow. The deck creaks softly beneath your feet, familiar now. Not a foreign vessel, but something that feels like your own.

You stand for a moment, catching your breath, looking back toward the island. Gratitude Shores glimmers under the moonlight, the lighthouse beam sweeping past before disappearing behind the curve of the bay.

Elaine sets the chest on the deck and rests her hands lightly on it. "You did well today," she says. "Not just because you found the key, but because you let yourself see."

You trace your fingers along the edge of the chest. "It feels different than I expected," you admit. "Not like accomplishment. More like… peace."

She smiles. "That's what true gratitude feels like. It doesn't rush. It doesn't demand. It just fills the space that used to be occupied by striving."

You let her words sink in as you move toward the railing. The sea stretches out in every direction, the moon painting a path of light across the water. The island is already fading into the night's shadow, but the sense of it, its lessons, its warmth, its quiet insistence that you remember yourself, remains.

After a while, you turn toward the cabin. Inside, the air smells faintly of salt and cedar. You set the treasure chest on the small table beside your bed, its lid closed over the treasures you found today: the mirror, the journal, the glasses. Beside it, you set the **Key of Gratitude** where the moonlight from the porthole catches its golden edge. A reminder that even in darkness, gratitude still shines. For a long moment, you just watch it gleam. A quiet promise that what you found on the island isn't something you can lose.

You change into dry clothes and sit on the edge of the bunk, the soft motion of the boat rocking you into calm. The moonlight glows on the surface of the water, silver and endless. You can still see the lighthouse beam in the distance, sweeping with slow, patient rhythm.

The day replays in fragments. The climb up the lighthouse, the trail to the waterfall, the tide pool, the reflection that made you cry and then made you smile. It's all still there, layered and alive inside you. You realize that transformation doesn't arrive in grand declarations or perfect clarity. It shows up quietly in softened edges, in easier breaths, in a willingness to see yourself without flinching.

You lie back on the narrow bed, pulling the blanket over you. Your body is tired, but it's the kind of tired that feels earned. The kind that comes after doing something honest and necessary.

Through the porthole, the lighthouse beam sweeps again. Steady. Unwavering. You close your eyes and feel its rhythm echo in your chest.

You whisper into the stillness, not sure if you're speaking to something that's been guiding you all along. "I'll keep the light."

And for the first time in a very long while, you believe it.

Sleep finds you easily.

The last thing you feel before drifting off is the faint hum of the *Golden Harmony* beneath you, her gentle rocking in time with the sea, the world breathing, the light continuing, gratitude alive in motion.

And as you drift into sleep, the thought comes softly, certain and true. Tomorrow, you'll set sail for what comes next.

III

INTUITIVE ISLAND

*"The intuitive mind is a sacred gift
and the rational mind is a faithful servant."*
— Albert Einstein

7

The Canyon

The morning after claiming your first treasure on Gratitude Shores, you wake to find Elaine already on deck, studying the charts spread across the navigation table.

"Sleep well?" she asks without looking up.

"Better than I have in months." You move beside her, drawn by the familiar calm of the sea and the quiet confidence she carries. Five islands are marked on the map, each distinct, each waiting. Your eyes trace from Gratitude Shores to the next destination. "Where are we headed?"

"**Intuitive Isle,**" Elaine says, tapping the chart. "But getting there takes more than sailing in the right direction. Its entrance is hidden behind a waterfall. Most people sail right past it without ever knowing it's there."

You lean in closer. The island's coastline rises in jagged cliffs, the inked outline showing what looks like a narrow slit of water almost invisible on the page.

"How do we find it?"

"Not with your eyes alone." Elaine opens the small drawer beneath the chart table and takes out the mariner's compass. Your compass, polished now, its brass face catching the early light.

She studies it for a moment before handing it back to you. "You already know how it works. It doesn't point north; it points true. This time, it will lead you inward as much as forward."

You take it from her, feeling the familiar weight settle into your palm. The metal is warm, as if it remembers you.

She nods toward the horizon. "You've trusted it before, but this journey will ask for more than that. This time, you'll have to trust yourself to follow it, even when the way looks impossible."

You slip the leather cord back over your head. The compass rests against your heart, steady and certain, as if it's waiting for you to begin.

You study the map, the morning light soft against the parchment. Beyond Gratitude Shores, the coastline of the next island looks different from the others, edged with steep cliffs and a narrow inlet barely visible on the chart.

Elaine adjusts a line, then nods toward the open sea. "We'll chart a course toward the cliffs."

You rest your hands on the wheel. "So we aim for what looks impossible."

She smiles. "That's usually where truth hides."

The wind shifts, full and clean. The sails fill, and the *Golden Harmony* begins to move, smooth, certain, alive beneath your hands.

It feels different this time. You're not waiting for direction or correction. You're already responding, feeling how the wind leans, how the hull adjusts.

Elaine watches from the rigging, her voice easy but warm. "Feels good, doesn't it?"

You nod. "Like I'm not just steering anymore. Like I'm part of it."

"She's been waiting for that," Elaine says. "So have you."

A quiet laugh escapes you, light and unforced. "Then let's see where she takes us."

Within the hour, the Golden Harmony is cutting through morning light, sails full, water gliding smooth beneath the hull. You stand at the wheel, hands steady on the polished wood, the mariner's compass warm against your chest.

Sailing feels different when you're fully responsible. Every gust and ripple asks for attention. Every tilt of the deck invites awareness. It's not control. It's communion.

Elaine joins you at the helm. "Look ahead. What do you see?"

You scan the horizon. The cliffs loom closer, tall and forbidding, their faces dark against the brightening sea. The sound of crashing waves swells around you, primal, pulsing, alive. Your body tenses, every instinct warning you to turn away.

But beneath that quick, protective fear, something steadier hums, the quiet certainty of the compass, the pull that doesn't shout or demand, only *knows*.

You hold steady.

Spray mists across your face, cold and sharp, but you keep the bow pointed toward the cliffs. Logic says this is wrong. Intuition says this is exactly right.

"Look for the waterfall," Elaine says. "It's there. You just have to see it."

You scan the gray expanse of stone and spray, searching. For a moment, there's nothing. Then, a flicker. A shimmer of falling water, so seamless with the sea mist it almost disappears.

"I see it," you breathe. "The waterfall." If you hadn't been searching, you would have missed it entirely.

"Then that's your way through. Straight through."

"Through it?"

"Through it," she confirms.

For a moment, you hesitate.

The words hang in the air. The mind lists reasons to stop: danger, damage, the risk of being wrong. But deeper than reason, something inside you steadies. The knowing you can't explain but can no longer ignore.

You take a slow breath and turn the wheel toward the waterfall. The bow shifts, cutting a clean line through the rolling water.

"Steady," Elaine says quietly. "Trust your hands. Trust the boat. Trust yourself."

The roar grows deafening. Spray mists across your face and arms. The air thickens with sound and salt. Your whole body vibrates with adrenaline as the bow strikes the waterfall.

A blinding rush of white, sound, and motion, and cold all at once. And you're in it. For a moment, everything disappears. There's no sky, no sea, only the roar and the sense of moving through something immense. Water pours over the deck, over you. Spray drenches your skin, salt stinging your eyes. You can't see the opening anymore, only the rushing curtain of water.

You can't think, only feel. For one impossible moment, it's chaos.

And then… silence.

The noise drops away. Light shifts. The water smooths beneath you.

You're through.

On the other side, the sea lies utterly calm, sheltered by towering cliffs that rise like sentinels. The air feels different here, cooler, softer, alive with echoing stillness. Behind you, the waterfall roars on, guarding the entrance you just crossed.

You did it. You trusted.

Elaine lets out a long breath beside you. "Well done, Captain."

You exhale too, a breath you didn't realize you were holding. Your hands tremble slightly on the wheel, adrenaline ebbing, replaced by the deep, certain calm that follows every act of real trust with a deep sense of rightness.

"I haven't done anything like that before," you say quietly.

"Like what?"

"Trusted myself when it didn't make logical sense. Followed my gut, even when I couldn't explain why."

"Then it's good you're remembering how," Elaine says with warmth. "Keep following the channel. Let the compass guide you. There's a lagoon ahead where we can anchor."

Behind you, the roar of the ocean fades into memory. Ahead, the lagoon opens wide, quiet and calm.

The air inside the hidden lagoon feels different; still, hushed, as though the world itself is holding its breath, almost sacred. The cliffs rise high on either side, sheltering the narrow channel you've entered. The water glows in the morning light, impossibly clear, reflecting the sky in perfect stillness.

You let your hands fall from the wheel, the ship gliding forward on her own momentum. For the first time since leaving Gratitude Shores, there's no wind tugging at the sails, no motion but the slow ripple of the current. The water mirrors the cliffs and sky so perfectly that you can't tell where reflection ends and reality begins.

"It's beautiful," you whisper.

Elaine nods, her expression thoughtful. "Most people never find this place. They get close, but they turn away before they reach the truth."

You look down at the compass, still warm against your chest, the needle now calm and centered. "It feels… different here."

"It should." She moves toward the bow, resting a hand on the rail. "You trusted what couldn't be proven. That changes how the world meets you."

The words settle over you like sunlight. You don't fully understand them, but they feel true in the way intuition always does, quietly, without argument.

"Drop anchor here," she says. "We'll go ashore."

You move through the motions you've learned, the clatter of chain echoing softly against the canyon walls. You know the anchor holds when you feel the boat's gentle sway as she comes to rest.

The two of you lower the dinghy and climb in, the oars slicing easily through water so clear it seems to glow from below. Small silver fish dart beneath the surface, disappearing into shadows that look like folds of silk.

"This feels hidden," you say quietly.

"It is," Elaine replies. "Intuitive Isle only shows itself to those who are ready to listen."

You glance at her, curious. "To what?"

"To themselves."

The answer lands like a pebble dropped into still water—ripples expanding through your mind long after the words fade.

When you reach the shore, you pull the dinghy onto the sand and take in your surroundings. The lagoon curves like a crescent moon, sheltered on all sides by tall, carved cliffs. At the far end, a narrow trail winds upward through the rock, leading inland.

"Where does it go?" you ask.

Elaine smiles faintly. "Somewhere that echoes."

You follow Elaine up the trail, one hand brushing the compass against your chest. Its steady warmth feels like a heartbeat guiding you inland.

The path's the incline, steady but manageable. The air is warm and clean, carrying the scent of minerals and salt. As you climb, the lagoon falls away behind you, shrinking into a circle of glassy light.

At the top, the path opens into a canyon unlike any place you've ever seen. The stone walls rise in smooth, curving layers, banded in shades of rust and rose and pale gold. Sunlight filters through narrow openings above, casting shifting patterns that move like living things across the walls.

The sound here is strange. Every movement, every word bounces back with a faint echo, slightly altered, as though the canyon is repeating your thoughts to you in a voice you almost recognize.

You stop walking. "It's… louder than I expected."

"That's what happens when you enter a place that echoes," Elaine says. "This is where the noise gathers. The voices that try to tell you who you should be, what you should want, what's safe."

You frown, listening. It's faint at first, like memory; half-heard, half-felt. But as you focus, the murmurs grow clearer.

Be careful. Don't get your hopes up. People will talk.

You're too old to start again. You should be grateful for what you have.

They come from nowhere and everywhere at once, overlapping until they blend into a low, familiar hum.

You press a hand to your chest. "It sounds like every thought I've ever had about why I can't."

Elaine's gaze softens. "That's because it is. Every voice you've absorbed over the years from parents, teachers, partners, friends. Even your own fears. They echo here until you can tell which ones belong to you and which ones don't."

You stand very still, feeling the weight of that truth. The air feels thick, vibrating with things you didn't know you'd been carrying.

"How do I know which voice is mine?" you ask quietly.

"You'll feel it," she says. "The one that doesn't argue or explain. It's quieter than the rest, but stronger. It's the one that never needs to prove itself right."

You nod, though doubt still flickers through you. The canyon's echo presses close, the overlapping whispers rising and falling like wind through hollow stone.

Elaine gestures toward a cluster of smooth rocks at the canyon's center. "Sit. Listen. Don't try to chase the noise away. Just notice it until it loses its hold."

You obey, lowering yourself onto the sun-warmed stone. The rock's heat seeps through your palms, grounding you. You close your eyes.

The echoes swirl. Fragments of judgment, self-doubt, and comparison. All the reasons you've held yourself back, disguised as wisdom or humility or practicality. For a moment, it's overwhelming. The noise is everywhere. But gradually, something shifts. You stop trying to quiet it.

You just listen.

And underneath the noise, you hear something else. Something small and steady, like a heartbeat deep below the surface. It doesn't speak in words. It doesn't demand attention. It simply exists, pulsing in rhythm with your breath.

When you finally open your eyes, the canyon looks different. The light seems softer. The echoes, quieter.

Elaine watches you. "You found it, didn't you?"

You nod. "It's strange. It's not a voice exactly. More like a feeling."

"That's intuition. It rarely talks in sentences. It speaks through knowing."

You look around the canyon, still half in awe. "It's been there all along."

Elaine smiles. "It always is. We just forget how to hear it."

You stay seated for a while, not speaking. The canyon hums with its own quiet pulse, and the longer you listen, the more it feels like your body is syncing with it. The rhythm of something ancient, patient, and alive.

When you finally rise, the compass presses lightly against your chest. Its weight feels different now, not heavy or demanding, but reassuring. You touch it without thinking, grounding yourself in the reminder of what you've just heard, or rather, what you've finally stopped ignoring.

Elaine stands nearby, her eyes warm but unreadable. "Ready?"

You nod.

As you walk out of the canyon, the air shifts. The echoes fade behind you, replaced by the softer sounds of wind through leaves and the low rush of the tide beyond the cliffs. The light grows warmer, gold sliding into coral. Everything feels less sharp, more fluid, as though the island itself has exhaled.

The trail bends, descending gently back toward the lagoon. The scent of salt grows stronger. You glance back once, half expecting to see the canyon walls move or shimmer, but they stand silent, holding what they've revealed.

By the time you reach the sand again, the tide has lowered, exposing smooth rock pools and coral-colored shells. The *Golden Harmony* sits anchored farther out, her reflection wavering in the calm water. You breathe in the salt air, the sound of the waves greeting you like an old friend.

Elaine pauses, turning toward a narrow side path that curves behind a cluster of low palms.

"There's one more thing to experience before we leave this island."

You follow, curiosity prickling through your fatigue. "Another canyon?"

"Not this time." She smiles. "Something deeper."

8

The Dive

The path opens to a smaller lagoon, tucked behind the main one, an enclosed basin with water so clear it looks lit from within. The late afternoon light glistens across the surface and sends small reflections up the rock walls. A short wooden dock reaches into the water. At the end of it stands a man with a set of diving tanks arranged at his feet.

Elaine lifts a hand. "Marcus."

He looks up and grins, his whole face warming. "Right on time."

You take in the gear, the quiet water, the faint scent of salt and sun on wood. Something in you tightens and expands at once. You already know what this is before anyone says another word.

"This is Marcus," Elaine says, leading you forward. "He has been waiting for you."

Marcus wipes his hands on a towel and offers one. His grip is sure and gentle, his skin cool from the sea. "You must be the new Captain."

You laugh lightly, the title still strange on your tongue. "So they tell me."

"I hear you are learning to trust your instincts," he says.

"I am trying."

"Good," he says, as if that is the only answer that matters. "Because that is what you will need down there."

You glance toward the lagoon. "Down where?"

"Beneath the surface." He gestures toward the calm, luminous water.

"Your next key is below. You'll find it by listening differently this time. Not with your ears, not even with your thoughts, but with what your whole body already knows."

A ripple of anticipation moves through you, part awe, part fear. "You mean, dive for it?"

"Exactly." Marcus's grin widens, but his voice stays calm and sure. "You'll have air, of course. And I'll be nearby if you need me. But the direction you take, the path you follow—that's all you. You'll know where to go when you stop trying to think about it."

You turn to Elaine. "Why diving? I've never done this before."

She studies you for a long moment, her expression kind but intent. "Because you've spent most of your life looking for answers on the surface. Sometimes, to hear yourself clearly, you have to go deeper than words."

The truth of that lands somewhere behind your ribs. You've been learning to trust what you feel, to listen beyond logic. But this asks for something more. Full surrender.

Marcus crouches by the gear, checking valves and clips with smooth, practiced movements. "When was the last time you did something purely for yourself?" he asks without looking up.

You think for a moment, realizing you can't remember. "A very long time ago."

"Then today's the day," he says simply. "No audience. No outcome. Just you and what's waiting to meet you down there."

For the next thirty minutes, he walks you through everything. How the regulator works, how to clear your mask if water gets in, how to equalize pressure in your ears as you descend, how to check your air gauge, and how to signal if you need help. His instructions are clear and thorough without being overwhelming.

He fits the tank into the harness and shows you how to adjust the straps.

"The most important thing," he says as he helps you into the buoyancy vest, showing you how to inflate and deflate it to control your depth, "is to keep breathing. Slow, steady breaths. Do not hold your breath. The ocean will hold you. You only have to let it."

The gear feels heavier than it looks. You adjust the weight belt he fastens around your waist. Elaine helps secure the final buckle.

"Keep your compass on," she says softly. "It doesn't work underwater in the usual sense, but it'll remind you where your real direction comes from."

You nod. "Trust what I know beneath what I see."

"Exactly." Her smile widens, touched with pride. "And remember, there's no rush. The ocean moves in its own time. So will you."

"How deep can I go?"

"The lagoon goes down about thirty feet at the center."

You gesture the 'okay' sign with your fingers.

"One more thing," Marcus says, handing you fins. "Trust yourself down there. Your body knows more than your mind gives it credit for. If something feels wrong, surface. If something feels right, follow it."

You slip the fins on and sit at the edge of the dock with your legs in the water. The lagoon stretches before you, inviting and slightly terrifying at the same time.

Elaine crouches beside you. "You've got this," she says, her hand on your shoulder. "You navigated through a waterfall this morning based on trust alone. This is more of the same. Follow what feels true."

You fit the regulator into your mouth and taste the rubber, feel the gentle resistance as you draw breath from the tank. It is strange and mechanical, but functional. Air flows steadily with each inhale.

Marcus checks your gear one last time, then steps back. "You are ready."

"Wait," Elaine says, her voice gentle and firm. "Before you go under, set an intention. Not what you will find, but how you want to move through this experience. With trust. With curiosity. With courage. Choose it."

The cool water laps at your calves. The words rise on their own. *"With trust. I intend to trust myself down there."*

Saying it feels significant, like a promise you are making to yourself. Not wishful thinking. A clear choice about how you will move through what comes next. Trusting yourself.

Elaine nods, satisfied. "Then go. The water is waiting."

You take one more breath through the regulator, steady and sure. Then you lean forward and slip beneath the surface.

The moment you submerge, the world transforms. Sound goes soft and far away. Your body feels weightless and supported. The water holds you the way Marcus promised.

You float at the surface for a minute and let your breath find a rhythm. In and out. Slow. Even. Your pulse settles into the same pace.

You press the vest's release and let a bit of air out. Your body begins to sink.

The descent is gentle. You remember to equalize, pinching your nose and blowing until your ears release. The water grows slightly cooler with depth, not uncomfortable, simply honest about where you are.

The underwater world reveals itself. The rocky bottom is covered with sea grass that sways with currents you cannot see. Small fish slip between rocks and do not scatter. Sunlight forms slow, moving ladders across the sand, as if the light itself is breathing.

It is beautiful. Peaceful in a way you did not expect.

You swim slowly and get used to the fins, to how you move when gravity lets go. You pass along the inside curve of the lagoon. You peer into crevices, watch little crabs tuck themselves out of sight, and find a shell that looks like porcelain and leave it where it belongs. Every few minutes you check your air. Still plenty. Still safe.

The lagoon is roughly circular. As you arc along the outer wall, you notice a darker seam in the stone. It is not a full opening, more a hint of one. You pause. Your mind speaks first. Unknown territory. Stay where you can see. Be sensible. Do not risk it.

Underneath that, something quieter rises. A pull. Not a command. An invitation.

You move closer, just to look. Light penetrates, dim but present. You can see the bottom and the contour of rock. It is navigable.

The competing voices begin their old chorus. Too risky. You do not know what is in there. You should turn back. This is how people get hurt.

Beneath them, the steady knowing. This is the way for you.

You check your air again. You are fine. You release a little more air from your vest and slide forward.

The passage narrows. The walls lift on both sides, not a trap, a tunnel. Small fish, the color of pale coins, hover along the rock. Anemones open and close like slow, breathing flowers.

You let yourself be carried by the rhythm of your breath. In. Out. In. Out. The sound of air through the regulator becomes a metronome for your attention. You are not scared. You are awake. You are paying attention.

The tunnel bends. You bend with it. A shaft of brighter light fans through a fissure, then fades. The current shifts against your forearms and calves, cool and clean. You hover and listen with your whole body. There. The faintest tug to the left.

You follow the tug and slip past a ripple in the rock where the stone shelves down like a stair. No key. Only a smooth basin and a spray of small shells. You circle once and keep going.

You reach a wider chamber where the roof lifts. The water here feels older, a little colder. A green parrot fish noses along the wall, unconcerned. You turn slowly, take the room in, and notice what is not obvious at first. A second seam, lower and to your right, half hidden by a fan of coral.

You angle down and pause. Your air is still good. Your breath is calm. Your shoulders drop another fraction. You let your attention widen until you are not searching anymore. You are letting the scene show you what matters.

The pull returns, smaller now, but clear. You angle again and deepen half a body length. There, tucked where two ridges meet, something catches light and then hides it.

You approach, careful not to kick silt into the water. It is not the key. It is a small shard of polished shell. Beautiful, but not it. You smile into your regulator. Not yet. You circle once more and notice the way the light changes across the rock when your body shifts. You are casting a shadow that reveals what glare kept hidden.

You move a hand and the shadow moves with it. In that small wedge of softened light, you finally see it. Not shining. Waiting.

A golden key rests on a ledge the size of your palm, almost flush with the wall. It is plain and elegant. It looks like something that has always belonged to the sea, yet somehow belongs to you.

Your heart lifts. You found it. Not by guessing. Not by forcing. By listening with your whole body and following what you knew.

You slide closer and curl your fingers around the key. It is cool at first, then warm in your hand. Underwater, you can't quite make out the engraving. You hold it to your chest for a breath, near the compass, and let the moment register. You did this.

You turn and begin back the way you came. The return feels shorter, as if the tunnel has relaxed around you. You do not rush. You do not show off. You keep the same steady rhythm you began with. Breath. Check air. Move with what is, not against it.

The tunnel mouth opens into the brighter water of the lagoon. You rise in a slow, safe ascent and break the surface with a sound that is half breath and half laughter.

Marcus and Elaine are waiting on the dock. The sun is lower now and paints the water with gold.

"You found it," Elaine says. Not a question. A recognition.

You swim to the ladder. Marcus reaches down and steadies you as you climb, the wet suit streaming water back into the lagoon. Your legs are a little shaky from effort and the thrill of it, but you feel more solid than you have in years.

You open your palm. The golden key gleams in the light. Now, in the daylight, you can clearly see the words engraved on the bow: **_Intuitive Intention_**

The Key of Intuitive Intention.

"I went into the passage," you say, still catching your breath. "Under the island. It was darker there, and I did not know what I would find, but I knew I had to go."

Marcus eases off your tank and vest and unclips the weights. His movements are efficient. His attention does not leave your face.

"You set an intention. You trusted yourself. You followed through. That is how intuition works in real life. It is not magic. It is paying attention to what you know and having the courage to act," he says.

"I was scared," you admit, sitting on the dock while he slips the fins from your feet. "The whole time I was swimming into that passage, my mind kept listing reasons to turn back."

"Scared and certain at the same time," Elaine says as she settles beside you. "That is what real intuition often feels like. Not the absence of fear, it's the presence of knowing in spite of it. Fear says that something bad might happen. Intuition says that this is the way forward. Both can be true at once."

You look at the key, then back at the water. "I have never done anything like that before. Not just the diving. Trusting myself that completely when I could not see what was ahead and had no proof I was making the right choice."

"And yet you did," Marcus says. "You chose trust, and when the moment arrived, you practiced it. That is how you build a kind of self-trust that does not shake. Not by thinking about it. By doing it."

He hands you a towel. You dry off slowly and let the words settle.

"There is a cave," Marcus says, nodding toward the canyon. "In the cliff where the echoes are quiet. That is where your treasure chest is waiting. You have the key. Now you get to discover what you earned."

You change into dry clothes and notice how tired your body is. Tired. But strong and present.

The three of you take the path that winds upward. The climb is steeper than you remember from the morning, but it is a good climb. The kind that comes from doing something real.

"I set an intention," you say as you walk, testing the words. "I have never thought about it that way. Like a choice about how I move through something, not just hoping it works out."

"Intention is everything," Elaine says beside you. "You cannot control what happens. You can always choose the way you show up. What you practice. Who you decide to be in any given moment."

The path levels. The cave entrance waits ahead, a dark mouth in pale stone where the canyon's noise fades to a hush.

9

The Cave

The cave is smaller than it appeared from outside. Shadows pool along the walls, swallowing the last traces of daylight. The air feels cooler here, damp and still, carrying the faint scent of salt and stone.

Marcus hands you and Elaine a small headlamp. "It gets darker the deeper you go," he says, slipping another around his forehead. His voice echoing softly. The beam of light shows a narrow path ahead, illuminating drops of water clinging to the ceiling like tiny stars.

You slip the band around your forehead and take a few careful steps inside. The floor is uneven, scattered with smooth pebbles. Each footfall sends a ripple of sound into the space, a low hum that seems to vibrate in your bones. The rhythmic water drips, keeping time with your own heartbeat

Elaine follows close behind, silent but steady, her presence a quiet anchor in the dark. The deeper you move, the more the outside world fades. No breeze, no gulls, no sound of the sea. Only breath, stone, and echo.

Your light catches something ahead. A glint of brass. You pause, heart quickening, and lift the beam higher.

The chest sits on a ledge carved from the rock, as though the cave itself made space for it. Dark wood, dulled fittings, edges worn smooth by time. And carved into the lid, a conch shell.

Marcus stops a few feet behind you. "I'll wait just outside," he says quietly. "What's inside is for you."

67

Elaine moves to your side. The two of you stand before the chest. You can feel the quiet pulse of the place, as if the cave itself is holding its breath, waiting.

Your hand trembles as you fit the key into the lock. It slides in perfectly. You turn it.

Click.

And lift the lid.

Inside, nestled in deep blue velvet, are three objects.

You have been building toward this all day. The navigation through the waterfall, the climb, the dive into dark water. Now everything you have learned seems to converge here, inside this chest.

You reach in and lift out the first item. A pendant on a delicate silver chain, rose quartz carved into a simple heart. It is warm to the touch, as though it has been waiting for your hands.

You lift the pendant carefully, the rose quartz catching the light. It rests warm in your palm, pulsing faintly, as if in sync with your own heartbeat.

Elaine watches quietly, waiting, saying nothing.

You don't need to ask what it is. You already know. You hold it a little longer, feeling the rhythm deepen inside you.

"It feels like remembering," you say softly.

"Your heart's wisdom," Elaine says. "But intuition alone isn't enough. You've learned to hear what your body knows, but the real power comes when you set intentions from that knowing. When you decide, consciously, to trust what you feel and act on it. That's why this key is called the **Key of Intuitive Intention**. Not just listening to your inner voice, but choosing to follow it. Making the intention to honor what your intuition reveals."

You think back to this morning, standing before the waterfall. How you intended to trust yourself through the crossing. How that conscious choice to trust made all the difference.

"I set an intention before the dive," you say slowly. "To trust myself. That's what made it possible to actually do it."

"Exactly," Elaine nods. "You've always had intuition. But now you're learning to pair it with intention, the conscious commitment to act on what you know. That's the key. Not just feeling, but choosing. Not just knowing, but doing."

She pauses, studying your face. "Tell me about your intuition. When have you felt it most strongly?"

You think about this morning, standing at the wheel, facing that waterfall, when something inside you steadied before your mind could explain it.

"This morning I felt something here." You press your hand to your chest. "Not a thought. A feeling. Like my heart understood something my brain was still figuring out."

"Has that happened before?" Elaine gently asks.

Something in you gives way, and the words begin to spill.

"All the time. I'll meet someone and just know I can trust them. Or shouldn't. I'll walk into a situation and feel like something is wrong even though everything looks fine." You tap your chest. "My heart says no, even when my mind lists reasons to say yes."

"And what do you usually do?"

"I ignore it. Tell myself I'm being irrational. That, feelings aren't reliable."

"And then?"

You pause. "I'm usually wrong. The thing that felt right from the beginning, the one I talked myself out of, that's what I regret."

Elaine lets the quiet stretch. The cave holds the silence like breath.

"I have this already," you say, looking at the pendant. "Don't I? I've always had it."

"Why do you say that?"

"Because it's not new. I remember feeling this way as a kid, knowing things I couldn't explain." You turn the pendant over. "I just stopped trusting it."

"Why?"

"Because no one else seemed to trust it. I was taught that real intelligence lives in the head, not the heart. That logic is reliable and feelings are noise." Your throat tightens. "Every time I tried to explain why I knew something, I couldn't prove it. So I stopped trusting it."

"And what has that cost you?"

You think of the choices you made by overriding what your heart knew.

Relationships you stayed in too long. Opportunities you turned down. Years of drifting.

"Everything," you whisper. "My confidence. My sense of direction. My ability to know what I actually want instead of what I think I should want."

You slip the chain over your head. The pendant settles against your chest, and immediately you notice your heartbeat. It feels like recognition, like your body remembering a language it once spoke fluently.

"And?"

"Like coming home," you say.

You reach for the second item, a conch shell, spiraled and gleaming, cream-colored with hints of pink. Its smooth surface catches the light and scatters it softly across the cave walls.

You raise the shell to your ear.

The sound isn't what you expect. It isn't a hollow echo or distant hum. It's movement, like the pulse of tide and current, the ocean breathing through stone.

Your breath catches.

"It's the same rhythm," you whisper. "Not something I heard down there… something I *felt*. When everything was dark and I couldn't see where I was going, it was like my heartbeat matched the sea's. And somehow, I knew which way to turn."

"What was that knowing?" Elaine asks.

You lower the shell. "It wasn't someone telling me what to do. It was more like a certainty. Like something inside me recognized the right direction even though I had never been there before."

"Has that happened before today?"

"Yes. So many times." You can feel the truth of it rising. "I'll be making a decision and suddenly just know what to do. Not because I've reasoned it out, but because something in me is sure. Or I'll take a turn without thinking and end up exactly where I need to be."

"And what do you call that?"

"Luck? Coincidence?" You look at the shell. "Intuition, maybe. But it feels deeper than that."

You think about all those moments when you knew something before you could explain it. The instinct to say no. The quiet pull to say yes. The moments that made no sense until later.

"It's always been there," you whisper. "This voice. This knowing. I just haven't been listening."

"Why not?"

You sit on a smooth rock. "Because it's quiet. My inner voice is so quiet compared to everything else. Everyone's opinions about what's smart, what's safe, what's expected, are so loud." You gesture with the shell. "This is a whisper beneath the shouting."

"Or maybe you let the shouting drown it out."

"Yes. Because it's easier to follow what others think than to trust what I know when I can't explain why." You meet her eyes. "If I follow someone else's advice and it fails, I can say it wasn't my fault. But if I trust this voice and I'm wrong, then it's on me."

"So you've been choosing other people's certainty over your own knowing."

"Yes."

"And what has that cost you?"

"I've made so many wrong choices. Not because I didn't know better. I did. This voice told me. Warned me. I just didn't listen." You lift the shell again. "It never stopped. Even when I ignored it, it never stopped trying to guide me."

You set the shell gently down.

Your hand hovers over the last object: a small brass compass, its surface worn smooth with time. You lift it carefully. It's beautiful in its simplicity. No ornate etching, no numbers marking degrees, only a single needle and a narrow band engraved with one word: **True.**

You turn slowly in a circle. The needle swings, then steadies. Not toward north, but toward something else, unseen, internal.

"It's not pointing to any direction," you say, your voice quiet in the stone chamber.

"Not one you'll find on a map," Elaine answers.

You study it more closely. The needle trembles slightly, then stills again. You take a few steps to the right, and it shifts almost imperceptibly.

"It's responding to me," you whisper. "Not to the earth, but to where I'm standing."

Elaine nods. "Your inner compass doesn't measure coordinates. It measures congruence. When you're aligned with what's true for you, it points steady. When you're not, it wavers."

You turn with the compass again. The needle flutters and steadies once more. You feel the shift inside your chest mirror it, tightening when you face one direction, softening when you turn another.

"How do I know which direction is right?" you ask.

"You already do," Elaine says gently. "You feel it. When something is right, your body knows. Your breath deepens. Your shoulders drop. You feel ease instead of tension. The mind complicates; the body recognizes."

You look down at the compass again. "That makes sense. I've always felt it. The way something feels off long before I can explain why."

"And what do you usually do when you feel that?"

You give a small, rueful smile. "I ignore it. Or try to explain it away. Tell myself I'm overreacting or being too sensitive."

Elaine's expression softens. "You've been taught to doubt your own navigation system. To hand your compass to everyone else."

You trace a finger over the engraved word, **True.** "Then no wonder I keep getting lost."

"You're not lost," she says. "You're just used to traveling by other people's directions. You forgot you had your own map."

You stand quietly for a moment, the compass warm now from your touch. The pendant rests against your chest, and the shell still gleams softly beside the open chest. Each object feels like a thread leading back to yourself, the heart that feels, the voice that whispers, the compass that aligns.

Slowly, you nod. "These aren't new gifts. They're reminders."

Elaine smiles. "Exactly. You're not collecting treasures; you're remembering truths."

You close your fingers around the compass, holding it to your heart. "It's strange," you say softly. "I thought these journeys were about learning something new. But it's more like… I'm peeling away everything that made me forget what I already knew."

"The deepest wisdom always feels like remembering," Elaine says. "It's the sound of your own soul recognizing itself."

You meet her eyes. "I want to trust this. I don't want to second-guess it anymore."

"Then don't," she says simply. "Trusting doesn't mean you'll never doubt. It means you'll listen anyway."

You sit for a moment longer, letting the quiet of the cave settle around you. Then you reach for the conch shell, hold it for one last breath, listening to the faint hum inside, steady, alive, and then place it gently back into the chest where it belongs.

You turn around once more with the compass in your hand, watching the needle quiver and steady, as if it knows you're ready to move again. Then you slip it into your pocket.

"I think I'm ready," you say.

Elaine nods once. "Then let's go show Marcus what you've remembered."

You take one last look at the chest before closing the lid. The carved shell on top catches the light of your headlamp, and follow Elaine back through the narrow passage.

Marcus is waiting. He's leaning against the canyon wall, arms loosely crossed, eyes half-squinting against the late afternoon sun. When he sees you, he straightens with an easy smile.

"Well?" he asks. "Did you find what you were looking for?"

"More than I expected," you say, handing back the headlamp. "I thought I was finding new treasures. Turns out I was remembering ones I'd lost."

Marcus nods slowly, as if he's heard that truth before. "That's usually how it works. We spend half our lives looking for things that were never gone. Just buried under noise."

You tilt your head. "You sound like someone who's done that himself."

He chuckles softly. "Oh, I have. I spent thirty-five years doing what made sense on paper. Everyone said it was the smart thing to do, the safe thing. But I woke up one morning and realized I'd built a life that didn't feel like mine. My body started to shut down. That was the only way it could get my attention."

"What did you do?"

He looks out toward the water, his eyes reflecting the shifting blue. "I listened. For the first time in my life, I actually listened. Quit the job. Sold everything. Bought a boat even though I'd never sailed before. I didn't know where I was going, but I knew I couldn't stay where I was."

"You found your way here."

He nods. "Eventually. The compass didn't lie."

Elaine joins him at his side, her expression soft. "Marcus helps remind travelers like you that intuition isn't a skill to master. It's a muscle you've already been using. Only you just forgot what it feels like to trust it."

You look at them both, the ocean gleaming behind them. "It's strange," you say. "Everything I've been given, the heart, the voice, the compass, they're all part of the same thing. It's like my intuition has different ways of speaking to me."

"That's right," Elaine says. "It speaks through what you feel, what you hear within, what your body knows before your mind agrees. Every time you trust one of those voices, the others grow stronger too."

You take a deep breath. The air smells of salt and sun-warmed stone. "So what now?"

Elaine glances toward the cliffs rising beyond the beach, their upper edge catching the fading light. "Now we climb. The lighthouse is waiting."

Marcus pushes off the wall and gestures toward the narrow path that winds upward between the rocks. "You'll want to see the view before sunset. It'll make everything you've learned today make sense."

You hold the chest closer, feeling the solid weight of it in your hands. "It already makes sense," you say, but your voice carries a softness, not finality. "Still… I want to see."

"Good," Marcus says.

The three of you start walking.

10

The Lighthouse

The path to the lighthouse winds along the northern coast, following the cliff's edge where land meets sea. The afternoon fades toward evening, the sun lowering in a haze of gold and amber. You can hear the waves but can't see them, just their breath against the rocks far below.

Marcus leads with the easy confidence of someone who's walked this path many times. He doesn't rush, doesn't fill the silence. His steady pace leaves space for you to think, to feel, to process all that's happened today.

You carry the treasure chest carefully, both hands around it. The pendant pulses gently against your chest with each step. *Trust your heart. Listen to your inner voice. Follow your true north.*

"How long have you been the lighthouse keeper?" you ask after a while.

"About seven years now." He glances back, smiling. "I found this island the same way you did. By following intuition, not logic. I was a corporate attorney once. Successful by every measure that doesn't matter."

The admission surprises you. He seems so grounded, so alive. It's hard to picture him in a suit, living a life of deadlines and argument.

"What made you leave?"

"I stopped sleeping," he says. "Every night I'd lie awake with this dull ache, like I was disappearing by degrees. Not in a dramatic way. Just fading. Until one day, I realized I couldn't hear myself anymore."

You know exactly what he means.

"So what did you do?"

"I quit. Sold everything. Bought a boat even though I'd never sailed. People said I was losing my mind. Maybe I was. But I was more afraid of losing my *life.* My real one. The one waiting beyond all the shoulds and expectations."

"Were you scared?"

"Terrified," he admits. "But I was more scared of staying. Of waking up one day and realizing I'd spent my life being someone I wasn't."

He turns back toward the cliffs, voice softening. "When I found this island, I knew. The way you know things when you finally start listening. I knew this was home."

"Do you ever regret it?"

He smiles faintly. "Never. I regret the years I spent not listening. But leaving? Finding this place? Becoming keeper of this light? That was the first true choice I ever made."

The lighthouse rises ahead. White stone against a darkening sky, the lamp already turning, casting slow arcs of gold across the sea. Up close, it's taller than you imagined, sixty feet maybe, the walls weathered by salt and wind. The red door gleams dully in the last of the light, and above it, carved words you can just make out:

SEE CLEARLY

Marcus opens the door and gestures you inside.

The air is cool, damp, smelling faintly of salt and oil. The room is simple: a small table, a logbook open to the current date, and the spiral iron staircase that climbs through the center, narrow and gleaming in the fading light.

"It's a climb," Marcus says. "But worth it. Take your time."

You begin to ascend, the chest secure in your arms. Elaine follows behind you, and Marcus brings up the rear. Each step rings softly underfoot, a rhythmic echo spiraling upward through the hollow tower.

As you climb, small windows open to the sea. Through the first, you glimpse the canyon, no longer intimidating, just ancient stone and shadow. Through the second, the inner cove glimmers dark and deep, the place where you dove and remembered trust. Through the third, the waterfall sparkles in the distance, both wild and calm. The path you once feared, now just another part of the island's rhythm.

Each window feels like a memory made visible. Proof of what you've crossed.

Your legs burn by the time the stairs open into the lantern room. But when out, breath catching, the world expands.

The room is all glass and light. The lens turns slowly in the center, magnifying the sun's last fire into brilliance. The light passes across your face like a benediction.

From here, you can see everything. The entire island unfurled below. The lagoon where the *Golden Harmony* rests at anchor, the canyon and cave, the path you climbed, the sea stretching to the horizon. Every piece of your journey visible in one sweep of light.

Elaine comes to stand beside you. "This is what clarity feels like," she says softly. "Seeing where you've been. Understanding why each step mattered."

You turn slowly, taking it in. "Every part was connected," you say. "The waterfall, the canyon, the dive. I couldn't have skipped any of it."

"The lighthouse doesn't create the light," Marcus says from near the lamp. "It just makes sure the light keeps shining. That's what drew me to this work. You don't have to be perfect or certain. You just have to keep the conditions clear so the light can do what it's meant to do."

You nod, the words resonating deep inside. You think of your own light, quiet, steady, always there beneath the noise. "I've spent my life being the ship," you say. "Chasing other people's lighthouses. But I have my own light. I just forgot to tend it."

Marcus smiles. "Exactly. Most people follow others' lights for a while. But at some point, you have to tend your own."

You set the chest down on a bench near the curved glass wall. Outside, the sun sinks lower, painting the sea in gold that fades to rose, then violet. The first stars appear. The beam sweeps across the waves again, constant, unhurried.

Elaine's voice is gentle. "What did you learn today?"

You pause. "That intuition isn't mystical. It's a way of knowing. My way of knowing. It lives in my heart and body as much as my mind. I stopped trusting it because I was taught to value logic and approval over truth."

You touch the pendant against your skin.

"I learned that intention creates direction. That the moment I said, 'I intend to trust myself,' everything began to shift. That fear doesn't mean I'm wrong. It just means I'm doing something that matters. And that I can be scared and still certain at the same time."

The beam sweeps over you again, lighting your face. "And I learned that I can't have real connection if I'm not being real."

Elaine's eyes shine. "Those are lived lessons, not just words. You didn't read them. You became them."

Marcus adds quietly, "The hardest part isn't learning this. It's remembering it when you leave the island."

You nod. "How do I not forget?"

"The gifts, Elaine says. "Your gifts," she corrects, gesturing toward the chest. "They're reminders of who you are. Each one brings you back to yourself."

"And keep setting intentions," Marcus says. "Before each choice, remind yourself who you want to be in that moment. That's how you keep your light tended."

You breathe in deeply, the salt and lamp oil mingling in the air. "A daily practice," you say softly. "Not perfection. Just returning."

Marcus smiles. "That's all the lighthouse does. It keeps returning to its rotation."

Looking out, the beam cuts across the night. The first stars shimmer in the vast dark sky. Elaine rests a hand lightly on your shoulder. "Time to head back."

The three of you descend together, your steps echoing softly down the spiral stairs.

When you descend again, you remember the small leather-bound logbook resting on the small table in the circular room: a delicate stained-glass table lamp casting a halo over the open pages.

"May I?" you ask, Marcus.

"Of course."

You turn to a blank page, past the signatures and reflections from travelers who've climbed to see the light before you. You pick up the pen, your hands trembling slightly, you write:

I came to this island thinking I needed to learn to trust my intuition. I'm leaving knowing it was always trustworthy. I just needed to remember I am too.

Marcus reads it and nods. "That's it exactly. Your intuition never stopped guiding you. You just stopped listening."

By the time you all step outside, the night has fully claimed the island, but the lighthouse keeps its promise, steady, radiant, marking the way for anyone searching for safe harbor.

"Thank you," you tell Marcus. "For keeping the light."

He smiles. "Keep yours, too."

The path back is silvered by moonlight. Your legs ache, your body weary from the day, but it's the good kind of tired. The kind that comes from living instead of thinking about living.

When you reach the beach where the dinghy waits, Marcus stops.

"This is where I leave you," he says. Safe travels to your next island."

Connection Cove, Elaine says. "That's where we're headed tomorrow."

Something flickers across Marcus's face: understanding, perhaps, or recognition. "Ah. That one's different. Lots of people. Lots of voices. You'll need everything you learned here," he says, pausing before continuing. "After the work you've done here, you're ready for it."

You shake his hand, feeling the solid warmth of his grip. "Thank you. For everything."

"Trust yourself," he nods, and then turns, following the cliff path back toward the lighthouse; his light, his calling, the rhythm of his choosing.

You and Elaine row the dinghy out across the lagoon in companionable silence. The oars dip and rise, silvered in moonlight. The air smells of salt and warm wood. The *Golden Harmony* waits within the lagoon, a soft reflection shimmering beneath her hull.

Once aboard, you carry the treasure chest down to your cabin. The first chest from Gratitude Shores sits where you left it, and you set the second beside it. Two islands, two keys, two treasure chests full of gifts.

You open the new chest. Inside, the conch shell glows faintly in the lamplight. You pick it up and hold it near your ear. Amid the ocean's echo you remember your own steady rhythm, guiding you now as it did today when advice seemed overwhelming.

Next, you pull the tiny compass from your pocket and set it beside it. A reminder that true direction is chosen from within, not imposed from without. You vow to check your inner compass often as your steps grow steadier.

The heart pendant, you keep, resting warm against your chest, steady with your heartbeat.

Your gratitude glasses and mirror come out too tonight. The lessons from Gratitude Shores deepen here. They ground your intuition in an ever-widening circle of awareness.

You take your gratitude journal from the first chest and begin to write.

Today I learned to trust myself. Not in theory, but in practice. I navigated through a waterfall because the compass—and my knowing—said it was right. I dove into unfamiliar water because I set an intention to trust myself, and I did. I found a key in the dark by listening to what I felt instead of what I feared. I learned that my heart is intelligent. That my inner voice is reliable. That my true north has been guiding me all along—I just stopped believing it could. The lighthouse showed me my whole journey from above. From that height, I saw the pattern, the clarity, the reason each challenge mattered.

You pause, pen still in hand. The cabin is quiet except for the gentle lap of water against the hull.

Tomorrow we sail to Connection Cove. Marcus said there will be more voices. But after today—after learning to hear my own beneath the noise—I think I'm ready. Or at least ready to find out.

You close the journal and tuck it into the chest. Then you lie back on the bunk, the pendant pulsing softly at your heart.

Through the glass of the porthole, you can see the cliffs glowing faintly in reflected light. High above, the lighthouse sends its beam out across the open sea beyond the lagoon, steady, rhythmic, unwavering. Its glow spills over the rock face like a heartbeat, a signal from shore to sea.

You exhale.

You did it. You found the second key, claimed the second treasure chest, and remembered how to trust yourself.

Tomorrow will ask you to practice it again, in new ways, among new voices. But tonight, you know it's possible. You have proof. You have gifts. You have your own inner light, and it's enough to find your way.

The last thing you feel before sleep is the pendant's gentle rhythm against your skin, keeping time with your breath. A quiet pulse reminding you:

You are trustworthy.

You are worth listening to.

You have everything you need to find your way home.

IV

CONNECTION COVE

"Connection is why we're here;
it is what gives purpose and meaning to our lives."
— Brené Brown

11

Changing Tides

Dawn breaks over the hidden cove with a clarity that mirrors your emerging inner certainty.

You wake naturally to the faint, rhythmic sway of still water aboard the *Golden Harmony.* The heart pendant, warm and steady against your chest. A rhythmic reminder of the authentic choices you're learning to make. Light slips past the rocks, casting long shadows over the tranquil surface of the water.

There's a quiet confidence in your chest. You realize you're not merely going through the motions anymore. You're truly here, fully present, and eager to embrace what lies ahead.

After dressing, you glance at the two treasure chests. They feel substantial now, tangible proof of real growth from both islands.

On deck, Elaine is preparing a simple breakfast.

"Good morning, Captain," she says. The title doesn't sound like formality anymore. It feels earned.

"Beautiful morning for the next adventure. How are you feeling today?" she asks, those perceptive eyes noticing everything.

"Different." The word surprises you with its ease. "More solid. Like I'm actually here instead of going through the motions. And excited. I keep waiting for anxiety about what happens next, but it isn't coming."

"That's what happens when you learn to trust your inner compass," Elaine smiles. "The future stops feeling like a threat."

Over breakfast, conversation turns to the next island.

"Your third destination, Connection Cove, is different," she says. "Not a single landmass, but a cluster of districts connected by elegant bridges spanning crystal-blue water."

She unfurls the treasure map across the chart table. A delicate weave of land and sea unfolds.

"Your mission," she continues, "is to cross the Bridges of Understanding before entering the Circle of Belonging."

"It's beautiful," you murmur, your eyes tracing the intricate lines. "But complicated."

" Family and Friends Relationships usually are."

Her finger taps the circle where all bridges converge. "Not all bridges will be safe. And you won't cross them all. Only the ones for your journey. Some appear sturdy but are unstable. Others seem fragile yet hold incredible strength."

That familiar flutter of anticipation stirs. "How will I know which bridges to trust?"

"The same way you found the hidden entrance here, and navigated the dive."

Her gaze meets yours. "Your inner knowing will guide you. But this time the stakes are higher. It's not just about trusting yourself. It's about learning to trust others and allowing them to trust you."

"I've spent so long protecting myself," you admit. "Building walls to avoid disappointment."

"And what did they keep out?"

"The good connections too," you reveal softly, touching the pendant. "I thought I had to choose between being safe and being close."

"That's what you'll discover here." Elaine begins raising the anchor. "Connection isn't about having clear boundaries that let the right people in."

"These first two islands have been personal journeys of discovery and growth," you say. "Connection Cove feels..." you hesitate, "...vulnerable."

"The courage to be vulnerable, to show your true self, and let others do the same, is where genuine connection lives," she says. "But it requires knowing you're worthy of being known, flaws and all."

You slip on the mariner's compass and help adjust the sails before taking the wheel. Your hands move with growing surety.

"What challenges should I expect in Connection Cove?" you ask as the ship glides from the hidden inlet.

"The kind most people spend lifetimes avoiding," Elaine replies calmly. "Being seen. Showing up authentically, even when it's scary. Learning which connections drain your soul and which nourish it."

The passage back through the waterfall is triumphant, not tense. Water splits and streams around the *Golden Harmony's* bow, affirming your growing mastery of uncertain seas.

Once in the open ocean, the sail toward Connection Cove feels different. The voyage to Gratitude Shores was an escape. The journey to Intuitive Isle was a discovery.

This one feels like needing to come home to yourself. Maybe, in a deeper way.

"Tell me about the bridges," you ask, watching them come into view on the horizon.

"They're different because connection wears many faces. Stone bridges are built slowly. Solid and dependable. Driftwood bridges sway with the tides but carry you well. seaglass bridges shimmer in the light, formed from fragments once broken, now smoothed by tide and time into something strong enough to hold truth.

Closer now, each district reveals its own character: a garden paradise, a peaceful forest, a lively cityscape.

"Where do we dock?" you ask.

Elaine grins. "That's part of your challenge."

You steer toward the central island. The lighthouse here is shorter than the one on Intuitive Isle, built low and sturdy to mark the channels rather than warn of cliffs. There's no dock in sight.

"Calm seas," you say.

Elaine nods. "Set the wheel lock, then find your way."

With the course steady, you unfurl the map. Connection Cove sprawls like a spiderweb of channels and bridges radiating from the central light.

You disengage the lock and steer the boat around to the other side, toward the nearest opening.

"Trust your knowing," Elaine says. "But remember, this journey is different."

"How?"

"It's inhabited," she answers simply. "You'll meet others on their own quests for authentic connection. Some will walk beside you, others will challenge you, but all will teach you something. Your task is to remain open and real."

Rounding the island, the air grows dense with life. Construction clatters in the distance where tall angular buildings loom. The noise stirs resistance in your chest, urging you elsewhere.

Then you see it. A quiet inlet between the central island and a stretch of meadow. Reeds sway at its edge, wildflowers nodding in the breeze. A simple dock waits, connecting the meadow and the lighthouse by a slender bridge.

With practiced ease, you drop the sails and let the boat glide to rest. The *Golden Harmony* nudges the dock, a peaceful haven wrapped in grass and light. Your heart beats faster. *Trusting yourself was hard. Trusting others will be harder.*

"Ready?" Elaine asks, securing the line.

The air is soft, carrying the scent of sun-warmed grass. The meadow stretches inland, open and calm.

It feels right, confirmed by that quiet certainty in your heart.

You take a breath.

"Yes. I'm ready."

12

The Meadow

As you step off the *Golden Harmony*, the weathered wood beneath your feet feels almost alive, as though it grew naturally from the reeds surrounding it. The air smells of fresh grass and salt carried softly from the open sea. The light here is different, golden, gentle, almost forgiving. Laughter rises faintly from beyond the trees, light and musical, drifting toward you on a mild breeze.

"This district is The Meadow," Elaine says, her voice calm beside you. "It's inhabited because connection requires other people. You can't learn authentic relationship in solitude."

You pause, your hand resting on the worn rail of the dock. The past two islands had been about your own strength. Trusting your intuition and finding gratitude. But this one feels different. Your stomach tightens. You've spent so much of your life trying to belong and never quite getting it right. Always the odd one out, even in familiar rooms.

"What if I mess this up?"

"What would messing up look like?" Elaine asks.

You hesitate. "Saying the wrong thing. Not being interesting enough. Being too quiet or too much."

Elaine studies you for a moment, then smiles. "Those sound like fears about performing, not about connecting. What if there isn't a wrong way to be yourself?"

You try to picture what that would even feel like. "I don't understand."

"That's all right. You're not here to know the answer yet. You're here to explore it."

The path through the meadow winds gently toward a grove of oak trees. It isn't paved or marked, just worn by countless feet before yours. The grass brushes against your ankles. Butterflies rise from wildflowers as you pass, and the sunlight dances between branches above you. Each step draws you closer to the sound of voices, low and steady, like a babbling brook.

"What should I do when we get there?" you ask, partly to stall, partly because you truly don't know.

"Show up. Notice what happens. Let yourself be here instead of trying to get it right."

You take a slow breath and continue walking beside her. The air changes as you near the trees. A clearing opens, wide, sunlit, and full of conversation. About a dozen people sit on blankets arranged in a loose circle. Their postures are relaxed, their expressions alive. You sense it immediately. *Presence.*

Elaine stops beside you. "I see them," she says softly. Then, with a reassuring hand on your back, "You've got this. I'll meet you back here this afternoon."

Before you can ask where she's going, she turns toward another path and disappears among the trees. You're left standing at the edge of the clearing.

You think about leaving. About finding some quiet corner and pretending you meant to explore alone. But before you can retreat, a woman with silver hair and kind eyes catches your hesitation. She smiles. Warm, knowing, and without expectation.

Something in you suddenly exhales.

She rises and walks toward you, every step unhurried. "Welcome to The Meadow," she says. "I'm River."

Her name fits her presence. Steady. Flowing. You can't help but notice her eyes: clear, bright, unguarded. Up close, you see laugh lines around her eyes and silver threading through dark hair. Her attention feels undivided, without judgment, just a genuine welcome.

"We're in the middle of our morning sharing," she explains, gesturing to the circle. "It's where we practice speaking from truth instead of from what we think others want to hear."

Your stomach flutters. A sharing circle. You've sat in these kinds of circles before. Structured, polite, just deep enough to feel meaningful, never deep enough to be real.

"I'm not sure I'm good at this," you admit quietly.

"What makes you think that?" River asks.

"I never know how honest is too honest. Or not enough," you finally admit.

River's smile is steady and reassuring. "You're not alone in that," she says. "Most people have learned to measure honesty by how it will be received. Here, we practice letting it simply be true."

She pauses, then tilts her head slightly. "You can't speak authentically here until you believe your worth."

"Worth?" you echo, unsure.

"Yes. You matter because you're here. Not because of how you speak, or how much sense you make. Just because you exist."

"Come sit," River offers. "You don't have to share until you're ready."

A woman shifts her posture to make room for you and smiles, her long, blond braid swinging. You sit carefully, feeling all eyes turn toward you, curious but not invasive. Your mind immediately begins calculating: *What should I say? How can I sound composed? How can I avoid oversharing?*

"Before we continue," River says gently, "let's welcome our newest visitor. Would you like to tell us your name and what brought you to the island?"

This is it. You could give a safe answer: *personal growth, deepening connection, self-discovery, or something thoughtful but guarded.*

You open your mouth, but nothing comes out. Your mind is blank under pressure as the silence stretches, and people wait.

"I don't know what to say." Your voice shakes. "I'm trying to think of something to share, but it all feels either boring or too much. I don't know what you want to hear."

Your words tumble out clumsily. Heat rushes to your face. You wish you could start over.

But the awkward silence never comes. Instead, the woman with gardener's hands smiles. "Thank you," she says. "That was honest."

"Honesty is how connection happens," a man sitting directly across from you adds. "If you had given a polished intro you'd planned, we would have nodded and learned nothing. What you shared let us really see you."

River nods. "See? You just practiced authenticity. Not the version you rehearsed, but the truth of the moment."

You blink, unsure how to respond. "But I failed. I couldn't even introduce myself properly."

"You didn't fail. You were honest," River says. "You said what was real for you. That's what matters."

"That doesn't make sense. In life, you have to prove your worth."

River's tone stays gentle. "Worth isn't tied to articulation. It isn't earned. It just is because you exist."

An older woman speaks next. "I spent years pretending I didn't need anything," she admits, "because I thought people would see me as weak and needy. But all it did was keep me from being known."

You nod, a tear escaping before you can stop it. She smiles, not with pity, but understanding.

The next person begins to speak, then another.

When someone speaks of struggle or uncertainty, others listen, nodding with recognition and sometimes adding their parallel experience. There is no advice-giving or competing for depth.

A young woman shares feeling exhausted from wearing many masks. "I try to be the life of the party with one group, serious with another, and nurturing at home," she shares. "I lost track of my real self."

A man laughs as he shares how he constantly apologizes for taking up space, saying, "I catch myself apologizing for apologizing." A burst of immediate, empathetic laughter quickly joins his own. Others nod, clearly recognizing the feeling.

Their stories differ, yet every one echoes something you've felt. The exhaustion of acting as if, the fear of not belonging, the quiet wish to be seen without having to earn it.

When River's gaze meets yours again, there's no pressure, only invitation. "Would you like to add anything?" she asks.

You hesitate, but the words come on their own. "I think I've spent most of my life trying not to take up space. I thought being quiet made me safe. Invisible. But I'm realizing it also made me disappear from my own life."

The admission lands like a small truth cracking open inside you. The circle stays still, holding space without comment. No one tries to soothe or analyze you. They simply see you.

River's eyes soften. "And here you are now," she says quietly. "Visible."

You breathe more easily than you have all morning. For the first time, you feel what it's like to be in a space where silence doesn't mean absence. Where being quiet isn't failure.

After what feels like both minutes and hours, River says gently, "It's time to close our morning circle, but you're all welcome to stay here, or go off on your own. Do whatever feels right."

Some stay on the blankets. Others drift toward quieter spaces, and a few pair off for more intimate conversations. You notice no one seems to be following social obligations or unspoken rules.

You stand. Elaine isn't back yet. Feeling uncertain what to do, you wander for a while to a sunny patch of meadow, sit, and lean back on your hands. The permission to simply be feels strange, like wearing a new skin. You've spent so long earning your place that stillness itself feels almost rebellious.

In the distance, an older man works alone near a woodpile, loading wood into a wheelbarrow. His broad shoulders move with steady, purposeful efficiency. You watch him for a moment, and something catches in your throat.

Your own father moved like that. Providing through action because words felt dangerous. You wanted him to tell you that you mattered, that you were special, that he saw you. But he built you a treehouse instead. Fixed your bike. Taught you to change a tire. Love in the only language he knew.

You never understood it was love until now. Until watching this stranger remind you that your father's silence wasn't rejection. It was the best he could offer with the tools he'd been given. He was doing what his father taught him: show up, work hard, provide. Never complain. Never burden others with feelings.

Worth doesn't need an audience, you realize. Your father taught you that, even if he couldn't say it out loud.

The sun is higher now, warming the meadow fully. You watch as people continue their natural patterns, recognizing a quality to the interactions. People being genuinely present with each other, rather than managing expectations.

Eventually, you stand, brushing grass from your clothes. Walking past the circle, you wander toward a trail where the ground seems to dip toward a body of water. The air carries the scent of damp earth and wild mint. Nearby, you hear laughter, light and unguarded. Turning your attention toward the sound, you notice a few people skipping stones across the glimmering surface, their reflections flickering within each ripple.

You stop, watching from a distance.

A middle-aged woman with curly red hair and freckles waves you over. "We need someone to break the tie," she calls out, her voice warm and teasing.

You hesitate. "I'm not very good at that."

"That's perfect," she says. "None of us are."

Something in her tone makes you smile. You step closer, the damp grass soft and springy beneath your feet as you near the water. A man with rolled sleeves and wet trousers up to his ankles nods toward the water. "All right, new rule," he says, holding up a stone. "Winner is whoever makes the most skips."

"Biggest splash," announces another voice.

The rules keep changing until no one is keeping track of them.

The woman who invited you hands you a smooth, flat stone. "Your turn."

You surprise yourself, a laugh escaping at your first attempt, sending the rock flying before it takes a nose dive. Without hesitation, you pick up another rock, crouch down, flick your wrist, and send it flying. This time, it bounces twice before sinking.

A roar of applause erupts, as though you've set a record, and something in your chest cracks open. Not breaking. Releasing.

You double over laughing, and it's the kind of laugh you haven't heard from yourself in years. The belly-deep, tears-streaming kind that shakes loose something that's been calcified.

Your body remembers this. Being a girl who wasn't monitoring every move. Who laughed without checking if it was too loud. Who played without performing.

When was the last time you laughed like this? Not the careful laugh you give at someone's joke, or the polite laugh that keeps conversation moving. This laugh—unguarded, full-bodied, alive.

You realize: *not since before you learned to be careful.*

It's ridiculous and joyful.

You pull out your phone, the impulse automatic to capture this moment, share this joy. Your thumb hovers over your husband's name. You imagine sending him a photo: grass-stained knees, flushed cheeks, this feeling of being fully alive.

But you already know what would happen. He'd text back "nice" or "having fun?" and return to watching TV. A polite acknowledgment that would somehow make this moment feel smaller. Less real.

When did you stop sharing your joy with him? When did you learn that your delight was an interruption rather than an invitation? That your aliveness was something to manage around his steady, controlled existence?

You pocket the phone and stay here, in this moment, with people who actually see the joy instead of tolerating it. Who laugh with you instead of at the fact that you're laughing. Who meet your energy instead of dampening it.

The realization sits quiet but firm: *some people can't hold your bigness.* That doesn't mean you need to make yourself smaller. It means you need to find people who can.

Others join in the fun. People make up victory dances. Someone slips in the mud and sends a spray of water across the group. Laughter breaks open, unguarded and contagious.

For a few moments, you let your guard down. There's no thought of what anyone thinks of you. No measuring up, or worrying how you sound or look. You're just being.

When the laughter finally softens, you all sit down on the bank, catching your breath. The man beside you shakes his head, grinning. "I don't think anyone actually won."

The younger woman glances over, smiling. "You've got a good laugh. You fit right in."

The words settle in gently. You look out at the water, the ripples catching the light. It feels strange and wonderful to be included for no reason at all.

The conversation drifts easily, full of simple things. Favorite places to walk, the wild mint that grows along the channel, where the herons nest this time of year. Some of the faces are older, weathered by sun and time, others young and bright. The mix feels natural, the kind of balance you didn't know you needed.

Eventually, a few people stand and begin to head back across the meadow. The middle-aged woman lingers. "If you follow the path up that way," she says, pointing toward a rise beyond the reeds, "there's an overlook. You can see all the bridges from up top. We usually watch the sunset there."

She pauses, looking at you with quiet curiosity. "You'd be welcome to join if you feel like it."

You meet her gaze and nod slowly. "Maybe I will."

"Good," she says, her smile soft and sincere.

"Can I ask you something?"

"Sure. Anything."

"I keep trying to figure out what the right way to be is, and everyone here seems to be saying there isn't a right way. How can I interact with people if there's no right way to do it?"

She smiles. "You just relax into it. Like you just did. You say what's true instead of what sounds good. You let yourself be uncertain instead of pretending to be confident."

"Easier said than done."

"It can be, at first," she acknowledges. "Because we've all learned that uncertainty and honesty are dangerous, that they'll lead to rejection or judgment. But in reality, the opposite is true. Being real with people leads to connection."

"Thanks," you smile.

"You're doing great. I'd like to get to know you," she adds.

You stand, pick up another stone, and toss it lightly. It skips once, then disappears.

"You've got this," the woman says as she walks away.

You stay for a while longer, watching the light shift across the water. You think about how easy it was to laugh, how natural it felt to join in without planning it.

Maybe friendship isn't something you have to earn. Maybe it's something that begins when you stop trying so hard to deserve it.

A familiar voice carries on the breeze. Elaine is walking toward you, her shadow long in the late afternoon sun.

"How was it?" she asks.

You stand, brushing off your hands. "Unexpected," you say. "But good. I think I understand what it feels like to belong, even just for a moment."

Elaine looks toward the ridge where the light has turned golden. "There's more of that ahead," she says softly. "Connection doesn't stop here. It grows, one small moment at a time."

Beyond her, you can see the stone bridge arching toward the next district. Its surface glows in the fading light, steady and strong.

You look back once toward the water, where the last ripples fade into calm. Then you turn toward the bridge, feeling both grounded and ready for what's next.

13

Community Square

The water below the stone bridge is crystal clear, and you can see schools of colorful fish swimming in synchronized patterns, together but distinct, each maintaining its own identity within the group.

"Stone bridges represent relationships built on solid foundations," Elaine explains, running her hand along the smooth stone railing. "They take time to construct, but once they're built, they can support real weight."

As you step off the bridge, Community Square reveals itself, bustling with activity. Unlike the contemplative atmosphere of The Meadow, this place hums with the energy of people engaged in shared pursuits. You can see gardens where people work side by side, outdoor workshops where groups collaborate on various projects, and cozy gathering spaces where conversations flow naturally among clusters of two or three people.

A young man approaches, paint splattered across his shirt and hands, a streak of blue across his cheek. He's grinning, energetic, maybe late twenties. He gestures enthusiastically toward a large wall where several people are painting a colorful mural.

"Perfect timing!" he says. "We could use more hands. I'm Tony."

"What are you painting?" you ask, studying the half-finished mural. Swirls of color, abstract shapes, what might be waves or wings.

"Community," he says simply. "Everyone adds what they feel. No plan. No rules. Just… contribution." He holds out a brush. "Want to try?"

You take the brush hesitantly, dip it into a container of paint, and walk to face the mural. The paint is thick, the color a deep coral pink. You add a stroke to the lower section. Tentative, uncertain if it belongs.

"Perfect," Tony says, and you can't tell if he's being kind or genuine.

Elaine picks up a brush too, adding her own marks, bold yellow streaks that somehow work with everything else. She's smiling, relaxed, clearly enjoying herself.

Tony steps back, surveying the wall. "The whole square is like this," he says. "Different groups, different activities. Try things. Notice how you feel. Some will energize you. Others will drain you."

"So I'm supposed to… wander around trying different groups?" you ask.

"Exactly. Find your people by noticing where you feel most yourself." He gestures around the square. "We'll be here all afternoon if you want to come back. No pressure."

Elaine touches your arm lightly. "I'm going to explore a bit. Find me later?"

You nod, and she disappears into the square's activity, leaving you standing with brush in hand, Tony already back at work on the mural, humming to himself.

You add another brushstroke. Then another. It's freeing, somehow, not knowing what you're making. Just contributing. After a few minutes, you set down the brush.

"Thank you," you tell Tony.

"Anytime," he says without looking up. "Really. Anytime."

You wander away from the mural, taking in the square's rhythm. Near a cluster of shaded tables, you spot a group of older women playing cards. They look comfortable, settled, talking quietly between plays. One of them notices you watching and waves you over.

"Need a fourth?" she calls. "We're just playing for fun."

You approach, grateful for the invitation. They make space, deal you in, and explain the game. Something simple, easy to follow. The cards are worn soft, the table scarred with years of use.

The women are pleasant. Kind. They ask about your journey, where you're from, make small observations about the weather. Surface things. Safe things.

You play a few hands. Smile. Nod. Contribute appropriate comments.

But something feels… flat. Not wrong, exactly. Just not right. These are nice people, but the conversation never deepens. Never becomes real. It skims along the surface, polite and careful, and you realize with surprising clarity: *this isn't your energy.*

You're not ready for boring. Not anymore.

After another hand, you set down your cards gently. "Thank you for including me," you say. "I think I'm going to keep exploring."

"Of course, dear," one woman says warmly. "Come back anytime."

They mean it. They're genuinely kind. But as you walk away, you feel lighter, not heavier. That's new. Leaving without guilt, recognizing that nice people can still be the wrong fit.

You find yourself drawn toward a community garden tucked behind the main square. The space is quieter here, more contemplative. Raised beds overflow with vegetables and herbs. A few people work among the rows, some chatting softly, others in comfortable silence.

You pause at the edge, watching. An older man tends tomato plants with careful attention, his movements deliberate and unhurried. A younger woman plants something in a far bed, earbuds in, working to her own rhythm. It's collaborative but not demanding. Purposeful but peaceful.

Different from the card table. Different from the mural. Just… different.

You're about to move on when someone passes by carrying a basket of harvested greens. She pauses, noticing you.

"Could you grab some of those tomatoes?" she asks, gesturing toward the plants the older man is working near. "We need them in the kitchen. Just the ripe ones. You'll see which ones are ready."

The request is so casual, so assuming of your competence, that you find yourself nodding. The older man looks up as you approach.

"Taking some for the kitchen?" he asks.

"If that's all right."

"Absolutely," he says simply, and returns to his work.

You pick carefully, choosing tomatoes that give slightly under your thumb, still warm from the sun. When your hands are full, you follow the woman's path toward where cooking smells drift through the air.

The cooking area is set up under a large pergola strung with lights. Several people work at different stations, chopping, stirring, and kneading. The smell of fresh herbs and simmering vegetables fills the air, and you notice the smell of fresh-baked bread, drawing you deeper in.

"Fresh tomatoes!" someone calls when they see what you're carrying. A woman with flour in her hair and a genuine smile takes them from you. "Perfect timing. Thank you."

"Want to help?" she asks, already rinsing the tomatoes. "We're making dinner for anyone who'd like to share a meal together."

You roll up your sleeves and find yourself naturally falling into the rhythm of chopping vegetables alongside others. The conversation flows easily, sometimes focused on the cooking, sometimes wandering to stories and experiences. What strikes you is how comfortable the silences are. No one feels compelled to fill every moment with chatter.

"I've never been good at cooking," you admit as you work on dicing onions, your eyes watering.

As the meal comes together, you notice people arranging tables under string lights that cast a warm glow over the gathering space. People bring dishes they've prepared, and soon there's a feast that no single person could have created alone, but that emerged naturally from everyone's authentic contributions.

During dinner, you find yourself seated between a quiet artist who shares profound insights in few words and an animated storyteller who makes everyone laugh with her observations about island life. The conversation moves organically from serious topics to playful banter, and you notice how everyone seems comfortable being exactly who they are. No one is performing. No one is trying to impress. The lack of pretense makes everything feel lighter, easier.

"This feels so different from dinner parties back home," you mention to Elaine, who's sitting across from you.

"How so?" she asks.

"There's no performance here. No one is trying to impress anyone or say what they think others want to hear. But somehow the conversation is more interesting, not less."

"That's what happens when people feel safe to be authentic," the artist you recognize from the mural, sitting beside you now, observes. "The real thoughts and feelings people have are always more fascinating than the socially acceptable ones most usually share."

Tony appears with a plate piled high, squeezing in at the end of the table. "Best part of my day," he announces. "Painting is good, but eating is better." He grins at you. "You didn't come back to the mural. Found something better?"

"I tried a few things," you say. "Card game. Garden. This felt right."

"That's the whole point," he says, mouth full. "Try. Notice. Choose."

After dinner, as people begin to clean up collaboratively, you notice how the work gets done efficiently and cheerfully. There's no awkwardness about who should do what. No resentment. Just natural, easy cooperation.

"I should probably help more with cleanup," you say, starting to feel guilty about not doing enough.

"You've been helping all evening," The lady, who asked you to grab tomatoes from the garden, points out gently. "Community isn't about keeping score or making sure everyone does exactly equal amounts. It's about everyone contributing authentically according to what they can offer."

The sun is lower now, painting the sky in shades of orange and pink. You remember the invitation from this morning, the overlook, the sunset.

"I think I'll go," you say to Elaine. "To that overlook."

"Mind if I join you?" Elaine asks.

"I'd like that."

The woman from stone-skipping is already waiting at the trail head, leaning against a tree, watching the square settle into evening. When she sees you approaching, she straightens, smiling.

"You came."

"Maybe turned into yes," you reply. "This is Elaine. Elaine, this is..." You pause, realizing. "I don't think I ever got your name."

"Clare," she says, extending her hand to Elaine. "We met at the water this morning. Throwing stones like children."

"The best kind of activity," Elaine says warmly, shaking her hand.

Clare links her arm through yours easily, and the three of you start up the trail together. It winds through trees, opens onto rock, and suddenly you can see everything. The cove below, the districts spreading out around the central island, the water catching the last of the light.

The three of you stand together at the edge, watching the sun sink lower, painting the water in shades of gold and coral. The lighthouse's lamp beginning to glow as dusk deepens.

No one speaks. The silence is comfortable, full. This is what you didn't know you needed. Not constant conversation, but presence. Being with people who don't require you to fill every moment with words.

When the sun finally slips below the horizon, Clare sighs contentedly. "Never gets old," she says.

As you start back down the trail, you notice a warm glow through the trees and catch the scent of wood smoke.

"Is that a fire?" you ask.

"The fire pit near the lighthouse," Elaine answers. "A gathering spot in the evenings."

You turn to Clare. "Want to come with us?"

Clare's face brightens. "I'd love that."

You walk over together, following the path toward the lighthouse. The fire pit's flames dance in the darkness ahead. A handful of people have gathered. Some you recognize from dinner, others you haven't met. Tony is there, guitar in hand, playing something soft and wandering.

And there, on a log bench, sits the older man from the woodpile this morning. The one who reminded you of your father.

You settle onto a bench with your new friend and Elaine, watching the fire, listening to Tony's music. The old man pokes at the fire with a stick, adjusting logs with the same quiet competence you noticed earlier. His movements are economical, purposeful. He doesn't speak, doesn't need to. His presence is enough.

You watch him, and something surfaces. Not the memory from this morning, but something older. Your father, at a campfire when you were small. The way he'd tend the flames.

"You all right?" Elaine asks quietly.

"Yeah," you say, and mean it. "I'm learning that people show love in different ways. And that's okay."

The fire crackles. Tony's music drifts into something brighter, and a few people start singing along softly. Your new friend smiles. You smile back. This is community. Not one thing, but many things. Trying and choosing. Leaving when it's wrong, staying when it's right. Being yourself and letting others be themselves. Contributing what you can. Asking for what you need.

After a while, Tony sets down his guitar, grabs a bag of marshmallows, and settles onto a log near you.

"Want one?" he offers.

You take one, and he hands you a long stick that's been resting by the fire. "So," he says, spearing his own marshmallow, "how'd your first day here treat you?"

"It's been a full day," you say, holding your marshmallow near the flames, watching it slowly brown. "Some things felt right. Some didn't."

"That's the idea," Tony says. "Most people never figure that out. They either try to fit everywhere and burn out, or they fit nowhere and give up. But you... You're learning to choose."

"Choose what?"

"Where to spend your energy. Who deserves your time. Boundaries."

The word lands differently than you expected. Boundaries. Sitting here, thinking about the card table you left, the kitchen you stayed in, it feels like... permission. To choose. To say yes to what fills you and no to what drains you.

"I always thought saying no made me selfish," you say quietly.

"Saying yes to everything means saying no to yourself," Elaine says.

"So finding my people is about trying things and paying attention?" you ask.

"Exactly," Tony says. "And then having the courage to leave what doesn't fit and invest in what does."

Your new friend squeezes your arm. "I'm glad you invested your time here," she says. "At the stones. At the sunset. Here."

"Me too," you say, and feel the truth of it settle in your chest.

The fire burns lower. People begin to drift away, heading back to wherever they're staying. You stand, brushing off your clothes, and look toward the water. The *Golden Harmony* sits peacefully in the channel, a lantern glowing on her deck.

"Ready?" Elaine asks.

You look back at the fire pit. Tony waves. The old man nods once, a small acknowledgment. Your new friend walks with you partway, then pauses at a fork in the path.

"I'll see you tomorrow?" she asks.

"Maybe," you say, then smile. "Probably."

She hugs you quickly, warmly, and heads off down the moonlit path.

You and Elaine walk the rest of the way in comfortable silence. When you reach the boat, you pause, looking back toward the lighthouse. Its beam sweeps across the water in a steady rhythm.

"What's next?" you ask.

"Tomorrow," Elaine says. "We'll explore more tomorrow. Tonight, rest. Let today settle."

You nod, suddenly aware of how tired you are. Good tired. The kind that comes from really living instead of just going through the motions.

Below deck, you change into a nightgown and lie down. Through the porthole, you can see the lighthouse beam sweeping past.

You found your people today. Some of them, anyway. Not all of them. But enough to remember what it feels like to belong without performing.

You don't lie awake wondering if you said the right things or made the right impression. You just rest, knowing you showed up as yourself. And that was enough.

14

The Forest

You wake to morning light streaming through your porthole, feeling rested. Last night's fire still warms your chest. The connections made, the laughter shared, belonging without performing. But as you dress and head to the deck, you notice something else beneath the warmth. A tightness.

Elaine is waiting at the rail, looking toward distant trees. "Morning," she says, studying your face. "How are you feeling?"

"Good," you say honestly. "Last night was… everything I needed." You pause, hand going to your chest. "But there's something else. Like something's waiting."

Elaine nods slowly.

"The Forest. And beyond it, Heritage Heights," she simply says, without explanation, as she continues to look toward the trees. Maybe… even beyond.

Your stomach tightens at the name, *Heritage Heights,* though you don't know why. Maybe, don't want to know. You only say, "Then let's go."

You help Elaine prepare the small rowboat.

As you push off from the dock, you notice the water ahead isn't open. Narrow canals spider-web every which way, creating a maze of passages. "Which way?" you ask.

Elaine points. "Follow the current. It'll show us." You row together through the twisting waterways.

The channels are barely wider than the boat in places, forcing you to navigate carefully. Mangrove roots reach into the water. Reeds brush the sides of the boat. The water itself shifts from deep blue to shallow green as the bottom rises and falls.

"Pay attention to the rhythm," Elaine says. "Water always knows where it's going."

You notice she's right. There's a pull, a subtle current threading through the maze. When you follow it rather than fight it, the rowing becomes easier. After twenty minutes of winding navigation, the channels open into a wider inlet. And there, spanning from one rocky shore to another, is the rope bridge. It's suspended high above the water, not over calm sea, but over a narrow gorge where tidal water rushes through with surprising force. The sound of it echoes off the rock walls.

"We have to cross that?" you ask, staring up at it.

"It's the only way into this part of the forest."

You row to the landing, tie up the boat, and climb the rough stone steps carved into the cliff face. By the time you reach the top, you're breathing hard. The rope bridge stretches ahead, swaying in the wind. Below, water churns white over rocks.

"Don't look down," Elaine advises. "Look where you're going."

As you step onto the first wooden plank, the bridge sways immediately beneath your weight. You grip the rope railings, your body tensing.

"Don't fight it," Elaine says behind you. "Feel how it moves. Work with it, not against it."

You take another step. The bridge sways more. Your instinct is to freeze, to make yourself rigid, to control the movement.

"Breathe," Elaine reminds. "Let your body move with the bridge. Trust it."

You exhale and soften your knees, allowing your body to respond to the bridge's rhythm instead of resisting it. You continue across. The bridge holds you, moves, adapts to your weight and the wind.

By the time you reach the other side, something in your body has shifted. You feel less tense. More fluid.

"Remember that feeling," Elaine says. "You'll need it today."

The forest path ahead is narrow, almost overgrown. Trees press close on both sides, branches reaching across the trail, roots breaking through the packed earth.

"It's dense," you observe.

"At first," Elaine agrees. "But watch."

You begin walking, and immediately you have to duck under a low branch, step carefully over an exposed root. The path demands attention. Presence. You can't rush through or zone out.

After a few minutes of careful navigation, you notice something.

"The trees," you say, pausing to look around. "They're close to the path, but they give each other space."

Elaine stops beside you, following your gaze. "What do you mean?"

You point to two massive oaks on either side of the trail. Their branches reach toward each other overhead, creating a canopy. But they don't tangle. Don't compete. Each tree has its own distinct space, even while being close enough to touch.

"They're near each other, but not crowding," you say. "Their roots must do the same thing underground. Taking what they need but not choking each other out."

"That's intimacy with boundaries," Elaine says simply. "Close enough to shelter each other from storms. Far enough apart to grow without restriction."

You keep walking, noticing more now.

A clearing where wildflowers bloom in the space between trees. Sunlight filtering down because the canopy isn't solid. There are gaps, openings, room for light.

"What happens when trees grow too close?" you ask.

"They compete for resources. Sunlight. Water. Nutrients. One usually dominates and the other suffers. Or they both become stunted, neither growing to full height." Elaine pushes aside a branch so you can pass. "The same happens with people. When there's no space between, someone always shrinks."

The words land quietly in your chest.

You think about relationships where you made yourself smaller. Compressed your needs, your voice, your presence to fit into spaces that had no room for your full self.

"I've been the one who shrinks," you say.

"Yes. But that wasn't generosity. That was survival."

The path winds deeper into the forest. You come to a stream cutting across the trail, water moving steadily over smooth stones.

"How do we cross?" you ask, looking for a bridge or stepping stones.

"Carefully," Elaine says, and steps directly into the water.

You follow, your feet sinking into the cold stream. The current pushes against your legs, not strong enough to knock you over, but present. Constant. You have to lean slightly into it to maintain balance.

"Notice the banks," Elaine says as you both reach the other side.

You turn to look. The stream has clear edges. Soil and stone and root systems create natural boundaries that contain the water, give it direction, keep it from spreading formless across the forest floor.

"Without banks, it would just be a swamp," you observe. "The water would go everywhere and nowhere."

"Exactly. Boundaries don't restrict the river. They give it somewhere to go. Power. Direction. Without them, the water loses its force, becomes stagnant."

You stand there dripping, understanding blooming. "I thought boundaries would make me less loving. Less giving. But maybe they're what let love actually flow instead of just… spreading thin and going nowhere."

"Yes."

You continue walking, clothes drying slowly in the filtered sunlight. The path climbs upward now, becoming steeper. Your breathing quickens. Your legs burn slightly.

"Why is the path getting harder?" you ask.

"Because you're going somewhere," Elaine says from behind you. "Easy paths that require nothing usually lead nowhere worth going."

You climb over a fallen log, bark rough under your hands. The obstacle forces you to slow down, to be more deliberate.

At the top of the rise, you pause to catch your breath. Looking back, you can see how far you've climbed, the path winding down through the trees behind you.

"I couldn't have rushed that," you say.

"No. Some things require effort. Discomfort. The willingness to be challenged." Elaine joins you at the summit. "That's true for boundaries too. Setting them is hard. Especially the first time. Especially with people who are used to you having none."

"What happens when you finally set one?"

"Some people respect it. Some people test it. Some people get angry because your boundary inconveniences them." She pauses. "That's when you learn who's safe and who isn't."

The path descends now, gentler. The trees begin to thin, letting in more light. You can hear something ahead… water, but different from the stream. Rhythmic. Steady.

"Is that the ocean?"

"The shore, yes. We're almost there."

As you walk, you notice something new. Mushrooms growing in a perfect circle at the base of a tree. Each one distinct, separate, but part of a connected network underground.

You kneel down, studying them. "They look independent, but they're actually all connected underneath, aren't they?"

"Mycelium network," Elaine confirms. "The whole forest floor is interconnected through fungal threads. Trees share resources through it. Warn each other of danger. Support each other's growth. But each tree is still distinct. Still itself."

"So connection doesn't mean losing yourself."

"No. Real connection requires you to be yourself. Otherwise, what's connecting? Just performances and personas. Not actual people."

You stand and keep walking, the sound of waves growing louder.

The forest opens suddenly onto a shore. Not a beach exactly, more like a rocky edge where forest meets water. Smooth stones, weathered driftwood, the scent of salt strong in the air.

The view is expansive. Water stretching to the horizon, reflecting morning light in a thousand shifting points.

"Come sit," Elaine says, settling onto a large, flat rock near the water's edge.

You join her, grateful to rest. Your legs are tired from the climb. Your mind is full of everything the forest showed you.

For a while, neither of you speaks. Just the sound of waves lapping against stone, birds calling from the trees behind you, wind moving through branches.

"Can I ask you something?" you finally say.

"Always."

"Why do I feel like I'm too much? Like my needs, my emotions, my... everything. Too much for people to want to deal with?"

Elaine is quiet for a moment, looking out at the water.

"Where did you learn that?" she asks gently.

"From people who needed me to be easier. Simpler. Less complicated."

"And what did you do with that?"

"I tried to become less. Need less. Feel less. Be less."

"How did that work?"

You almost laugh, but it comes out bitter. "Terribly. I felt invisible. Resentful. Like I was shrinking myself into nothing and still somehow being too much."

Elaine picks up a smooth stone, turns it over in her hand. "Here's what I want you to understand. The people who made you feel like you were too much? They weren't telling you the truth about yourself. They were showing you their limits."

The words settle into you like stones dropping into still water.

"What do you actually need?" Elaine asks. "Not what you've been told you should need, but what you genuinely need to feel secure and connected."

You think about this honestly. "I need reassurance sometimes when I'm feeling insecure. I need to be able to talk through my feelings when something's bothering me. I need to know that someone's actually choosing me, not just tolerating me."

"Do those needs sound excessive to you?"

When you hear them spoken aloud, they don't. They sound basic. Human. "No."

"But how do I know what I deserve?"

"Think about last night. The people around that fire. When they shared vulnerabilities and struggles, did you think they were too much?"

"No. I thought they were being honest and brave."

"So why do you hold yourself to a different standard than you hold everyone else?" Elaine's question hangs in the salt air. "You extend understanding and acceptance to others' needs, but you can't imagine that you might deserve the same."

The truth of it lands like a physical blow. "I don't know how to believe I deserve that."

"Then that's the work. Not becoming less needy or less complicated or less emotional, but learning to believe that you're worthy of love exactly as you are."

She pauses, picking up another stone.

"The forest taught you about boundaries this morning. Trees that give each other space. Rivers that have banks. Networks that connect while staying distinct. That's what healthy relationships look like. Not you shrinking yourself to fit. But both people maintaining their own space, their own needs, their own identity, while also being close."

You watch the waves, letting her words sink in.

"I've been afraid of having boundaries," you admit. "Afraid it would make me difficult. Selfish. Push people away."

"Boundaries don't push the right people away. They filter out the people who need you to be boundary-less in order to feel comfortable. The people who need you to not be yourself."

She stands, brushing sand from her clothes. "Come on. There's more bridges to cross today."

You stand too, looking where she's pointing.

In the distance, a bridge made entirely of driftwood spans from this shore to another part of the island. Each piece of wood is different, weathered by salt and time into distinct shapes and shades. Yet somehow they all fit together to create a stable pathway.

"That leads to Heritage Heights," Elaine says. "Where you'll face the foundation. The beliefs carved into you before you knew to question them."

Your stomach tightens. But something is different now. You're not going there empty or unprepared. The forest filled you with lessons. The shore gave you words for wounds you couldn't name.

"I'm scared," you admit.

"Good. That means you're paying attention." She looks at you directly. "But you're ready. You know about boundaries now. You understand that your needs aren't burdens. You see that you've been trying to fit into spaces too small for your fullness. That knowledge will matter when you face what's ahead."

You take a breath, looking at the driftwood bridge.

"Will you be with me?"

"Every step."

Together, you begin walking across the rocky shore toward the bridge. Each piece of driftwood is unique, fitted together with obvious care. Some pieces are smooth and pale, others dark and gnarled. But they create something beautiful and functional together, not despite their differences, but because of them.

As your feet touch the first weathered plank, you think about what the forest taught you.

Space and closeness. Banks and flow. Distinct and connected. All at once.

The bridge sways slightly but holds firm. You keep walking, Elaine beside you, the afternoon sun warming your back as you cross to Heritage Heights.

Whatever waits there, you're ready to face it. Not alone. Worthy of taking up exactly the space you need.

15

Heritage Heights

Halfway across the driftwood bridge, you feel something shift in your chest. Not painful. More like something that's been caged suddenly testing the bars.

Your hand goes to your sternum.

"What is it?" Elaine asks, noticing.

"Something's changing. Moving." You search for words. "Like something waking up."

"Keep walking. Sometimes the journey itself begins the healing."

You continue across, one weathered plank at a time. With each step, that sensation in your chest loosens slightly, then tightens again, then loosens more. Like something breathing for the first time in years.

By the time you reach the other side, something fundamental has shifted. Not resolved. But opened.

The shift from forest to city is immediate and jarring. One moment, natural wood beneath your feet. The next, smooth stone. Deliberate. Constructed. Built.

The plaza is paved with stone placed with obvious intention. You look down and see words etched into some of the pavers right beneath your feet:

not enough

too much

must be earned

dangerous to speak

invisible

don't matter

Hundreds of them, worn smooth by countless feet walking over them without seeing.

"Everyone walks on their beliefs," Elaine says quietly, "until they choose to look down."

You stand there, reading the words beneath your feet. Each one familiar. Each one something you've thought about yourself at some point.

The buildings around the plaza rise in layers. Some foundations look ancient, weathered stone holding up gleaming modern structures. Others are actively under construction, scaffolding everywhere, workers moving with purpose. And the glass. So much glass. Every building surface reflects and refracts, creating layers of images that shift as you move.

"It looks different from the other districts," you observe.

"Because this is where beliefs become visible. Where you can see the architecture of what you've been living inside." Elaine gestures toward the buildings. "Everything here is constructed. Nothing is natural or organic. That's the point."

You notice people moving through the streets with intention. Some entering buildings, others gathered at construction sites, still others standing before glass walls as if studying their own reflections.

"Where do we start?" you ask.

Elaine points across the plaza to a wide staircase that descends beneath the city streets. "Down. You can't understand what's been built until you see the foundation."

As you walk toward the staircase, you notice words carved into the sides of buildings, etched into cornerstones and door frames:

Children should be seen, not heard.

Don't be difficult.

Stop making a fuss.

What will people think.

Family comes first.

Good girls don't.

"These aren't the beliefs we carry about ourselves," Elaine observes. "These are the words other people use to build walls around us."

Your throat tightens with each one you recognize.

Passed down through generations. Installed in childhood before anyone knows to question them." Elaine pauses at the top of the stairs. "Some people carry them their whole lives without ever seeing they're there. You're choosing to look."

The widening staircase spirals down, descending underground. The walls are carved too. Layer upon layer of inherited beliefs, passed down through generations.

At the bottom, the space opens vast and dim. The walls here are ancient bedrock, the place where the deepest beliefs live.

You walk slowly, running your hand along the cool stone. Reading what's been carved here:

*I am **not enough***

***Love** must be earned*

*My needs are **burdens***

I am too much

Some words carved deeper into the stone than the others, each hitting you harder than the surface words in the plaza. These are the roots.

Then you see it.

One section of wall, darker than the rest, the words carved so deeply they cast shadows even in the dim light:

I am not important

Your breath stops. The tightness in your chest feels like a fist clenching.

"This is mine," you whisper.

You reach out with shaking fingers, touch the cold stone. The carving is old. Ancient, almost. The letters are deep, as if they've been believed for a very long time.

Movement catches your eye.

Suddenly, in the shadows, you sense something small shift.

You move toward it slowly, drawn by recognition deeper than memory.

Your heart pounds as your eyes adjust to the darkness.

A child sits there. Knees pulled tight to chest. Arms wrapped around herself. Back pressed against the stone wall. Alone among all these carved beliefs.

She looks up slowly, and the world tilts.

Her eyes are your eyes. The shape of her face, the way she holds herself small. You know her immediately because she is you.

The you who learned these words were true. Who believed them so completely she came down here to live with them. Because if they're true, at least there are no surprises. No hope that turns to disappointment.

For a long moment, neither of you moves. Neither of you breathes.

Then you crouch down very slowly, making yourself smaller, less threatening. Keeping distance between you.

"Hi," you say softly.

She watches you with careful, wary eyes. Not hostile. Just guarded.

"My name is…" you start, then stop. She knows who you are. She is you. "I came to find you."

She doesn't speak. Just watches.

Elaine remains near the stairs, a quiet presence. Not interfering. Just holding the space.

"How long have you been down here?" you ask gently.

The child doesn't answer."

Her eyes fill, but the tears don't fall. She's learned not to let them.

"Can I sit with you?" you ask. "I won't come closer. I'll just sit here for a while. Would that be okay?"

She studies you for a long moment. Then gives the smallest nod.

You settle onto the cold stone floor, back against a different wall, giving her space and control. The silence stretches. You don't rush it. She needs to know you're not going to force anything.

Finally, the child speaks. Her voice is so quiet you have to strain to hear it.

"Did you come to tell me to leave?"

"No."

She looks surprised.

"I came because I wanted to understand. Why are you here. Why you stayed."

"I'm supposed to be here." Her voice is flat. Matter-of-fact. "This is where I belong."

"Why do you think that?"

She gestures to the carved wall behind her without looking at it. "Because it's true. It says so right there."

You look at the words. ***I am not important***

"And you believe them?"

"Of course. Why would they be carved in stone if they weren't true?"

The logic is perfect. Heartbreaking. A child's understanding of permanence.

"Can I tell you something?" you ask gently.

She waits, still wary but listening.

"I've been living with that belief my whole life. Up there." You gesture toward the stairs, toward the world above. "And it's made everything so hard. So lonely. I thought if I just tried harder, performed better, made myself more useful, then maybe I would matter. But it never worked. Because the belief was always there."

The child is very still, absorbing this.

"So I came down here," you continue, "because I wanted to understand where it came from. And I found you."

"I didn't ask you to come."

"I know. But I came anyway. Because you've been carrying this alone for a long time, and I thought maybe..." you search for words. "Maybe we could figure it out together. Where this belief came from. Whether it's actually true. Whether you have to stay here."

"It's safer here," she says with an edge to her voice. Something fierce and protective. "I tried, you know. I tried to matter. I was brave sometimes. Sometimes I felt like maybe I did matter. But then someone would overlook me, or dismiss me, or not see me, and I'd fall back down. Harder each time."

She pulls her knees tighter to her chest. "Eventually I just... stopped. I came down here, where I already knew the answer. It hurt less to accept the belief than to keep fighting it over and over. I got too tired to keep trying."

The truth of it hits you in the chest. This is exactly what you've been doing. Protecting yourself from disappointment by not expecting to matter.

"That makes sense," you tell her honestly. "You're not wrong for thinking that way. For protecting yourself. When you're small, you find ways to make it hurt less."

She looks at you with something like recognition. Like someone finally understands.

"But can I ask you something?" You keep your voice gentle. "Has it worked? Does it hurt less down here?"

Her face crumples slightly before she controls it. "No," she whispers. "It hurts all the time. But at least I'm not surprised by it."

"What if there was another way?"

"There isn't."

"How do you know?"

"Because I've tried. I've tried mattering, and it doesn't work. I've tried being seen, and nobody sees. I've tried speaking up, and nobody listens. So I came down here, where at least the stone is honest about what's true."

You're quiet for a moment, feeling the weight of her experience. The accumulated dismissals taught her this lesson.

"Will you show me something?" you ask. "You don't have to go anywhere or do anything scary. Just come to the wall for a moment. Stand beside me. Can you do that?"

Suspicious but curious, she says, "Why?"

"Because I want to understand these words better. And I think maybe you remember things about them that I don't. Will you help me?"

After a long, measured pause, she unfolds herself slowly and stands. Staying just far enough away that you can't touch her. Still in control of the distance.

You stand too, moving slowly to the carved wall. Your hand reaches out, fingers tracing the deeply cut *I am not important* letters.

"These words," you say. "Do you remember when they first got carved?"

"They've always been here."

"But before they were in stone. When they were just… feelings. Or experiences. Do you remember?"

The child is quiet. Then her small hand reaches out tentatively, touches the stone below yours. Her fingers trace the letter *I*.

"Pieces," she whispers. "I remember pieces."

"Show me," you encourage gently. "Tell me what you remember when you touch them."

Her finger traces the curve of the letter. She closes her eyes.

"Dinner table," she says quietly. "Lots of voices. Everyone talking over each other. I had something to say. Something I was excited about. But every time I started to talk, someone else would talk louder. After a while, I stopped trying. I just sat there being quiet. And nobody noticed that I stopped."

Your throat aches.

"How old were you?"

"Five, maybe. Or six. It happened a lot."

"What did you decide in that moment? When you stopped trying?"

She's quiet, thinking. "That my words must not be important. If they were important, people would stop to hear them."

You move your finger to the next letter. "What about this one?"

The child's finger joins yours on the ***a***. Her eyes close again.

"Being excited. Having something to show someone. A drawing, I think. Something that felt special. I ran to find it, and when I got back, they were busy. They said, 'Not now. Later.' I waited and waited. But later never came."

"And what did you decide then?"

"That what I cared about wasn't important enough to see."

You continue this way, moving letter by letter. With each one, a memory surfaces. Not dramatic. Not traumatic. Just accumulated moments of being overlooked, dismissed, and told to be different.

Being told you were *"Too loud. Too much. Why can't you be quiet?"*

Having your feelings minimized. *"You're making a big deal out of nothing."*

Having your needs treated as inconvenient. *"Can't you see I'm busy?"*

Learning that other people's comfort mattered more than your voice. Each memory, small by itself. But together, they built this belief stone by stone, word by word, until it became bedrock.

The child is crying now, silent tears streaming down her face as she traces the letters.

"So these words," you say gently, "they were… conclusions you drew from what happened. You decided you weren't important because people couldn't see you clearly."

You pause before continuing, "Can I tell you something?" You don't wait for an answer. "Their blindness doesn't mean you aren't important. It just means they couldn't see."

She looks up at you with those tear-filled eyes. "But how do I know what's true? That I'm not important, or that they just couldn't see? How do I know what to believe?"

It's the most important question.

"I don't know yet," you admit. "But maybe we could find out together. Would you be willing to come upstairs with me? Just to see what's there. If it's too scary or too hard, we can come right back down. You're in control. But I think there might be answers up there. Things that could help us understand."

She looks at the carved walls. Her safety. Her prison.

Then she looks at the stairs leading up.

"I'm scared," she says.

"I know. Me too."

Elaine steps forward then, her presence gentle but steady. She kneels down so she's at the child's level, though still giving her space.

"What if finding out makes things better?" Elaine asks softly. "My name is Elaine. I've been guiding her" she gestures to you "through this journey. And I'd like to help guide you too, if you'll let me."

The child looks at Elaine with those careful, measuring eyes.

Elaine assures her. "You're in control. We're just offering to walk with you."

The child considers this. Then looks back at you.

"Will you stay with me? The whole time?"

"Yes. I promise."

"And if I want to come back down, you won't try to stop me?"

"You can come back whenever you want."

Another long pause. Then, barely perceptible, she nods.

"Okay," she whispers. "I'll try."

You extend your hand, not expecting her to take it. Not forcing.

She looks at your hand for a long time. Then, so slowly, she reaches out. Her hand is small and cold in yours, but solid. Real. Her pulse beats fast against your palm.

You walk together toward the stairs, Elaine leading the way but giving you space. With each step, you feel the child's grip tighten.

"You're safe," you murmur. "We're together. You're safe."

The climb is quiet. Just your breathing and hers. The sound of footsteps on stone. Slow and steady.

You emerge into sunlight.

The child gasps slightly, squinting against the brightness. Her hand grips yours almost painfully.

"Too bright," she covers her eyes with her other hand.

"I know. Your eyes need time to adjust. We can wait here as long as you need."

You stand at the top of the stairs, at street level, just breathing. Letting her eyes adapt. Letting her realize she's still here, still safe, still in control.

When she's ready, she looks around slowly.

The street ahead is busy but not chaotic. People moving with purpose between buildings. And directly in front of you, close enough to watch, is a construction site.

The child's grip loosens slightly as curiosity overtakes fear. "What are they doing?"

You watch as one worker lifts a brick. Words are carved into its surface: *You're too loud.* Another worker adds a brick on top: **Stop making a fuss.** A third cements another in place: ***Other children don't act like this.*** Brick by brick, they're building a wall.

The child studies them. They're focused, methodical. Not cruel. Not angry. Just doing what they know how to do.

"They look like they think they're helping," she says slowly. "Like they think walls keep things safe."

"Maybe that's all they knew," you add softly. "Maybe walls were built around them too, and they're just doing what was done to them. They couldn't teach you something they never learned."

As you watch the workers continue their careful construction, one of them steps back to wipe her brow. Something about the gesture, the exhaustion in it, the way she carries herself stops your breath. She reminds you of your mother. Not literally, but in essence. The weariness. The determination to do what she thought was right, even when depleted. Your mother, building walls with words because that's all she could do at the time.

"Does that make it okay?"

"No," Elaine says. "But it makes it understandable."

"I don't think they knew," she says finally. "What they were building."

"You're right. Good intentions and harm can exist together," Elaine says quietly. "People can only give what they have. If they never learned to value their voices, to make space for their bigness, then they couldn't teach you those things either."

The child is quiet, processing.

"So it wasn't because I was bad?"

"No. It was never because you were bad."

"Or too much?"

"You were never too much. You were exactly right."

"Come on," you say gently. "Let's walk a little more. See what else we can find out."

You move slowly through the street, the child staying close. Her hand in yours. Her pulse still quick but steadier now.

You pass other construction sites. Some building new structures. Some tearing down old ones. Some renovating.

"Changing things," you say. "Building new beliefs. Removing old ones.

It's possible to change what was built."

Her eyes widen slightly at this.

You turn a corner and the street opens into a wider square.

In the center stands something massive and bronze, catching the afternoon light. As you move closer, you realize what it is.

A coin.

A giant bronze coin, standing vertical like a wheel, taller than you are.

The child's grip loosens as curiosity overtakes wariness. She pulls you forward, drawn to it.

"It's a coin," she breathes. "A giant coin."

You walk around it slowly, taking it in. The bronze has aged to a deep patina, green and gold, beautiful in its weathering. One side faces the square where you entered. The other faces away.

At its base, carved into the stone pedestal, one word: **TRUTH**

The child reaches out tentatively, touches the bronze surface. It's been rubbed smooth by countless hands before hers. Her fingers trace the engraving on this side.

"There's a picture," she says, studying it closely. "A wheel. Like on a ship."

You lean in to see. She's right. The engraving shows a ship's wheel, perfectly detailed, with spokes radiating from a central hub.

The child counts them, touching each one. "One, two, three, four, five." She looks up at you. "Five spokes. Why five?"

You study them, wondering. "I'm not sure yet."

She continues exploring the engraving with her small fingers, tracing the rim of the wheel, following each spoke to the center. "It's beautiful. All the pieces fitting together."

You walk around to see the other side of the coin. The child follows, still holding your hand.

This side shows something different. A compass rose, intricate and detailed, with all the directions marked. North, South, East, West, and all the points between.

"A compass," you say, touching it. The bronze is warm from the sun.

"Which way does it point?" the child asks.

You study it more closely. "All of them. Every direction at once."

She frowns. "But that doesn't make sense. A compass is supposed to show you which way to go."

"Maybe this one is different," you say, though you don't understand it either.

Elaine has been watching quietly. Now she steps closer, looking up at the massive coin.

"What do you know about coins?" she asks.

The child thinks. "People throw them in fountains and make wishes."

You add, "They have two sides. Heads or tails."

"They're worth something," the child says. "You can buy things with them."

"Yes," Elaine says. "All of that." She pauses, letting you both look at the coin again. "But what else? What do coins really do?"

You think about this. "They let you choose. You decide what to spend them on."

"And?" Elaine prompts.

"Invest," you say slowly. "Save. Trade. Exchange."

The child looks at the word carved at the base. "Truth. Why is it called truth?"

Elaine gestures to the coin. "What do you notice about it?"

"It's big," the child says.

"Besides that. What about its structure?"

You walk around it again, studying. "It has two sides."

"Two different sides," the child adds, moving from the wheel to the compass and back. "But it's one coin. Not two coins. One."

"Yes," Elaine says softly. "Two sides. But one coin. Not two separate things. One whole thing with two faces."

Something in her tone makes you stop. Look at the coin differently.

"You've been living like two separate coins," Elaine continues quietly. "The child in the darkness. The adult trying to reach upward. Split apart. Fragmented. Two coins that can't touch, can't connect, can't become whole."

The child looks at you across the width of the coin. Her eyes are wide with understanding.

with understanding.

"But we're not two coins," she whispers.

"No," you say, your voice catching. "We're two sides of one coin."

Elaine nods. "And you can't spend half a coin. Both sides are necessary. Both sides make up the whole."

The child moves back to the wheel side, studying it with new intensity. "The wheel," she says. "Five spokes."

"You'll understand what those represent later," Elaine says. "For now, just notice them. Count them. Remember them."

"One, two, three, four, five," the child repeats, touching each spoke.

You return to the compass side. "And this? All the directions at once? What does that mean?"

"Your true north is inside you," Elaine says. "But you can't find it while fragmented. The compass only works when you're whole. When both sides of the coin are integrated."

The child sits down at the base of the coin, pulling her knees to her chest, making herself small again. The contrast is stark. The massive coin above her, standing tall and complete. The child below, curled into herself, divided and trapped.

"This is what the belief did," she says quietly, gesturing to her curled position. "It made me small like this. I thought if I stayed down here, stayed small, I wouldn't get hurt again."

You crouch down beside her, not touching, just present.

"I wished so many times," she continues, and her voice breaks. "I wished to matter. To be important. To be seen. I threw pennies in fountains. I wished on birthday candles. I wished and wished and nothing changed."

"Because wishes don't work," you say gently.

She looks up at you, tears streaming. "What does?"

You place your hand on the coin, feeling the solid bronze beneath your palm. "Choices. Action." You look at the wheel engraved on this side. "Not wishing. Doing."

The child unfolds herself and stands, placing her small hand on the coin beside yours. "I've been wishing my whole life. Wishing the belief wasn't true. Wishing someone would see me."

You stand and walk around to the other side of the coin, looking at the compass engraving. "And I've been trying to live without you. Trying to be honest, to connect, to create. But I kept getting pulled back and losing my way."

"Because I was still down there. Holding the lie."

The child starts to walk around, stopping at the edge of the coin.

"Two sides," you say, looking at her at the edge of the coin.

"One coin," she finishes, meeting your eyes.

You walk to meet her at the edge of the coin. Kneel, and look into her eyes. "I left you in the darkness," you say quietly. "I thought I could heal without you."

"And I stayed there," she says. "Because I was scared."

"I'm sorry," you say, tears escaping from somewhere deep. "I'm sorry I abandoned you."

"I'm sorry too," she whispers. "For giving up. For holding onto the lie."

Her tiny hand reaches up to wipe your tear, and in one swift swoop, you pick her up, to hold each other tight.

"I forgive you," you say into her hair. "For being scared. For protecting yourself the only way you knew how."

"I forgive you too," she says. "For leaving me. For trying to heal without me."

You pull back just enough to look at her face. "And I forgive myself. For not understanding that healing meant being whole."

"I forgive myself too," she says quietly. "For not knowing there was another way."

Tears stream down both your faces.

"A coin isn't just for wishing," you say. "It's for choosing what has value. For investing in what matters."

She reaches around and places her small hand on the compass side of the coin.

"For believing the truth," she nobs, knowingly.

You place one hand on the wheel side of the coin.

"One coin," you say.

"Our truth," she finishes.

"I need you," you tell her. "I need your joy. Your spontaneity. Your capacity to hope even when it's scary. Your creativity that doesn't calculate whether it's good enough first. Your wonder. Your play."

"I need you too," she says. "Your strength. Your wisdom. Your ability to keep going when I want to give up. Your understanding that comes from experience. Your determination. Your courage."

And as you both hold the coin, the bronze catches light.

It feels solid. Real.

And the boundaries dissolve.

You feel her fear becoming your fear, acknowledged instead of suppressed. Her pain becoming your pain, validated instead of minimized. Her young perspective becoming your renewed wonder. Her protective strategies becoming your conscious choices.

And she receives from you: your hard-won wisdom, your capacity to navigate complexity, your strength that comes from survival, your understanding that comes from experience.

The integration happens in waves of light and warmth and recognition. Your body responds dramatically. Your chest expands so fully it almost hurts, breath reaching places that haven't moved in years. Your shoulders drop and straighten simultaneously, finding their true position. Your spine lengthens vertebra by vertebra. Your jaw unclenches.

Your free hand moves to your heart. It beats stronger, steadier, with a rhythm that feels ancient and right. Energy floods through you. Not frantic energy. Whole energy. The kind that comes from being complete. You feel taller. More solid. More present. More real.

When you open your eyes, the light has settled into something softer.

The child is gone. Not lost. Integrated. Home.

You stand alone in front of the bronze coin, both your hands now touching it. One on the wheel. One on the compass.

"Welcome back," Elaine says simply.

You look down at your hands on the coin, feeling the profound difference in your body. "She's here. She's really here. Not separate. Not hidden. Just... here. Part of me."

"How do you feel?"

"Solid," you say. The word doesn't feel adequate. "Like I'm allowed to exist. Like I take up exactly the right amount of space. Like I'm finally real."

You step back from the coin, looking at it fully. The wheel with its five spokes. The compass with all its directions.

"I don't understand everything about this coin yet," you say.

"Five spokes for five islands, though you haven't visited them all yet," Elaine says.

You look down at the word carved in stone at the base of the coin: **TRUTH**

"Not the lie carved in the foundation," you say. "This. Wholeness. Integration. Being complete."

"Yes." Elaine smiles. "That's enough for now. The rest will reveal itself when you're ready."

You nod, knowingly, and together you walk out of the square. Your stride is longer, more certain. Your shoulders are back but relaxed. Your chin is level. Your gaze is direct without being aggressive.

People seem to see you differently. Or maybe you're just finally allowing yourself to be seen.

As you approach the plaza, you pause at the stairs. "The words are still down there, aren't they," you say, gesturing toward the foundation stairs. "Carved in stone. *'I am not important.'* They didn't disappear."

"No. The past doesn't disappear. But your relationship to it has changed. You're not defined by it anymore. You're not living from it anymore."

You cross the plaza, looking down at the carved words in the pavers beneath your feet. All those limiting beliefs worn smooth by countless people walking on them unconsciously.

But you see them now. You acknowledge them. And you choose differently.

At the far edge of the city, Elaine points to a bridge. "You couldn't see this bridge before," she says. "It was here all along."

A seaglass bridge stretches ahead, transparent and shimmering in the afternoon light. And beyond it, the lighthouse stands waiting.

"Ready?" Elaine asks.

You nod, taking the first step onto it carefully, still feeling the wholeness from integration humming through your body. The glass holds you. Light, creating rainbows on the water. Through it, you can see straight down to the water below.

Everything looks different now. Clearer. True.

You cross toward the Circle of Belonging, whole at last.

16

The Arbor

"It's like walking on light," you say, taking another careful step. "I can see straight down through the surface to the depths beneath."

The light through the sea glass creates patterns on your skin as you move. Shifting colors. Blue, green, amber.

"This bridge is beautiful," you say.

"Honesty, even when it reveals difficult truths, can be beautiful," Elaine says, walking beside you. "Seeing clearly through to what's underneath creates strength."

You realize you're not running anymore. You're walking toward something with clear eyes. Integrated. Whole.

When off the bridge, just ahead, nestled in a gentle hollow, is a fragrant rose garden. The garden is a perfect circle, bordered by an impossibly dense wall of climbing roses. The air carries a sweet, layered perfume. You see the boundary clearly: every velvety bloom is guarded by a wickedly sharp, black thorn.

The beauty of belonging is inseparable from the pain it sometimes inflicts. You pause at the garden's edge, studying the roses more closely. Each bloom, velvet and radiant, grows alongside its thorns, sharp, dark, unyielding. You cannot pluck the flower without risking the cut. You cannot have the beauty without the protection, the softness without the defense.

"Roses and thorns," Elaine says quietly. "You can't separate them. Every relationship that matters has both. The people who gave you life also gave you wounds. The friends who brought you joy also brought you pain. That's not a flaw in the design. That's the nature of being human."

You reach out, letting your finger hover near a thorn without touching it. "I had wanted only the petals. To reject the whole plant because of the thorns."

"And now?"

"But now I am realizing that family and friends, all relationships that matter, come with both beauty and pain."

"Yes. The question isn't whether there are thorns. It's whether the roses are worth it."

"I understand that my birth family gave me life, even when they couldn't give me everything I needed. And my chosen family, my friends, give me belonging, seeing me clearly and choosing me anyway."

"Yes. The key isn't choosing between them. It's honoring both. Forgiving the limits of one while celebrating the gifts of the other. Family and friends together create the web of belonging you've been seeking all along.

"I see how they come together. The thorn protects the rose. The wound and the beauty grow from the same stem."

Elaine nods. "Forgiveness doesn't remove the thorns. It accepts that they exist alongside the petals. It stops demanding that love come without edges."

In the exact center of the circle stands an arbor, made of smooth, ancient, pale wood. Functional and strong, held up by two massive round pillars, connected by a single solid beam overhead. The silence here feels like it's holding its breath. The quiet before a final, profound undertaking.

You reach out to brush aside a rose to reveal the word carved into the rough, warm wood, FAMILY. The wood feels rough, but warm. Rooted. The pillar, a permanent anchor. You close your eyes, and the memories surface. They aren't painful flashes anymore. They are quiet, grainy photographs. Your mother's tired but trying face in the kitchen light. Your father's silence. A sibling's jealous word, regretted instantly. You see their limits. The flaws. The humanity. The thorns in those most intimate roses.

"I forgive you," you whisper, pushing through a physical ache in your throat. "I forgive you for your limits. I forgive you for what you couldn't give me. I forgive you for the mistakes that carved beliefs in me where doubt grew.

Feeling something land on your hand, obviously carried by the soft wind, you open your eyes and see that it's a rose petal, the color of your birthstone. The lingering ache of forgiveness fades, replaced by an intense warmth that isn't about excusing their actions but accepting their beings.

A deeper voice, your own fundamental truth, follows: "And I thank you. For my life. For my breath. For my existence. Without you, I wouldn't be here."

You cross the small space in the entrance and place your hand on the second pillar. This one is smoother, polished by friction and time. The memories here are sharper: friends who drift, their goodbyes uncomplicated but final. A sudden, crushing betrayal. And the memory of your own impatience, your own critical words that pushed someone you cared about away.

Here, the forgiveness is shared.

And you say to those roses, "I forgive you for leaving," you say, your voice stronger now. It isn't a whisper. It is a decree. "I forgive myself for leaving. I release you with love. Our paths served their purpose."

You trace your finger along the tangled vines, following their curve. Below a knot in the wood, in a space between two roses, you notice the word FRIENDS.

As you back away from the second pillar, looking up at the solid beam connecting them both, you notice how this overhead beam holds the weight of everything, not just family, not just friends, but the wider world. It frames the sky above. A clear blue canvas. The memories here are less personal and more pervasive. A coach who said you weren't strong enough. A teacher who dismissed your idea with a sigh. The endless roar of media messages insisting you weren't thin enough, smart enough, successful enough. The entire cultural chorus planting a relentless rhythm of "not enough."

"I forgive you," you speak up toward the setting sunlight. "I forgive you for planting seeds you didn't know were weeds. You gave what you had. The beliefs that were given to you."

You extend your hands, palms up, reclaiming the power of decision. "I pull the weeds now. I choose what to plant. I choose what grows."

Taking a deep breath, you walk through the arbor, moving past the pillars, just beyond the frame, resting on a waist-high stone stand, is the chest. It looks ancient and carved with swirling vines, smelling faintly of cedar and earth.

You reach for it, your fingers tracing the metal fixtures. Curiously, the chest has no latch. No mechanism. No lock. You feel like you've won the lottery.

Without hesitation you lift the lid, where inside, nestled in silk, are the three items: A ring with your birthstone that catches the last light of day.

"Unity," Elaine says. "Belonging is your birthright."

And beside a pouch, you save for last, you see a delicate bracelet with several charms already attached, space for more.

"Friends collected over time. My chosen family," you say. "People who feel like home."

"Let's see what's inside the pouch," Elaine urges. You reach your hand into the velvet pouch and pull out a single seed. "For planting a tree, with new roots, creating something that belongs to you, but will outlast you for generations to come. Your legacy tree," Elaine smiles.

And there, beneath, at the bottom of the chest, lies the golden key. You lift it, feeling its weight, and read the engraving that winds around the bow: *Family and Friends*

The Key of Family and Friends.

You lift it, feeling its weight.

"This Key was never locked away from you. It was always here, waiting for you to become whole enough, forgiving enough, and clear enough to see it."

"I always belonged. I just needed to release what was blocking me from receiving its gifts."

You slide the ring onto your finger. It fits perfectly.

You fasten the bracelet around your wrist. The charms catch light.

You hold the seed in your palm, feeling your potential. A sharp, clear understanding floods your consciousness. The key, the only key that ever matters, is not an object to be found but the simple, unearned recognition of your own worth. The treasures are not earned. They are inherent. They have always been within you.

"I focused so much on the pain, the rejection, the doubt planted by others, that I couldn't see the deep, rooted beauty and pure truth of those relationships," you say quietly."

You look at the birthstone ring on your finger. A quiet acknowledgment of your birthright to exist, to breathe, to simply *be*.

The missing charms don't feel like loss. They represent potential. An ongoing story of my chosen family, with space for new, bright metal charms to be added.

You gently place the seed back into the pouch and return it to the chest for later planting. Close the chest lid and follow Elaine out of the Circle of Belonging toward the lighthouse steps.

You stand before the lamp and know what to do. You shine your light. The light isn't a searchlight aimed at the world. It is the light from within your own integrated, whole self. It blazes through the massive lens, illuminating the vast, darkening sea.

Through the glass, you turn your gaze, looking out over the island, past the dense circle of the rose garden. And you understand. You are the one who crossed all the bridges, navigated the tides of doubt, and completed the difficult, essential work of forgiveness. Not just of others, but of the story you have told yourself.

"My light matters," you whisper, your voice steady and clear, echoing in the glass lantern room. "I belong in this world."

You descend the lighthouse stairs slowly, each step deliberate. At the bottom, you pause and look back up at the light still blazing above you.

"That light doesn't stop when I walk away," you say to Elaine.

"No. Your light keeps shining whether you're watching it or not."

You walk together back toward the rose garden, passing through it once more. This time, you don't flinch from the thorns. You see them clearly. The sharp alongside the soft, the pain woven with the beauty. Both real. Both necessary.

Just ahead, the *Golden Harmony* waits, steady as always.

That evening, you sit on deck as the sun sets, the birthstone ring catching the last light on your finger, the charm bracelet gentle against your wrist, and the heart pendant warms your chest. Jewels of belonging. Aware of how much has changed since you first boarded this boat.

That night, you sleep deeply. Peacefully held by the gentle swaying of the *Golden Harmony.*

V

TREASURE ISLAND

"What lies behind us and what lies before us
are tiny matters compared to what lies within us."
— Ralph Waldo Emerson

17

The Storm

You wake to the gentle rocking of the *Golden Harmony*, morning light streaming through your porthole. Through the glass, you can see Connection Cove beyond—the meadow, the square, the forest, the arbor where you forgave and claimed belonging. And rising from the center, visible even from here, your own lighthouse beam still rotating in the dawn light.

But today, you're leaving.

On deck, Elaine is already moving with unusual intensity. Not her typical calm efficiency. Something sharper. More focused.

"Big sailing day ahead," she says when you emerge. No preamble. No gentle morning greeting.

"To Treasure Island?"

"Yes. But this passage is different." She secures a halyard with practiced hands, testing the tension. "Longer. Two full days of open water if conditions hold. Maybe three if they don't."

You look out at the calm water of the cove, the gentle morning breeze. "It looks peaceful."

"It won't stay that way." Elaine points to the horizon where you can just make out a thin line of darker clouds. "There's weather coming. A real storm. Not the squalls we've navigated through. Something bigger."

Your stomach tightens. You've steered through fog, navigated the waterfall approach to Intuition Isle, and threaded the channels into Connection Cove.

139

But those were different. Shorter passages. Protected waters.

"Can we wait it out?" you ask.

"We could. Anchor here until it passes." Elaine meets your eyes. "But that's not what you need. What you need is to learn how to handle difficulty head-on. How to prepare. How to execute. How to hold steady when everything in you wants to let go."

She gestures you closer to the mast. "Before we go anywhere, you're going to learn what a captain needs to know. Really learn it. Because on Treasure Island, you'll be alone. And I need to know you can handle whatever comes."

"I've steered through rough water before," you say, thinking of the fog, the waterfall.

"You have. But this is different. Those were navigation challenges in protected areas. This is open ocean. No landmarks to guide you. No shelter. Just you, the boat, the wind, and the sea." She pulls a coil of rope from a locker. "And it starts with preparation. Show me a bowline."

You tie one, fingers remembering the pattern from previous lessons.

"Good. Clove hitch."

You demonstrate.

"Figure eight. Reef knot. Sheet bend."

One by one, you tie them, muscle memory taking over.

Elaine nods in approval. "Your hands remember. That's good. But knowing knots won't be enough if you don't understand why we use each one." She points to various lines. "This is the mainsheet. This controls the boom. If we need to reef, reduce sail area in heavy wind—you'll use the reef lines here." She indicates lines running along the boom. "We'll practice that in a minute. But first, I need you to understand something fundamental."

She walks you to the life jacket locker and pulls out two personal flotation devices. Hands you one.

"Put it on. Now."

You slip it over your head, fastening the buckles.

"When we're preparing for heavy weather, this isn't optional. I don't care how good a swimmer you are. I don't care if you feel silly wearing it. In a storm, if you go overboard, this is the only thing between you and drowning.

Understood?"

The seriousness in her voice makes your mouth go dry. "Understood."

"Good. Now, reefing the sails." She moves to the main halyard. "In a storm, sail area becomes your enemy. Too much sail and the wind will overpower the boat. We'll be knocked down. Possibly capsized. So we reef early—before we think we need to—to reduce that risk."

She demonstrates how to ease the halyard, lower the mainsail partway, and secure the reef points along the boom. "Your turn. Lower it, tie off the reef points, tension the halyard again."

Your hands fumble at first. The lines are stiff, the reef points awkward to reach while the boom swings slightly in the breeze.

"Again," Elaine says when your first attempt is sloppy.

You do it again. And again. Until your fingers know the sequence without thinking.

"Why are we doing this now, while it's calm?" Elaine asks.

"So I know how when it's not calm."

"Exactly. In a storm, you won't have time to figure it out. You'll be cold, wet, scared, and exhausted. Your hands will shake. Your brain will be screaming at you to just hold on and survive. But if your body already knows what to do, you can do it anyway."

She walks you through storm preparation with methodical precision. How to secure everything on deck—jerrycans of water, loose lines, the dinghy. How to close hatches and dog them down. How to check bilge pumps. How to plot a storm course that keeps wind at an angle that won't broach the boat.

"Show me how you'd secure the dinghy," she says.

You work through it, lashing it down with lines run through the bow and stern eyes, testing the tension.

"Tighter. If a wave hits that, it'll rip free and take someone's head off."

You adjust, pulling harder, doubling the lines.

"Better."

The sun climbs higher as you work. Elaine drills you relentlessly. Plot a course. Trim the sails. Read the wind. Anticipate shifts. React to gusts.

"What's your heading?" she snaps.

You check the compass. "Two-seven-five."

"Wind direction?"

You look at the telltales streaming from the shrouds. "Southwest, maybe fifteen knots."

"Good. Now we're going to practice leaving the cove. Show me how you'd navigate out."

You move to the wheel, feeling its familiar weight under your hands. This is your fourth time steering, and your body remembers. You ease the boat forward, using the jib to catch wind, feeling how she responds.

The channel out of Connection Cove is narrow, the lighthouse standing guard at its entrance. You've done this approach in reverse—coming in. But going out requires threading between rocks on one side, shallows on the other, timing your tack to catch the current.

"Talk me through it," Elaine says, not touching anything, just watching.

"Current is running out," you say, reading the water. "I'll use it. Stay center channel until we're past the lighthouse, then come about to port to catch the wind for open water."

"Why port?"

"Because the wind is southwest. If we come about to starboard, we'll be too close to the rocks."

"Good. Execute."

You do. The Golden Harmony responds to your hands, threading the channel, passing the lighthouse with room to spare, coming about smoothly as you clear the entrance.

And suddenly, you're in open water.

The difference is immediate. The gentle swell of the cove becomes rolling waves. The protected breeze becomes steady wind. The horizon stretches endless in all directions.

"This is where it gets real," Elaine says quietly. "No islands to hide behind. No shortcuts. Just the sea."

You grip the wheel tighter, feeling the boat respond to the waves differently out here. Bigger movements. More power in the water.

"You're doing fine," Elaine observes. "But look at the sky."

You do. The thin line of clouds you saw earlier has grown. Darker now. Spreading across the horizon like a bruise.

"How long until it hits?" you ask.

"Three hours. Maybe four." She moves beside you at the wheel. "Which gives us time to get far enough from land that we have sea room to maneuver, but not so far that we're caught in the worst of it without preparation."

"What do we do?"

"We sail smart. We prepare early. We don't panic. And when it hits, you steer us through."

Your heart pounds. "Me?"

"You. I'll be here. I'll help if you need it. But you're the one at the wheel. This is your storm to navigate."

The next three hours pass in a strange mixture of calm sailing and mounting tension. The wind builds steadily. The waves grow. The sky darkens not just with clouds but with something heavier. More ominous.

Elaine watches everything with the eyes of someone who's done this a hundred times. "Time to reef," she finally says. "Not because we need to yet, but because we will soon. And I'd rather do it now while we can still think clearly."

Together, you lower the mainsail partway, secure the reef points, and raise it again. The reduction in sail area is immediately noticeable. The boat feels more balanced. More controllable.

"Good," Elaine says. "Now secure yourself. Clip your safety harness to the jackline."

You do, the tether running from your life jacket to the line running the length of the deck. If you slip, if a wave takes you, the line will hold.

"Check bilge?"

You drop below, check the pump. Dry. Good.

When you return to deck, the storm is visibly closer. You can see the rain now. A gray wall moving across the water toward you.

"Here it comes," Elaine says. "Take the wheel."

You grip the spokes—five of them, you notice suddenly, radiating from the hub like the bronze coin, though you can't think about that now—and brace yourself.

The storm hits like a physical blow.

One moment, manageable wind and waves. The next, roaring chaos.

Wind slams into the sails with a sound like thunder. Rain doesn't fall—it drives horizontally, pelting your face so hard it stings. The waves that seemed large before now tower, dark mountains of water that lift the bow and send the stern crashing down.

"Hold your heading!" Elaine shouts, her voice barely audible over the roar. "Two-seven-five! Don't let her come about!"

You grip the wheel with everything you have, feeling it buck and pull under your hands like a living thing trying to escape. The boat wants to turn into the wind—it's her natural instinct—but that would put you broadside to the waves. That would roll you.

"I can't!" you shout back. "It's too strong!"

"Yes you can! Smaller movements! Feel the wave before it hits! Anticipate!"

A wave crashes over the bow, sending water cascading across the deck. You're drenched instantly, salt water stinging your eyes, filling your mouth.

You can't see. Can't breathe. Can't think.

But your hands hold the wheel.

"That's it!" Elaine's voice cuts through. "You held! You're still on course! Keep going!"

Another wave. Bigger. The bow climbs up, up, up—so steep you think you'll flip backward—then crashes down with bone-jarring force.

Your hands slip. You overcorrect. The boat swings ten degrees off course.

"Steady!" Elaine calls. "Bring her back! Small adjustments!"

You correct, pulling the wheel back, finding the heading again.

Your arms are already burning. Every muscle screaming. But you can't let go.

The storm rages around you. Rain so thick you can barely see the bow. Wind so loud it's like standing inside a jet engine. Waves that seem impossible, that physics says shouldn't exist but do anyway.

And through it all, you hold.

You learn to read the rhythm. To feel a big wave coming in the way the boat lifts differently. To brace before it hits. To adjust the wheel a spoke or two, not yanking but guiding.

Time loses meaning. Could be thirty minutes. Could be three hours.

Your hands are numb. Blistered. Raw.

Your arms shake with exhaustion.

Rain has soaked through every layer. You're cold in a way you didn't know was possible.

But the wheel is steady in your hands.

"You're doing it," Elaine says, and she's not shouting anymore. Her voice is normal volume. Which means—

You look up. The rain is lighter. The wind has dropped from a roar to a howl to merely strong.

The waves are still large, but not mountainous. Not life-threatening.

The worst has passed.

"You can ease off now," Elaine says gently. "The storm is behind us."

But you can't let go. Your hands have been gripping so long, they've locked in place. Cramped around the wheel.

Elaine steps forward and carefully pries your fingers free, one at a time.

You stumble back to the cockpit bench and collapse, legs giving out.

"I did it," you say, and your voice sounds strange. Distant.

"You did."

"I actually did it."

"You held steady through the worst of it. Never panicked. Kept adjusting. Kept learning in real time. That's what captaining is. Not knowing everything. But staying present when everything is chaos."

You look at your hands. They're wrecked. Blisters opened and bleeding in places. Rope burns across the palms. Bruises forming on your knuckles from gripping so hard.

But they held.

"What you just did," Elaine says, settling beside you, "that's the hardest thing you'll do on this journey. Harder than anything waiting on Treasure Island. Because this required you to hold on when everything in you screamed to let go. To trust yourself when there was no one else to trust. To keep going when you thought you couldn't."

"But you were here," you say.

"I was. But I didn't touch the wheel. I didn't make any decisions. You did all of it. I could have taken over if you'd failed. But you didn't fail."

You sit in silence, watching the last of the storm clouds disappear behind you. Ahead, the sky is lighter. Clearing.

The sea still rolls with large swells, but they're gentle compared to what you just navigated. The kind of waves that rock you instead of trying to capsize you.

"Look," Elaine says, pointing ahead.

On the horizon, barely visible in the afternoon light, is land.

An island.

"Treasure Island," she confirms. "We're ahead of schedule. The storm pushed us faster than we would have sailed in calm seas. We'll make landfall by sunset."

Pride swells in your chest, almost painful in its intensity. You navigated through a storm. You held course. You brought the boat through.

"Rest now," Elaine says. "You've earned it. I'll take the wheel for the final approach."

You want to argue. To stay at the wheel. To finish what you started.

But your body has other ideas. The moment Elaine takes over, exhaustion crashes over you like its own wave.

You go below, peel off soaking clothes, wrap yourself in a blanket, and collapse into your bunk.

You sleep hard. Dreamless. The kind of sleep that comes after pushing your body and mind past every limit.

When you wake, the motion of the boat feels different now.

18

The Arrival

On deck, the quality of light has changed. Golden. Late afternoon. The air smells different. Not just salt, but something else. Garden flowers. Tilled earth. The scent of a place that's been cultivated.

"Welcome back," Elaine says from the wheel. She looks tired but satisfied, her hands resting easily on the spokes. "We'll dock in about thirty minutes. Ready to take the helm again?"

You move beside her, studying the island ahead. Your hands find the wheel almost automatically now, and Elaine steps aside, letting you take control for the final approach.

The *Golden Harmony* glides toward Treasure Island as the sun descends, painting the marble structures in shades of amber and rose. Your hands rest on the wheel with newfound confidence. The storm taught you that. The blisters have started to heal, but the memory remains sharp: the moment you discovered you could hold steady when everything tried to break you loose.

"Look at that," you say softly, nodding toward the island.

Elaine stands beside you, following your gaze.

"It's so different from the others."

"Yes, Gratitude Shores was wild beauty, untamed beaches with its lighthouse rising from ancient stone. Intuitive Isle hid behind waterfalls, secret coves, and mysterious depths. Connection Cove spread itself in organic clusters, bridges connecting naturally formed districts. But Treasure Island is intentional. Constructed. Every element is deliberately placed."

Ahead, you see magnificent gardens cascade down terraced hillsides in geometric precision, as if each plant was chosen, each pathway purposefully designed. And rising from the center, dominating the landscape, stands a palace.

"It's beautiful," you say, though the word feels inadequate.

"It's intimidating," Elaine observes with characteristic honesty.

Your stomach tightens. She's named what you were trying not to feel. The previous islands invited you in with their wildness, their imperfection, their sense of discovery. This one feels like walking into a museum where you're not sure you're allowed to touch anything.

"There's a dock ahead," Elaine points. "The main harbor."

You guide the *Golden Harmony* toward it, your movements sure. Docking is second nature now. After Connection Cove's narrow channels and navigating through a literal storm, this calm harbor feels almost too easy.

The wheel responds to your slightest touch, the boat answering like she knows you now. Like you've earned each other's trust through the storm. You ease her alongside the dock with barely a bump, and Elaine secures the first line before you've even fully stopped.

"Well done, Captain," she says, and the title carries weight now. Not courtesy. Recognition.

As you secure the remaining lines, you notice the dock itself. Not weathered wood like the others, but smooth stone with brass fittings. Clean. Maintained. Nothing left to chance or nature's whim.

"Someone takes care of this place," you observe.

"Someone takes care of everything here," Elaine replies. "That's the point."

Before you can ask what she means, a figure appears at the top of the dock stairs. A woman, perhaps seventy, moves toward you with the kind of grace that comes from a lifetime of intentional practice. She's tall, her silver hair pulled back in an elegant twist, wearing flowing linen that manages to look both casual and formal simultaneously.

Her face is striking. Not beautiful in a conventional sense, but arresting. Deep lines around her eyes and mouth that speak of decades of expression. Hands that look strong despite their age, moving with purpose as she waves.

"Welcome to Treasure Island," she says, her voice carrying easily across the space. Not loud, just clear. Practiced projection. "I'm Sage," she continues, walking down the stairs to meet you.

"Thank you," you manage, suddenly aware of your windblown hair and lingering exhaustion in your bones, as she approaches. Next to this woman's composed presence, you feel distinctly unpolished.

Sage's eyes, gray and sharp, missing nothing, travel from you to Elaine and back. "You look like you've had quite a journey."

"We came through a storm," you say. "It was…"

"Difficult?" Sage supplies when you trail off.

"Yes. But I held steady. I steered through it."

Something in Sage's expression shifts. Not quite a smile, more like recognition. "Then you've already learned something valuable. The question is, what will you do with what you've learned?"

The question hangs in the air, heavier than it sounds.

You glance at Elaine still on deck, suddenly uncertain about what happens next. "Your belongings are safe on the boat," Sage says, noticing your hesitation.

"Everything you need will be taken care of," Elaine says reassuringly.

"Aren't you coming?" You ask.

"Not this time," Elaine says, settling back against the rail. "This island is your work to do alone. I'll be here on the Golden Harmony, tending to repairs and resupply. You'll see me at meals if you need me, but the discovering… That's yours."

Something in her tone is both reassuring and final. This is a threshold you cross alone. You exchange a glance with Elaine, who gives a small nod of encouragement. Whatever this is, you're meant to walk into it.

"Come. Let me show you what awaits," Sage gestures.

Following Sage up the stairs, you emerge onto a wide promenade. The stones beneath your feet are smooth, each one fitted perfectly to the next. No weeds pushing through cracks, no moss softening edges. Everything deliberate. Everything maintained.

"Treasure Island," Sage begins, gesturing broadly, "is where visitors discover what they have to offer the world. It's the transition point between internal work and external expression."

"What do you mean by offer?" you ask.

Sage stops walking and turns to face you fully. "I understand you're on the five-island voyage. Is that correct?"

"Yes," you answer.

"The first three islands you visited, Gratitude Shores, Intuitive Isle, and Connection Cove, those were about receiving. Learning to see what you have. Trust what you know. Integrate who you are. Yes?"

You nod. "Yes. Exactly that."

"This island is different." Sage resumes walking, her pace unhurried but purposeful. "Here, you give. Here, you discover what unique gift you carry. What wisdom you've gathered through your lived experience. What you have that the world needs."

Your chest tightens. "I'm not sure I have anything worth..."

"Don't," Sage interrupts, but not unkindly. "Don't finish that sentence. I've heard it a thousand times from a thousand arrivals. I'm not sure I have anything worth sharing. Who am I to think I'm special? Others are so much more qualified. The words change slightly, but the fear underneath is always the same."

She pauses before a fork in the path. To the left, the gardens. To the right, the palace rises above manicured lawns. She takes neither path, instead leading you to a bench positioned between them.

"Sit," she says. It's not a command, but you sit anyway.

Sage settles beside you, her posture straight but not rigid. "Tell me about the storm."

The shift in topic surprises you, but you find yourself responding. "It was terrifying. The waves were... I didn't know waves could get that big. And the wind, it felt like it was trying to tear the boat apart."

"But you held the wheel."

"I did. For hours. My hands," you look down at them, at the healing blisters, the rope burns still visible. "My hands wanted to let go so many times. But I couldn't."

"Why didn't you let go?"

You consider the question. "Because I'd learned everything I needed to know before the storm hit. Because…If I let go, we'd have capsized, and Elaine trusted me to steer." You pause, searching for the truth. "Because something in me refused to give up. Even when I was terrified, even when I thought I couldn't do it, I held on."

Sage nods slowly. "That's your first gift. Endurance. The capacity to hold steady when everything is chaos. Most people let go. They panic, they freeze, or they abandon the wheel and hope someone else will take over. You didn't."

"But that's not special," you protest. "That's just survival. Anyone would have done the same."

"Would they?" Sage's gaze is penetrating. "Tell me honestly. How many people in your life, when faced with storms, have let go? How many have given up, numbed out, or refused to take the wheel in the first place?"

The question lands hard. You think of your husband, checking out in front of the TV instead of navigating the rough waters of your finances. Your mother, who handled her own pain by building walls instead of working through them. Friends who chose comfortable numbness over uncomfortable growth.

"Most people," you admit quietly. "Most people let go."

"Exactly. So when I say endurance is your first gift, I'm not talking about something everyone has. I'm talking about a capacity you've developed through lived experience. Through refusing to abandon yourself even when it would have been easier. That's treasured wisdom. That's what you have to offer."

You sit with this, feeling it settle somewhere in your chest. Not quite believing it, but not immediately rejecting it either.

"But," Sage continues, standing and gesturing for you to follow, "knowing you have a gift and knowing how to share it are very different things. That's what the next three days are for."

"Three days?"

"Yes. That's how long you have on this island. To discover what your unique offering is. To create something that demonstrates your treasured wisdom. To contribute rather than just consume."

Your heart rate picks up. "Create something? Like what?"

"That," Sage says with a slight smile, "is for you to discover. Come. Let me show you the Gallery of Gifts. It might give you some ideas. Or it might terrify you completely. Either way, you need to see it."

She leads you down the right hand path, toward the palace. As you climb the wide marble stairs, you notice details: carved reliefs along the railing supports showing various scenes. A woman writing, a man teaching, someone painting, another gardening. Each scene different but united by something you can't quite name.

"What are these carvings?" you ask.

"Previous visitors. People who discovered their gifts here and chose to leave a mark. A record of their contribution."

"All these people found their gifts in just three days?"

"Not found," Sage corrects gently. "Uncovered. The gift was always there. They just needed time and space to let it emerge."

The palace doors stand open. Tall, wide, welcoming despite their grandeur. Inside, the entrance hall is circular, domed, with light streaming through windows set high in the walls. The floor is polished marble, and your footsteps echo softly.

But it's what lines the walls that stops your breath.

Displays. Hundreds of them. Each one showcasing something different.

To your left, a manuscript rests in a glass case, its yellowed pages still visible through the glass: *My Journey from Silence to Voice*. Below it, a small placard reads: *Eleanor, age 62. Found her gift of written truth after 40 years of staying quiet to keep the peace.*

To your right, a painting. Abstract, all blues and golds, somehow conveying both chaos and calm simultaneously. The placard reads: *Marcus, age 58. Found his gift of expressing emotion through color after a lifetime of being told men shouldn't feel.*

You walk slowly along the curve of the hall, taking in each display. A recipe book, hand written, with annotations in the margins. A photograph series documenting a community garden project. A wooden figure, powerful and compelling. A teaching curriculum for helping women find their voices. A business plan for a non profit. A collection of poems. A quilt stitched from fabric scraps, each square telling a story.

"This is overwhelming," you whisper.

"Why?" Sage asks, genuinely curious.

"Because they're all so accomplished. So complete. So clearly valuable."

"And yours won't be?"

"I don't know." The admission feels like defeat. "I don't know what mine would even be. I don't paint. I'm not a great writer. I can't build things or start organizations. What could I possibly create in three days that would belong here?"

Sage doesn't answer immediately. Instead, she guides you to a particular display near the center of the hall. It's simpler than the others. Just a single journal, open to a page of handwritten text.

"Read it," Sage instructs.

You lean closer. The handwriting is shaky, uncertain, crossing out words and starting again. But the message is clear:

I came to this island thinking I had to prove I was special. Thinking I had to create something impressive to earn my place. But what I learned is that my gift isn't about being impressive. It's about being honest. About sharing the messy truth of what I've lived through and what I'm still learning. Maybe that's enough. Maybe that's more than enough.

Below, the placard reads: *Catherine, age 49. Found her gift of witnessing others by first witnessing herself.*

"Catherine arrived six months ago," Sage says softly. "She spent her first two days trying to write the perfect inspirational memoir. Trying to paint despite never having held a brush. Trying to create something she thought would impress people. She was miserable. Blocked. Convinced she had nothing to offer."

"What changed?"

"On the morning of the third day, she stopped trying. She sat in the garden, wrote in her journal, not for anyone else, just for herself, and a younger woman approached her. Asked if she was okay. Catherine started talking. Just being real. Sharing where she'd been, what she'd learned, how hard it still was. And the younger woman wept. Said it was exactly what she needed to hear. That Catherine's honesty gave her permission to be honest too."

Sage gestures to the journal. "That's when Catherine understood. Her gift wasn't creating content or art or programs. Her gift was presence. Authentic witnessing. The willingness to be vulnerable first so others feel safe being vulnerable too."

You stare at the journal, something loosening in your chest. "So she didn't have to be impressive?"

"No. She had to be real. There's a difference."

You turn away from the display, looking around the hall with new eyes. The manuscript from Eleanor, you notice now that it's not perfectly bound, just pages held together with a simple clip. Marcus's painting has visible brushstrokes, places where colors bleed into each other messily. The quilt has uneven stitching in places.

"They're not perfect," you say, realizing.

"No. They're authentic. That's what makes them valuable." Sage moves toward a door at the far end of the hall. "Come. Let me show you the studios. The spaces where people explore and discover. You'll spend tomorrow there, trying different things, seeing what resonates."

You follow her through the door into a long corridor lined with windows.

Through them, you can see various buildings scattered across the palace grounds. Some traditional, some modern, some barely more than open air pavilions.

"The writing studio," Sage points to a building with floor to ceiling bookshelves visible through windows. "The art studio. The teaching pavilion. The maker's workshop. The garden space. The movement studio. Over there," she indicates a cluster of smaller buildings, "individual reflection spaces. Private rooms where people can think, process, create without interruption."

"I'm supposed to go to all of these?"

"You're supposed to explore. Try things. Notice what calls to you and what doesn't. Notice where you feel alive and where you feel like you're performing. Notice what feels like yours and what feels like you're trying to inhabit someone else's gift."

You stop walking, the weight of it settling on your shoulders. "What if I don't find anything? What if I try everything and nothing feels right?"

Sage turns to face you fully. "Then you'll know what your gift isn't. That's valuable too. Most people spend their whole lives trying to force themselves into gifts that aren't theirs because they think they should. You have three days. The first two are for exploring and eliminating. Trying things, seeing what resonates, discovering what clearly isn't yours. The third day is for offering what is."

"And if I can't create something worth displaying?"

"Who said anything about displaying?" Sage's tone is sharp now, cutting through your spiral. "This isn't about creating something for the gallery. That's just what some people choose to leave behind. This is about discovering what wants to come through you. What expression of your lived wisdom wants to emerge. Whether anyone else ever sees it is irrelevant."

She softens slightly. "The key appears when you offer something authentically. Not when you create something perfectly. There's a difference."

"The key?" Your hand goes instinctively to your chest, where the rose quartz heart still hangs.

"Yes. The **Key of Treasured Wisdom**. But it's different from the others you've found. This key reveals itself differently."

"How?"

"When you make your authentic offering, when you share your gift from truth rather than performance, you'll know. Something shifts. The key finds you in that moment. Sometimes it's physical, appearing in a pocket or on a table where it wasn't before. Sometimes someone hands it to you. Sometimes you simply realize you've been holding it all along."

Sage's expression is gentle.

"The form doesn't matter. What matters is the moment of recognition. When you stop trying to prove your worth and simply share what you have, the key makes itself known."

"So I can't search for it?"

"No. You can only become ready to receive it."

The sun has dropped lower, casting long shadows across the corridor. Through the windows, you can see lights beginning to glow in various studios. Other people working on their discoveries, presumably.

"Are there other visitors here now?" you ask.

"Several. You'll likely encounter them tomorrow. Some have been here a day, others are on their last day. Everyone's at a different stage of their discovery."

"Do they all find their gifts?"

"Most do. Some leave without the key, but even they leave changed. Sometimes the lesson of Treasure Island is learning what you're not meant to carry. That's valuable too."

You absorb this as Sage leads you back outside and down a different path. This one winds through the gardens, less formal than the main walkways. Here, the landscaping relaxes slightly. Still beautiful, but more natural. Less controlled.

"You'll stay in one of the guest cottages," Sage explains. "Private space. Quiet. You'll need it. This work is intensive, even when it doesn't look like much from the outside."

The cottage she indicates is small but perfect. Stone walls, a thatched roof, a single window overlooking the sea. Inside, it's simple: a bed, a table, a chair, a small bathroom. Nothing unnecessary. Nothing to distract.

"Your things from the boat have been brought here," Sage says. "Including your treasure chests from the previous islands. You might want to spend time with them tonight. Remembering what you've learned. Integrating what you've claimed."

She moves to the door, then pauses. "One more thing. Tomorrow morning, come to the main garden at sunrise. There's something you need to see before you begin exploring the studios."

"What is it?"

"A question," Sage says simply. "The question that will guide your three days here."

Before you can ask more, she's gone, footsteps fading down the stone path.

You stand in the doorway of your cottage, watching the last light fade from the sky. In the distance, you can see the *Golden Harmony* still tied to the dock, her mast silhouetted against the deepening blue.

And rising, barely visible, the lighthouse. This island has one too. They all do. But you haven't climbed it yet. Haven't learned what it's meant to teach. That will come later.

For now, you're alone with the weight of Sage's words: *What unique gift do you carry? What wisdom have you gathered? What do you have that the world needs?*

The questions feel both exciting and terrifying.

Because what if the answer is nothing?

What if you search for three days and come up empty?

What if your lived experience, your hard-won lessons, your endurance through storms both literal and metaphorical, what if none of it translates into something you can offer?

You push the thought away, step inside, closing the door behind you.

On the table, someone has already placed a pitcher of water and a simple meal. Beside it, a note in elegant script:

Rest tonight. Tomorrow, you begin the most important discovery of your journey: what you're here to give, not just receive. Trust the process. Trust yourself.

Sage

You eat slowly, tasting nothing. Your mind is already spinning ahead to tomorrow. To the studios. To the exploration. To the moment, if it comes, when you'll finally understand what your gift is.

You notice the quiet, a sharp contrast to the day's bustle. Beside your bed, your four treasure chests lie waiting, the tangible echoes of your journey, each holding stories, lessons, and fragments of your true self.

You open the chest containing the conch shell. Its spiral smooth and weathered by countless tides. Picking it up, you bring it to your ear. The faint, steady pulse of the ocean whispers within, a rhythm older than time.

This shell doesn't shout answers or commands. It offers something subtler: a reminder that guidance is not always loud or clear. Sometimes, it's a quiet current beneath the surface, steady and persistent, waiting for you to trust it.

Setting the shell down gently, you allow a deep calm to settle. These gifts aren't just souvenirs; they are parts of you, tools and touchstones on this island and beyond, helping you navigate the vastness of your own unfolding story.

Outside, full darkness has fallen. Through the window, you can see stars beginning to emerge. More stars than you've ever seen, away from city lights. A whole sky full of light that was always there, just waiting to be visible.

Maybe that's what tomorrow is about, not creating light. But finally letting yours be seen.

You finish eating and move to the bed. It's comfortable, the sheets clean and cool. But sleep feels far away.

Instead, you lie there thinking about the gallery. About Catherine's journal with its crossed-out words and shaky handwriting. About how her gift wasn't impressive. It was real. About how maybe that's enough..

Your eyes grow heavy despite your racing thoughts. The day's exhaustion, both from the storm and from arriving here, finally catches up.

And as you drift toward sleep, your last conscious thought is a question that feels both like fear and hope:

What if I've had something worth sharing all along?

<h1 style="text-align:center">19</h1>

The Question

You wake before dawn, pulled from sleep by something you can't name. Not anxiety exactly. More like anticipation humming just beneath your skin.

The cottage is still dark, but through the window you can see the first hint of light touching the horizon. That pale gray that comes before the world remembers color.

You dress quietly, as if the silence itself is something sacred you don't want to disturb. Your feet find the stone path outside without hesitation, drawn toward the main garden like there's a thread pulling you forward.

The air is cool, damp with morning mist. Everything feels suspended, waiting. The kind of moment that exists between what was and what will be.

You follow the path Sage showed you yesterday, past the palace, past the gallery entrance, toward the gardens that cascade down the terraced hillsides. But you're not going to the formal gardens with their geometric precision. The path curves left, leading you to something different.

The main garden reveals itself gradually as the light grows. It's circular, maybe a hundred feet across, surrounded by low stone walls. Not manicured like the others. Wilder. More alive. Plants grow in natural clusters, seemingly random but somehow perfectly placed. Flowers you don't recognize. Herbs releasing their scent into the morning air. Small trees providing shade without blocking light.

And in the center, a fountain.

Not elaborate. Just a simple stone basin, water flowing from a central spout in a steady, musical rhythm. The sound fills the space, echoing softly off the surrounding walls.

Sage is already there, sitting on one of several stone benches arranged around the fountain. She's wearing simpler clothes than yesterday, a long tunic and loose pants, both in shades of cream and gray. Her hair is down now, long and silver, catching the growing light.

"You came early," she says without turning around. Not surprised, just observing.

"I couldn't sleep." You move closer, taking in the garden. "This place is beautiful."

"It's honest," Sage replies. "That's why I prefer it to the formal gardens. Those are designed to impress. This one just exists."

You settle onto the bench beside her, both of you facing the fountain. For a long moment, neither of you speaks. Just the water, the birdsong beginning in the trees beyond the walls, the slow unfurling of morning.

"I promised you a question," Sage finally says.

"Yes."

"Before I ask it, I want you to understand something." She turns to face you now, her gray eyes serious. "The next three days will be uncomfortable. Not because the work is physically difficult, though it might be. But because you're going to bump up against every story you've ever told yourself about not being enough. Every comparison. Every moment of self doubt. Every voice that says who do you think you are."

Your chest tightens. "That sounds terrible."

"It is," Sage agrees. "And it's also necessary. Because your gift, your real gift, is buried under all those stories. And the only way to reach it is to dig through them."

"What if I can't?"

"Can't what? Dig through them? Or can't find anything underneath?"

Sage is quiet for a moment, considering. "Let me tell you something about this garden. When I first arrived on this island, thirty years ago, this space was empty. Just dirt and rocks. Nothing grew here. The soil was poor, full of clay and stones. Most people would have said it was worthless."

She gestures around the thriving space. "But I saw something different. I saw potential. Not because I'm special, but because I was willing to do the work. Breaking up the clay. Removing the stones. Adding compost, year after year. Planting, failing, learning, planting again. It took five years before anything really took hold. Five years of looking at mostly dirt."

"Why are you telling me this?"

"Because your gift is like this garden. It's there. But it might be buried under poor soil. Under stones that were thrown at you. Under clay that hardened around your heart. The work isn't creating something from nothing. It's removing what's blocking what's already there."

You look around the garden with new eyes. All this abundance grew from dirt and stones.

"So the question," you prompt.

Sage stands and walks to the fountain. She reaches into the water, her hand disappearing beneath the surface, and pulls out something small. A stone, smooth and dark, roughly the size of her palm.

She returns to the bench and places the stone beside you.

"This," she says, "is the question stone. Every visitor to this garden receives one. It's yours now, for the next three days. Keep it with you. Let it remind you."

You pick up the stone. It's heavier than it looks, still cool and wet from the fountain. Completely smooth, like it's been worn down by years of water moving over it.

"What does it remind me of?"

"The question." Sage settles back on the bench. "Are you ready?"

Your heart beats faster. "Yes."

"What wants to be born through you?"

The question lands softly but somehow fills the entire space.

You turn it over in your mind, searching for the right answer, the impressive answer, the answer that will prove you belong here.

"I don't know," you finally admit.

"Good," Sage says. "If you knew already, you wouldn't need these three days. The question isn't looking for an immediate answer. It's looking for your attention. Your willingness to stay with it even when you don't know."

"What wants to be born through you," you repeat quietly, feeling the weight of each word.

"Not what you think you should create," Sage clarifies. "Not what would impress people. Not what your mother wanted or your husband needs or your children expect. What wants to come through you. Through your specific life. Your specific wounds. Your specific wisdom."

You hold the stone tighter. "How will I know?"

"You'll feel it. When you stop trying to figure it out with your head and start listening with your whole body. When something makes you feel both terrified and alive at the same time. When you think I can't possibly do this immediately followed by I have to do this."

The daylight has grown stronger now, touching the tops of the garden walls, making the fountain water sparkle. Other people are beginning to appear, walking the paths toward the various studios. Early risers, like you.

"Come," Sage says, standing. "Let me introduce you to some of the others. Not everyone. Just a few whose journeys might illuminate yours."

You slip the question stone into your pocket, feeling its weight settle against your leg. A constant reminder.

Sage leads you along a gravel path that winds through the garden toward a cluster of people gathered near a large oak tree. Three of them, sitting on blankets spread across the grass, steam rising from cups they're holding.

"Morning circle," Sage explains. "Some visitors gather here before heading to the studios. To ground themselves. To remember they're not alone in this."

As you approach, one of them looks up. A woman, maybe sixty, with short gray hair and paint stained hands. Her face is kind, open, the kind of face that makes you feel like you could tell her anything.

"Sage," she greets warmly. "Bringing us a newcomer?"

"This is our latest arrival," Sage says, gesturing to you. "She survived a storm to get here."

"Ah," the woman nods knowingly. "Then you're stronger than you think. I'm Patricia." She gestures to the others. "This is James and Zoey."

James is younger, maybe late thirties, with nervous energy that shows in how he can't quite sit still. He gives you a quick smile and a wave.

Zoey is harder to read. Older, perhaps seventy, with the kind of stillness that comes from years of practice. She inclines her head in greeting but doesn't speak.

"Sit," Patricia invites, patting the blanket beside her. "We were just talking about resistance."

You settle onto the blanket, grateful for the warmth of the sun that's now fully clearing the garden walls. Sage remains standing, observing but not joining.

"What kind of resistance?" you ask.

"The kind that shows up right when you're about to do something real," James says, his leg bouncing slightly. "I've been here two days. Yesterday I had this moment, this clarity about what I wanted to create. And then immediately, every reason why I couldn't. Why it wouldn't work. Why I wasn't qualified. Why no one would care."

"What did you do?" you ask.

"I froze," he admits. "Spent the whole afternoon trying to convince myself I could do it. Wasted the entire day arguing with my own head."

"Today's different though," Patricia says gently. "Today you know what you're up against."

James nods, though he doesn't look entirely convinced.

"What are you working on?" you ask Patricia.

"A series of paintings," she says. "But not pretty paintings. Honest ones. About aging. About becoming invisible. About the rage I feel at being dismissed because I'm no longer young." She laughs, but there's an edge to it. "Turns out I have a lot to say about that."

"How long have you been here?"

"This is my last day. I found my key yesterday evening." She pulls it from her pocket, holding it up to catch the light. It's golden, ornate, beautiful.

"Took me right up until the last moment. I was convinced I'd leave empty handed."

"What changed?"

Patricia thinks about this. "I stopped trying to make art that would make people comfortable. I made something that made me uncomfortable. And somehow that was the key. Literally."

You look at the golden key in her hand, trying to imagine holding your own. "What does it open?"

"The treasury," Sage answers. "Where the treasure chests are kept. Each one holds the gifts specific to this island. But you can't receive them until you've given something first."

Zoey speaks for the first time, her voice soft but clear. "Gift for gift. Offering for offering. You cannot receive what you're not willing to give."

"That's beautiful," you say.

"It's terrifying," Zoey counters. "I've been here two days and I still don't know what my offering is. I keep trying things that feel safe. Small. Controllable. And nothing shifts."

"What are you afraid of?" Patricia asks gently.

Zoey is quiet for a long moment. "That if I offer what's really true, what I really have to say, people will reject it. Reject me."

The vulnerability in her admission makes your chest ache with recognition.

"That's everyone's fear," Sage says from where she's standing. "The fear of being seen fully and found wanting. But that's also where your gift lives. On the other side of that fear."

James groans. "Why can't the gift be on the safe side of fear? Why does it have to be terrifying?"

"Because gifts that cost you nothing to give are worth nothing to receive," Sage says simply. "Real gifts require real risk. That's what makes them valuable."

The group falls into contemplative silence, each person sitting with their own version of that truth.

You reach into your pocket, feeling the smooth weight of the question stone. What wants to be born through you.

"I don't even know where to start," you admit quietly.

"The studios," Patricia suggests. "That's where I started. Just trying things. Seeing what felt alive and what felt dead. Process of elimination."

"That's where I spent yesterday," James adds. "Trying everything. Writing, painting, clay work, even dancing." He shakes his head. "I felt ridiculous the whole time."

"But you learned what you're not," Sage points out. "That's valuable."

"I guess," James says, not sounding convinced.

"Today you try again," Sage says, her tone both kind and firm. "With what you learned yesterday. That's how this works. Try, fail, learn, try differently."

She turns to you. "You'll do the same. Spend today exploring. Notice what draws you and what repels you. Notice where you feel alive and where you feel like you're performing. Tomorrow, you'll refine. Eliminate what's clearly not yours. Day three, you'll offer what is."

"That's not much time," you say, anxiety rising in your chest.

"It's exactly enough time. Too much time and you'll overthink it. Too little and you won't go deep enough. Three days is the threshold where real work happens."

Patricia stands, brushing grass from her clothes. "I should get to the studio. Want to finish one more piece before I leave this afternoon."

"I'll come with you," James says quickly, like he needs the company to face whatever he's avoiding.

Zoey rises more slowly. "I think I'll sit by the fountain for a while longer. Quiet helps me hear what's underneath the noise."

They disperse, leaving you alone with Sage again.

"Overwhelmed?" she asks.

"A little," you admit. "They all seem so far ahead of where I am."

"Patricia was exactly where you are three days ago. Convinced she had nothing to offer. James was paralyzed by comparison. Zoey was hiding behind politeness, afraid to speak her truth. You're all on the same journey, just at different points along the path."

She helps you to your feet. "Come. Let me show you the studios more thoroughly. Then you're on your own. To explore. To discover. To fail safely."

"Fail safely?"

"Yes. That's what this island provides. A space where failure is expected. Where you can try things badly without consequence. Where making a mess is part of the process, not proof that you shouldn't be doing it."

You follow her out of the garden, along a different path than yesterday. This one leads directly to the cluster of studio buildings you saw from the corridor.

The first building you come to is the writing studio. Through the large windows, you can see several people already inside, some at desks with paper and pens, others with laptops, one woman pacing while speaking into a recording device.

"You can write anything here," Sage explains. "Your story, lessons learned, poetry, fiction based on your truth, letters you'll never send. The form doesn't matter. What matters is whether the act of writing opens something in you or closes it."

"What if I'm not a good writer?"

"Then you'll discover that writing isn't your primary gift. But you might discover it's a useful tool for accessing what is. Some people write their way to their truth even when words aren't their final offering."

You move to the next building. The art studio. This one is more chaotic, gloriously so. Canvases lean against walls. Paint splatters mark the floors. Easels stand at various angles. Sculptures in progress occupy tables. Everything smells of oils and turpentine and creative mess.

Patricia is already inside, tying an apron around her waist, studying a large canvas.

"Not everyone here creates visual art professionally," Sage notes. "Some have never picked up a brush before. But sometimes the act of putting color on canvas, of making something with your hands, bypasses the critical mind and lets truth emerge."

The teaching pavilion is next. It's open air, covered but with no walls. Several people sit in a circle, one woman standing and talking while the others listen. You can't hear what she's saying from here, but her body language is animated, passionate.

"Teaching reveals what you know that you don't know you know," Sage says. "When you try to explain something to someone else, you discover the depth of your own understanding. Or the gaps in it."

The maker's workshop is full of tools. Woodworking, metalworking, clay, fiber arts. The sound of sawing and hammering drifts through the open door. James is visible inside, standing at a workbench, looking uncertain about which tool to pick up.

"Making something physical can ground abstract wisdom," Sage explains. "Sometimes your hands know things your mind hasn't caught up to yet."

The garden space is exactly that. Plots of earth, some planted, some freshly turned. A woman kneels in one, hands deep in soil, her face peaceful.

"Growing things teaches patience," Sage says. "And the wisdom that everything has its season. You can't force a seed to sprout faster. You can only provide conditions for growth and wait."

The final building is the movement studio. Through windows you see people in various forms of motion. Some dancing, some doing yoga, one person simply walking in slow circles.

"Your body holds wisdom your mind can't access," Sage says. "Sometimes you have to move to remember what you know."

You've completed the circuit, standing now back near the main path.

"These are your options," Sage says. "Explore them. Try them. Notice what happens in your body, not just your thoughts. Notice what makes you feel more alive and what deadens you. Notice what scares you in an exciting way versus what scares you in a this isn't mine way."

"How will I know the difference?"

"The exciting fear feels like standing at the edge of something. Like you might fall but you might also fly. The wrong fear feels like forcing yourself into clothes that don't fit. Both are uncomfortable, but they're different kinds of discomfort."

She pulls something from her pocket. A small cloth bag tied with a cord. "One more thing. Inside this bag are cards. These cards hold words of wisdom. You can use them to set an intention for the day or anytime you need guidance, just pull one. Don't think about which to choose, just let your intuition guide you. The word that comes is the word that needs your attention in that moment. A kind of oracle, if you will."

You take the bag, feeling the weight of multiple cards inside.

"Now," Sage says, stepping back. "I leave you to it. You won't see me again until tomorrow morning, same time, same place in the garden. Unless you need me. Then ask anyone. They'll know where to find me."

"Wait," you say, suddenly not wanting her to leave. "What if I do this all wrong?"

"There is no wrong. There's only what you learn." She smiles. "Trust the process. Trust yourself. And remember the question." She taps your pocket where the stone rests. "What wants to be born through you."

Then she's gone, walking back down the path toward the palace, leaving you alone at the threshold of discovery.

You stand there for a moment, overwhelmed by the options. All those studios. Infinite possibilities. Three days.

Where do you even start?

Your hand finds the question stone in your pocket. What wants to be born through you.

You don't know yet.

But maybe that's okay.

Maybe not knowing is exactly where you're supposed to begin.

20

The Studios

You take a breath, look at the studios spread before you, and make a choice.

The writing studio.

Not because you're a writer, but because words have always been how you process things. How you make sense of chaos. Maybe starting there will help you find your way.

You push open the door and step inside.

The room is larger than it looked from the outside. Natural light floods through tall windows. The space smells of paper and coffee and possibility.

Several people work at scattered desks, each absorbed in their own process. No one looks up when you enter. This isn't a social space. This is a working space.

You find an empty desk near a window and sit. Paper, journals, and pens wait in a neat stack. A cup full of sharpened pencils. Everything you need.

Except the words.

You pick up a pen, open a blank journal, and stare at the empty page.

What wants to be born through you.

Your mind spins through possibilities. Your story? Lessons from the journey? Something inspirational about motherhood and empty nests, and finding yourself again?

But none of it feels true. It all feels like what you think you should write, not what wants to be written.

170

You put the pen down and just sit. Looking out the window. Watching clouds move across the sky. Listening to the scratch of other people's pens, the quiet tap of keyboards, the occasional sigh or satisfied hum.

After what might be ten minutes or an hour, time losing meaning, you pick up the pen again.

And instead of trying to write something meaningful, you write what's actually true right now:

> *I don't know what I'm doing. I'm sitting in a room full of people who seem to know what they're writing and I have no idea. I'm terrified that I'll spend three days trying things and leave with nothing. That I'll discover I don't actually have a gift to share. That all the work I've done on the other islands, all that growth and integration, will amount to nothing because I can't figure out how to give it away.*
>
> *I keep thinking about Catherine's journal. How messy her handwriting was. How honest her words were. How that was enough.*
>
> *But what if it's not enough for me? What if my honesty is boring? What if my truth doesn't help anyone?*
>
> *What if I'm just not special?*

You stop writing, looking at what you've put on the page. It's not beautiful. It's not inspiring. It's just real.

And somehow, seeing it written down makes the fear a little less suffocating.

You keep going.

> *The storm taught me I can hold on when everything tries to make me let go. But holding on and offering something are different things. One is about endurance. The other is about generosity.*
>
> *Can you be generous when you're still afraid? Can you give when you're not sure you have anything worth giving?*
>
> *Sage says my gift is buried under stories I've told myself. Stories about not being enough. About being too much. About needing to be*

perfect before I'm allowed to be seen.

What if I stop trying to write something impressive and just write what's true?

What if the gift isn't about being special? What if it's about being honest?

You look up from the page, surprised by what's emerged. Not answers, exactly. But questions that feel alive.

Across the room, a woman closes her laptop and stands, stretching. She catches your eye and smiles. Not intrusive, just acknowledging. We're both in this.

You smile back.

Then you look down at your page again and realize something.

You've been writing for the past hour.

Not because you were trying to create something for the gallery. Not because you were trying to prove you belonged here.

But because writing helped you think. Helped you see what you actually felt underneath the performance.

Is this your gift? Writing?

Maybe. Maybe not.

But it's a tool. A way to access truth.

And maybe that's enough to start with.

You close the journal, slip it into your bag along with the pen. You'll come back to this. But right now, you want to try something else.

You leave the writing studio and walk toward the art studio, drawn by the smell of paint and possibility.

When inside, Patricia looks up from her canvas. Her hands are covered in paint, and there's a streak of blue across her cheek.

"How's it going?" she asks.

"I don't know yet," you answer honestly. "I'm just trying things."

"Good," she says, turning back to her canvas. "That's exactly what you should be doing."

You find an empty easel, a blank canvas already. Paint supplies arranged neatly on a nearby table. Everything waiting.

Though you helped paint the mural with many hands before, this is the first time you sit alone before a blank canvas, with only your own vision to guide you. You pick up a brush, dip it in blue paint without thinking about why, and make a stroke across the canvas.

It's terrible. Uneven. Amateurish.

But it's something.

You make another stroke. Then another.

You're not trying to paint anything in particular. Just letting the brush move. Seeing what happens.

After a while, a shape emerges. Not planned. Just appearing from the accumulation of strokes.

A wave.

Dark blue, rising, about to crest.

You stare at it, recognition flooding through you.

The storm. You're painting the storm.

Without consciously deciding to, you pick up white paint. Add the foam at the wave's crest. Then gray for the sky. Dark swirls for the wind.

You lose track of time. Brush moving, paint layering, the canvas slowly filling with the memory of holding that wheel, of staying steady when everything wanted you to let go.

When you finally step back, the painting is crude. Unsophisticated. Nothing like Patricia's skilled work at the next easel.

But it's true.

You painted what you survived. What you endured. What you held through.

"That's powerful," Patricia says softly from beside you.

You startle. You didn't realize she was looking.

"It's not very good," you say automatically.

"It's honest," Patricia corrects. "That's better than good."

You look at the painting again, trying to see it through her eyes. The wave does look powerful. Dangerous. And in the corner, barely visible, a small dark shape. The boat. Still afloat.

"Is this your gift?" you ask. "Painting?"

Patricia considers this. "Painting is the medium. But the gift is the willingness to show what's usually hidden. The rage, the grief, the truth nobody wants to talk about. The paint is just how I share it."

"So the form doesn't matter as much as what's being expressed."

"Exactly." Patricia rinses her brush in a jar of murky water. "James has been trying to find the perfect medium. Spent all yesterday jumping between studios, looking for the one that would make him feel talented. But that's backwards. The gift isn't about talent. It's about truth. Once you know your truth, you find the form that best expresses it."

"How do I find my truth?"

Patricia laughs. "You just painted it, honey. That wave. That storm. That tiny boat still afloat. That's your truth. You endure. You hold steady. Now the question is, how do you want to share that truth with others who need to hear it?"

She leaves you with that question hanging in the paint scented air.

You look at your painting. At the storm you survived. At the boat still floating.

Is this your offering? A painting?

It doesn't feel complete. It feels like part of something, but not the whole thing.

You clean your brushes, leave the painting to dry, and step back outside.

The sun is high now. You've been exploring for hours. Your stomach reminds you that you haven't eaten since the small meal last night.

You follow the scent of food to a covered pavilion where lunch is being served. Simple fare. Bread, cheese, fruit, soup. You fill a plate and find a seat at one of several long tables.

James drops into the seat across from you, his plate piled high.

"Hungry?" you observe.

"Starving. I've been in the maker's workshop all morning trying to build something. Anything. I'm terrible at it." He takes a huge bite of bread.

"How's your day going?"

"I wrote some. Painted some. Still don't know what I'm doing."

"Same," he says around a mouthful of food. "But Sage says that's normal. The first couple days are for exploring and eliminating. Trying everything, learning what's not yours. Day three is for offering what is."

"Do you feel any closer to knowing what your offering will be?"

James shakes his head. "Not really. But I'm learning what it's not. It's not woodworking. Definitely not metalwork. Probably not painting, though I haven't tried that yet. Maybe teaching? I think I might try the pavilion this afternoon."

"What do you do? In your regular life, I mean."

"I'm an accountant." He says it like an apology. "Numbers, spreadsheets, tax returns. Nothing creative. Nothing that matters."

"It matters to your clients."

"Maybe. But it's not my gift. It's just what I'm good at. There's a difference."

You think about this. Being good at something versus it being your gift to share. They're not the same thing.

"What made you come on this journey?" you ask.

James is quiet for a moment, chewing slowly. "I turned forty last year. Had this moment where I looked at my life and realized I'd never done anything that felt like mine. Everything was safe. Responsible. Expected. And I just thought, is this it? Is this all I get?"

"What do you want?"

"I don't know. That's why I'm here. To figure out what wants to come through me instead of what I think I should be doing."

The question. What wants to be born through you.

"Have you pulled a card yet?" you ask, remembering the bag Sage gave you.

"A card?"

"Sage gave me this." You pull out the cloth bag. "Oracle cards with words on them. You pull one at the end of each day. The word you get is what needs your attention."

"May I?"

You hand him the bag. He reaches in without looking and pulls out a card. Written on it is one word: **VOICE**, over a soft, watercolor rainbow arching across a serene landscape.

James stares at it. "Huh."

"What?"

"I've been quiet my whole life. Literally. I'm the youngest of five kids. Never got a word in edgewise growing up. Just learned to be quiet, let everyone else talk. Even now, I barely speak up in meetings. Just nod along with whatever everyone else thinks."

"Maybe that's what you're here to discover. Your voice. What you have to say when you're not being quiet."

He pockets the card, looking thoughtful. "Maybe."

You finish eating together in companionable silence. Then James heads off to try the teaching pavilion, and you're left alone again with the afternoon stretching ahead.

You decide to try the movement studio. Not because you're a dancer, but because your body feels restless. Like it needs to process something your mind hasn't caught up to yet.

The movement studio is quieter than the others. Just three people inside, each in their own space, moving to music only they can hear through headphones.

You find a spot near the back, kick off your shoes, and just stand for a moment. Feeling your feet on the floor. Your breath moving in and out. The weight of the question stone in your pocket.

Then, without music, without any plan, you start to move.

Slowly at first. Just swaying. Feeling the rhythm of your own breathing.

Then bigger movements. Arms reaching up, stretching wide. Your spine curling and extending. Your feet stepping, turning, finding new ground.

You're not dancing, exactly. You're just moving. Letting your body do what it wants to do without your mind controlling it.

And something shifts.

You feel the storm again. Not thinking about it, but feeling it. Your arms become the wheel, pulling, adjusting, holding. Your body becomes the boat, rocking, tilting, finding balance.

You move through the memory, and your body knows things your mind forgot.

How terrifying it was. How your hands shook. How many times you almost gave up.

But also how strong you were. How you adjusted, adapted, kept going.

You dance it all out. The fear, the endurance, the triumph.

When you finally stop, breathing hard, sweating, you realize you're crying.

Not sad tears. Release tears.

You've been holding the story of the storm as proof of your strength. But you haven't felt it. Haven't let your body remember what it accomplished.

Now you have.

You sit down right there on the floor, letting the tears come, letting your breath slow, letting the realization settle.

Your gift has something to do with this. With endurance. With holding steady. With surviving storms and teaching others they can too.

But how?

You don't know yet.

But you're closer.

You leave the movement studio and step outside into late afternoon light. The world feels different now, softer somehow, like the crying opened something that had been sealed shut.

Your legs are shaky, your body exhausted in that deep bone-tired way that comes from real release. But your mind feels clearer than it has all day.

You don't want to go straight to your cottage yet. You need to walk, to let your body finish processing what it started in the studio.

You follow a path that winds through the gardens, not the formal ones near the palace, but the wilder ones that cascade down the terraced hillsides. The sun hangs low, turning everything golden. That magic hour when light seems to come from inside things rather than falling on them.

Your hand finds the question stone in your pocket. You've been carrying it all day, feeling its weight shift with each movement. Now you pull it out, hold it up to the fading light.

What wants to be born through you.

In the writing studio, words helped you see your fear.

In the art studio, paint helped you remember the storm.

In the movement studio, your body helped you feel your strength.

Three different forms. But the same truth underneath: endurance. Holding steady. Surviving and teaching others they can too.

But that still doesn't tell you how to share it. What form your offering should take.

You walk until you find yourself back at the fountain in the main garden where the day began. Full circle. The water still flows in its steady rhythm, catching the golden light.

You sit on the same bench where you sat with Sage this morning. It feels like a week ago. So much has happened in just one day.

The garden is empty now, everyone dispersed to studios or evening meals or private reflections. Just you and the fountain and the growing shadows.

You close your eyes, listening to the water, and let yourself simply be. Not trying to figure anything out. Not pushing for answers. Just breathing. Being. Trusting that what needs to emerge will emerge when it's ready.

"Thought I might find you here."

You open your eyes to see Elaine standing at the garden entrance, two plates of food balanced in her hands.

"I brought dinner," she says, moving toward the bench. "Figured you might need some company after your first day."

Relief floods through you. You didn't realize how much you needed to see a familiar face until this moment.

"How did you know where I was?" you ask as she settles beside you, handing you one of the plates.

"Lucky guess. You tend to return to water when you're processing things. The boat, the ocean, the fountain. Water calls to water."

You look at the plate. Simple food again. Bread, roasted vegetables, some kind of grain salad. But it smells incredible and your stomach reminds you that you haven't eaten since lunch.

You eat in comfortable silence for a while, just the sound of the fountain and evening birds settling into trees.

"So," Elaine finally says. "Tell me about your day."

Where do you even start?

"I tried three studios," you begin. "Writing first. I thought maybe I could write about the journey, about what I've learned. But it felt forced. Like I was trying to sound wise instead of just being honest."

"What happened when you stopped trying to sound wise?"

"I wrote what was actually true. That I'm scared. That I don't know what I'm doing. That I'm afraid I'll leave here with nothing." You take another bite of bread. "It wasn't impressive. But it was real."

Elaine nods, chewing thoughtfully. "And then?"

"Then I painted. I've never really painted before, but I just picked up a brush and started. And somehow I ended up painting the storm. The wave, the boat, the whole thing."

"How did that feel?"

You think about this. "True. Like I was remembering something my mind had stored but my body hadn't processed yet. The painting was terrible, technically. But it was honest."

"Honest seems to be your compass today."

"Patricia, another visitor here, she said something similar. That the gift isn't about talent or skill. It's about truth. Once you know your truth, you find the form that expresses it."

"Do you know your truth yet?"

You look at the fountain, watching water arc and fall in its endless pattern. "I think my truth has something to do with endurance. With holding steady through storms. With being willing to keep going when everything wants you to stop." You pause. "But I don't know how to share that. How to make that useful to anyone else."

"What happened in the third studio?"

"I danced." The word feels strange in your mouth. "Or moved, I guess.

I'm not a dancer. But I just let my body move without thinking, and I ended up dancing the storm. Feeling it instead of just remembering it. And I cried. A lot."

"What did the crying release?"

"I think…" you search for the words. "I think I've been holding the storm as proof that I'm strong. Look what I survived. Look what I endured. But I hadn't actually felt it. Hadn't let my body remember how terrifying it was. How many times I almost gave up. And also how I didn't. How I held on anyway."

Elaine is quiet for a long moment. "You keep describing moments where you're remembering your strength. What if that's the thread? Not what you did, but how you help others remember their own strength?"

The words land somewhere deep.

"I don't understand," you say slowly. "How do I help others remember their strength?"

"By being willing to show them yours. Not the polished, impressive version. The real version. The part where you're terrified and crying and not sure you can do it. And then the part where you do it anyway." Elaine sets down her empty plate. "People don't need heroes who make it look easy. They need witnesses who make it look possible."

You sit with this, feeling it settle.

"I think that's what Catherine did," you say, remembering her journal in the gallery. "She shared her honest struggle, and it helps others."

"Yes."

"So my gift might be the same as hers? Witnessing? Being present?"

"Maybe. Or maybe yours takes a different form. Maybe you witness through writing. Or teaching. Or creating spaces where others feel safe to be honest. The form doesn't matter yet. First you need to own the truth: you've survived things that broke you open and made you stronger. That's treasured wisdom. That's what people need."

You look down at the question stone still in your hand. "What wants to be born through me," you say quietly.

"And?" Elaine prompts.

"Maybe it's not a thing I create. Maybe it's a way I show up. A willingness to be real so others feel safe being real too."

"Now you're getting somewhere."

The light has nearly faded now, the garden settling into dusk. A few lanterns begin to glow along the pathways, casting soft pools of light.

"I should let you get back to your cottage," Elaine says, standing and collecting both plates. "You need rest. Tomorrow's another full day."

"Elaine?" you call as she starts to walk away.

She turns back.

"Thank you. For bringing dinner. For listening. For helping me see the pattern I couldn't see alone."

She smiles. "That's what I'm here for. Well, that and keeping the *Golden Harmony* in good repair. She needed some attention after that storm."

"Is she okay?"

"She's perfect. Strong. Ready for whatever comes next." Elaine pauses. "Just like you."

Then she's gone, footsteps fading down the path, leaving you alone in the deepening evening.

You sit for a few more minutes, not ready to leave the garden yet. The fountain continues its song, water catching the lantern light now instead of sunlight.

Your body feels heavy with exhaustion, but your mind feels lighter. The day gave you pieces, not answers. But pieces are enough.

You finally stand and make your way back to your cottage through paths lit by lanterns and stars. The night air is cool, carrying the scent of jasmine and something else you can't name. Mystery, maybe. Possibility.

Inside your cottage, everything is as you left it this morning, though it feels like years have passed since then. Your treasure chests sit on the table, waiting.

You open them one by one, slowly, touching each gift inside.

The gratitude glasses from Gratitude Shores. You slip them on briefly, looking around the cottage. The simple beauty of it. The care someone took to prepare this space for you. The privilege of being here at all. You set them aside gently.

Each gift rests heavy with quiet power. More than mere reminders, they carry fragments of your story, pieces of your heart, and echoes of the truths you've uncovered. They embody both your past growth and the emerging light within you. They don't hand you a map or a clear path forward. Instead, they invite you into the unfolding mystery of your own offering, something only you can discover in time.

The path for tomorrow is not about answers handed down, but about stepping fully into the questions the gifts awaken inside you.

But, tonight is for letting the day settle into your bones.

You pull out your gratitude journal from the first treasure chest and open it to a blank page. The pen feels familiar in your hand after this morning's writing.

You write:

Today I learned that my gift might not be a thing I create but a way I show up. That honesty is more valuable than impressiveness. That my body knows things my mind hasn't caught up to yet. That crying in a dance studio can be as important as any finished product.

I painted a storm. I danced a memory. I wrote my fear. None of it was perfect. All of it was real.

Tomorrow I'll explore more and eliminate what's clearly not mine so I can focus on what is.

Tonight I'm grateful for: Elaine bringing dinner. The fountain teaching me to return. Patricia showing me that rough edges are where truth lives. My body remembering its strength. The question that has no answer yet.

You close the journal and remember the oracle cards Sage gave you. You pull the deck from your bag, noticing for the first time how beautiful they are. Watercolor backgrounds, each one different, each word carefully lettered.

You shuffle them slowly, letting your fingers get familiar with their texture. Then you spread them face down on the table and hover your hand over them, feeling for the one that wants to be chosen.

Your hand stops over one card. You flip it. The image shows a delicate ladybug, painted in soft watercolors, perched on an outstretched hand. And below it, one word in elegant script: **TRUST**

You stare at the card, at the tiny creature resting so confidently on the open palm. Such a small thing. So vulnerable. But trusting enough to land.

Trust.

Trust what? The process? Yourself? That tomorrow will reveal more? That you don't have to know everything now?

All of it, probably.

You prop the card against the lamp on your bedside table where you can see it and set the question stone beside it, as a reminder for tomorrow.

Then you change into sleep clothes, slip between the sheets, and lie there watching stars through your window.

Your body aches in the best way. Used, stretched, asked to remember things it had stored away.

Tomorrow you'll continue exploring, trying what you haven't tried yet, eliminating what's clearly not yours.

But tonight, you just need to rest. To let everything you learned today weave itself into the fabric of who you're becoming.

As you drift toward sleep, you think about Elaine's words: *People don't need heroes who make it look easy. They need witnesses who make it look possible.*

And the ladybug on your oracle card, trusting enough to land.

And the question: What wants to be born through you?

You don't have the answer yet.

But you're learning to trust that it will come.

And somehow, that's enough.

21

Process of Elimination

You wake to birdsong and soft morning light filtering through your cottage window. For a moment, you lie still, feeling the difference in your body from yesterday. Sore muscles from the movement studio. A looseness in your chest that wasn't there before. The sense of having cracked something open without knowing yet what's inside.

The **TRUST** oracle card still leans against your bedside lamp, the watercolor ladybug catching the morning light. You pick it up, studying it while your mind slowly surfaces into full wakefulness.

Trust the process. Trust yourself. Trust that what needs to emerge will emerge.

You dress, slip the question stone into your pocket, and step outside. The air is cool and fresh, carrying the scent of flowers and dew-wet grass. Your feet find the path to the main garden automatically, drawn by the same pull as yesterday morning.

Sage is already there, sitting on the same bench by the fountain. This time she's holding a cup of tea, steam rising in delicate spirals.

"Good morning," she says as you approach. "There's more tea if you'd like some." She gestures to a small table nearby where a pot and extra cups wait.

You pour yourself a cup and settle beside her, both of you facing the fountain in comfortable silence.

"How was day one?" Sage finally asks.

"Overwhelming. Clarifying. Confusing. All of it at once."

"Good. That means you're doing the work." She takes a sip of tea. "What did you learn?"

You think about this. "That I'm looking for something. But I don't know if I'm looking in the right places."

"Tell me what you tried."

"Writing. Painting. Moving. Each one showed me something different. Writing helped me see my fear. Painting helped me remember the storm. Moving helped me feel my strength."

"And?"

"And I still don't know what my gift is. What form it should take."

Sage is quiet for a moment, watching the water. "You're still thinking about form. What if form is the last thing that matters?"

"I don't understand."

"Yesterday you discovered that your truth has something to do with endurance. With holding steady. With surviving storms and coming out stronger. That's your essence. That's what you have to offer. The form, how you share that, comes later. First you have to own the essence fully."

You cup your hands around the warm tea, feeling its heat seep into your palms. "Elaine said something similar last night. That people don't need heroes who make it look easy. They need witnesses who make it look possible."

"Elaine's wise," Sage observes. "What did that land for you?"

"That maybe my gift isn't about creating something impressive. Maybe it's about being willing to show the messy truth of survival. The scared part and the strong part. Both."

"Now you're seeing it." Sage sets down her empty cup. "Today, keep exploring. Try what you didn't try yesterday. But pay attention to something different. Instead of asking 'am I good at this,' ask 'does this help me access my truth.' Those are very different questions."

"What if nothing does? What if I try everything and it all feels wrong?"

"Then you'll know your gift doesn't live in the studios. Maybe it lives in conversation. In presence. In the spaces between formal creation.

Catherine's gift was witnessing. She didn't create anything for the gallery. She simply sat with someone and was real. That was enough."

You think about Catherine's journal with its crossed-out words and shaky handwriting. How it was the most powerful thing in the whole gallery precisely because it was so honest.

"So I might leave here without creating anything tangible."

"You might. Or you might discover your offering in the last hour of the last day. The timeline doesn't matter. The willingness does."

Sage stands, brushing invisible dust from her linen pants. "Today, try what you didn't try yesterday. The teaching pavilion. The maker's workshop. The garden space. See if any of them open doors. And if they don't, that's information too. Elimination is as valuable as discovery."

"Will I see you tomorrow morning?"

"Same time, same place. Unless you need me sooner. You know where to find me."

She walks away, leaving you alone with the fountain and your thoughts.

You finish your tea slowly, watching light shift across the water. Today feels different than yesterday. Less frantic. Less desperate to find the answer. More willing to trust the process of elimination.

You pull out your oracle deck and shuffle, letting your hands move without thinking. One card slides out, almost jumping from the deck.

You flip it over.

The image shows a vibrant rainbow arching across a watercolor sky, colors bleeding into each other in beautiful imperfection. Below it, one word: **VOICE**

Voice.

You think about James pulling this same card yesterday at lunch. How he'd been quiet his whole life, never speaking up, always letting others talk.

What does voice mean for you?

You've had a voice. You've spoken up, sometimes. But have you spoken your truth? Or just the version of truth that felt safe to share?

You pocket the card and head toward the studios.

The teaching pavilion calls to you first. Maybe because of the card. Maybe because it's what scares you most.

The pavilion is open-air, just a roof supported by columns, benches arranged in a loose circle. Several people are already there. You recognize Zoey sitting quietly on one bench, and a few others you haven't met.

A man stands in the center, middle-aged, gesturing as he speaks. You catch the tail end of his sentence: "…and that's when I realized my whole career had been built on what I thought I should do, not what I actually wanted to do."

People nod, some making notes in journals.

"Thank you, David," a woman facilitating says. She notices you hovering at the edge. "Please, join us. We're in the middle of sharing circles. Everyone gets a chance to share something they've learned through lived experience. No teaching required, just truth-telling."

You settle onto an empty bench, your heart already beating faster.

David sits down, and the woman turns to the next person. "Zoey? Would you like to share?"

Zoey hesitates, then stands. Her movements are careful, controlled. When she speaks, her voice is soft but clear.

"I spent forty years being polite," she says. "Never disagreeing. Never making waves. Always smoothing things over, making sure everyone else was comfortable. And I thought that was kindness. But yesterday I realized it was fear. Fear that if I showed my real opinions, my real feelings, people would reject me."

She pauses, looking down at her hands. "I don't know how to stop being polite. But I'm learning that kindness and honesty can coexist. That real connection requires real truth, even when it's uncomfortable."

She sits down quickly, as if she's used up all her courage.

The facilitator nods appreciatively. "Thank you for that honesty, Zoey. Who's next?"

A younger woman stands. "I'm Megan. This is my last day." She takes a breath. "What I learned is that I spent my whole life waiting for permission. Permission to take up space. Permission to want things. Permission to say no. And nobody was going to give me that permission. I had to give it to myself."

One by one, people share. Not teaching, exactly. Just offering what they've lived through and what it taught them.

When the circle comes to you, your throat tightens.

"I don't know if I have anything worth sharing," you begin, and several people smile with recognition.

"I came on this journey because I felt invisible. Like I'd spent twenty-five years being a mother, and when that role changed, I didn't know who I was anymore. I thought I had nothing to offer the world."

You pause, surprised by what's coming out. "The first three islands taught me to see differently. To trust myself. To integrate the parts of me I'd abandoned. But this island is asking something harder. It's asking me to believe that what I've lived through, what I've survived, matters. That it's worth sharing."

Your voice cracks slightly. "And I still don't know if I believe that. But I'm trying."

You sit down, heart pounding, face flushed.

The facilitator's eyes are kind. "That's the work right there. Thank you."

The circle continues, but you barely hear the others. Your own words keep echoing. *I'm trying.*

When the sharing ends and people begin to disperse, Zoey approaches you.

"What you said," she begins quietly. "About not knowing if what you've lived through matters. I feel that too."

"How do you push through it?"

"I don't know yet. But hearing you say it out loud helped. It made me feel less alone in the fear."

You look at her, this woman who spoke her truth about politeness and fear, and realize something. You didn't teach anyone anything in that circle. You just told the truth. And somehow that was enough.

"Maybe that's the point," you say slowly. "Not teaching people lessons, but showing them they're not alone in the struggle."

Zoey nods. "Maybe."

You leave the teaching pavilion feeling shaken but also strangely energized. Speaking your uncertainty out loud didn't make you look weak. It created connection.

Voice isn't about having answers. It's about being willing to speak your truth, even when that truth is I don't know yet.

The maker's workshop is next. You're drawn by curiosity more than any sense that this is yours, but Sage said to try everything.

Inside, the space smells of wood and metal and oil. Tools line the walls, workbenches occupy the center, and the sound of sawing and hammering creates a rhythmic music.

James is there, looking frustrated at a piece of wood he's trying to sand.

"How's it going?" you ask, approaching his bench.

"Terrible," he admits. "I have no idea what I'm doing. I thought maybe if I built something with my hands, something tangible, it would feel more real than words or paintings. But I'm just making a mess."

You look at his project. It's rough, uneven, clearly the work of someone who's never done this before. But there's something earnest about it.

"What is it supposed to be?"

"A box," he says. "Just a simple box. Somewhere to keep things that matter. But every cut is wrong, every edge uneven. It's garbage."

"Or it's honest," you counter. "Perfect boxes are easy to find. But a box that someone made with their own hands, even if it's imperfect, that's different. That has meaning."

James looks at the box with new eyes. "Maybe."

A woman working at a nearby bench looks up. "You know what I learned here? That making something with your hands is humbling. You can have all these big ideas in your head, but when you actually try to bring them into form, you discover how hard it is. How much you don't know. How much patience is required."

"Is that your gift?" you ask. "Making things?"

"I don't think so," she admits. "But the process of making taught me about my relationship with perfection. How much energy I waste trying to make everything flawless instead of just letting things be good enough."

You pick up a piece of scrap wood from a bin, feeling its texture, its weight. Without thinking too hard about it, you find sandpaper and begin smoothing the edges.

There's something meditative about it. The repetitive motion. The gradual transformation from rough to smooth. The way your body knows what to do even when your mind doesn't.

You sand for maybe twenty minutes, not making anything, just smoothing this one piece of wood. Making it pleasant to hold.

When you finally set it down, you realize something. Your mind went completely quiet while you were sanding. No anxious thoughts about your gift or your offering. Just the sensation of wood grain under your fingers and the sound of sandpaper against surface.

"How do you feel?" the woman asks, noticing.

"Quiet," you say. "Like my brain turned off and my body took over."

"That's what working with your hands does. It gets you out of your head."

You thank them and leave, slipping the piece of wood in your bag. You're not a maker. That much is clear. But the experience taught you something about quieting mental noise.

The garden space is last. You've been avoiding it, not sure why.

When you arrive, only one person is there. The same woman you saw yesterday, kneeling in soil, her hands buried in earth.

"Mind if I join you?" you ask.

She looks up, face peaceful. "Please. There's always more weeding to do."

She gestures to a plot that's obviously been neglected. Weeds have overtaken whatever was once planted here.

"Start anywhere," she says. "Just pull what doesn't belong so what does can grow."

You kneel in the dirt, feeling it cool and slightly damp beneath your knees. You start pulling weeds, their roots resisting before giving way.

"I'm Margaret," the woman says from her plot. "This is my last day. I found my key this morning."

"Congratulations. What's your gift?"

"Cultivation," she says simply. "Creating conditions for growth. Not forcing things to happen, but tending what wants to grow naturally."

"Is that what you do in your real life?"

"I'm a therapist. Or I was. I retired last year and felt lost. Thought I had nothing left to offer. But being here, working in this garden, I realized my gift isn't about the specific profession. It's about the essence. Creating safe space. Tending growth. Removing what blocks flourishing."

You pull another weed, thinking about this. "So you might still be a therapist? Or something different?"

"I don't know yet. But I know the essence of what I'm meant to do. The form will reveal itself."

You work in comfortable silence for a while. The sun climbs higher, warming your back. Your hands get dirty, earth wedging under your fingernails. Sweat beads on your forehead.

And something in you relaxes.

This isn't your gift either. You're not meant to be a gardener. But the metaphor is teaching you something.

You're pulling weeds in your own life too. Removing what doesn't belong, beliefs that choke out growth, so something truer can flourish.

"What are you learning?" Margaret asks, as if reading your thoughts.

"That I've been so focused on what I should plant, I haven't finished pulling the weeds."

"What are the weeds?"

You sit back on your heels, looking at the pile of pulled weeds beside you. "The belief that I have to be impressive. That my offering needs to look a certain way. That I should know already what my gift is instead of trusting it to reveal itself."

"Those are big weeds," Margaret observes. "Deep roots."

"Yeah."

"But you're pulling them. That's the work."

You stay in the garden another hour, just weeding, letting your body do simple work while your mind processes everything.

By the time you leave, the sun is high and your stomach is growling. You head to the dining pavilion, hands still dirty from soil.

After attempting to get your soil stand hands clean, you head inside, and find James and Patricia sitting together. Patricia waves you over.

"How's day two?" she asks as you fill a plate and join them.

"I tried the teaching pavilion, the maker's workshop, and the garden."

"And?" James prompts.

"And none of them are my gift. But each one taught me something."

"Like what?" Patricia asks, genuinely curious.

"The teaching pavilion taught me that speaking my uncertainty out loud creates connection. The workshop taught me that my mind goes quiet when my hands are busy. The garden taught me I'm still pulling weeds, removing beliefs that block growth."

Patricia nods thoughtfully. "That's elimination. Learning what you're not so you can focus on what you are."

"But what if I eliminate everything? What if nothing is mine?"

"That's impossible," Patricia says firmly. "You have a gift. Everyone does. You just haven't recognized it yet because you're looking for something formal, something you can point to and say 'this is it.' But gifts are often quieter than that."

James picks at his food. "I still haven't found mine either. I'm running out of time."

After lunch, you find yourself walking with no destination in mind. Your body needs to move after all the sitting and kneeling.

You end up back at the fountain in the main garden. It's become your anchor point, the place you return to when you need to think.

You sit on the bench, pull out the question stone from your pocket, and hold it in your palm.

What wants to be born through you.

You've tried writing, painting, dancing, teaching, making, and gardening.

You've explored different forms of expression. And while each one taught you something, none of them felt like *it*. None of them made you think yes, this is mine.

Maybe that's the point.

Maybe your gift isn't about creating something in a studio. Maybe it's something else entirely.

You think about the moments yesterday and today that felt most alive:

When you wrote honestly about your fear in the journal.

When you painted the storm without trying to make it good.

When you danced and cried and let your body remember.

When you spoke your uncertainty in the teaching circle and Zoey thanked you for it.

When you just sat with Margaret in the garden, pulling weeds.

The moments that mattered weren't about skill or talent. They were about presence. About being real. About showing up authentically and letting that be enough.

Is that your gift? Presence?

It sounds too simple. Too unimpressive.

But maybe that's the point.

You sit with this thought as the afternoon sun moves across the sky, casting longer shadows.

A voice interrupts your reverie. "Mind if I sit?"

You look up to see a young woman, maybe late twenties, standing nearby. She looks uncertain, like she's not sure she should be interrupting.

"Please," you gesture to the bench.

She sits, leaving space between you. For a moment, neither of you speaks.

Then she says quietly, "I saw you in the teaching circle this morning. What you said about feeling invisible, about not knowing if what you've lived through matters. That was exactly what I needed to hear."

Your chest tightens. "Really?"

"Really. I'm on day one. I got here yesterday evening. And I've been spiraling since I arrived, convinced I don't belong here, that I have nothing to offer, that everyone else is so much further ahead than me." She wipes at her eyes quickly. "And then you spoke and I realized I'm not the only one who feels that way."

You turn to face her more fully. "You're definitely not the only one."

"Can I ask you something?" She's still not quite looking at you, focusing on the fountain instead. "How do you keep going when you're not sure? When you don't know if you have a gift or if you're just fooling yourself?"

The question lands in your chest like something heavy and familiar.

"Honestly?" you say. "I don't know. I'm making it up as I go. But I think that's the point. We're all making it up. The people who look like they have it figured out, they're probably just better at hiding their uncertainty."

She nods slowly. "That helps. Just knowing I'm not alone in feeling lost."

You sit with her in silence for a while. Not trying to fix anything or teach anything. Just being present with her uncertainty because you know how it feels.

Eventually she stands. "Thank you. For being honest. For not pretending you have all the answers."

"Good luck with your journey," you say.

She smiles. "You too."

After she leaves, you sit very still, feeling something shift inside you.

That moment. That simple, unplanned conversation. When you weren't trying to be helpful or wise or impressive. When you were just honest about your own struggle. That helped her.

Is this what your gift looks like?

Not creating something formal. Not teaching or painting or writing something profound. Just being willing to be real so others feel less alone.

Your heart beats faster. This feels like something. Not the full answer yet, but a piece of it.

You pull out your oracle deck and draw a card without looking.

When you flip it over, the image shows a seedling pushing up through dark soil, painted in soft greens and browns. The word below reads: **EMERGENCE**

Emergence.

Something pushing up through darkness toward light. Not forced.

Natural. Inevitable when conditions are right.

You stare at the card, feeling truth resonate in your bones.

Your gift is emerging. It's been emerging all along. You just had to stop forcing it and let it surface naturally.

The sun is lowering now, late afternoon turning to evening. You should head back to your cottage, but you're not ready yet.

Instead, you slip the card into your pocket and walk to the art studio. Not to paint, but to look at the painting you made yesterday.

It's still there, propped against the wall where you left it. The storm wave, dark and powerful, the small boat barely visible in the corner.

You stare at it with new eyes.

This painting isn't impressive. It's not technically skilled. But it's true. It shows what you survived. And more than that, it shows the boat still afloat.

That's what people need to see. Not just the storm. But the fact that you can survive it.

Not because you're special or talented or have some secret knowledge. But because you held on. Because you endured. Because you didn't let go even when everything in you wanted to.

You notice Patricia gathering her paintings. She's leaving in the morning, heading back to the mainland.

"Looking at your work?" she asks, coming to stand beside you.

"Trying to understand it."

"What do you see?"

"Survival," you say. "Endurance. Proof that the storm doesn't have to destroy you."

Patricia is quiet for a moment. "You know what I see? I see someone who painted their truth even though they thought they weren't an artist. Someone who was brave enough to make something real instead of something good."

She puts her hand on your shoulder briefly. "That's your gift. Not the painting itself. The willingness to be real. To show the hard parts. To witness yourself and others without judgment. That's rarer than you think."

She leaves with her wrapped canvas, and you stay a moment longer with your storm painting.

Tomorrow is day three. Offering day.

You still don't know exactly what form your offering will take. But you're starting to understand its essence.

Presence. Honesty. Witnessing. The willingness to be vulnerably real so others feel safe being real too.

That's what wants to be born through you.

Not a thing you create. A way you show up.

You leave the studio as dusk settles over the island. Your stomach reminds you that you haven't eaten since lunch. You head toward the dining pavilion, drawn by warm light and the low murmur of conversation.

Inside, the evening meal is in full swing. Simple fare as always, but the room feels alive with people processing their days.

You fill a plate and scan for a familiar face. Elaine sits at a corner table, and when she sees you, she waves you over.

"Day two," she says as you settle across from her. "How did it go?"

"Different than yesterday," you say, taking a bite of warm bread. "I tried three more studios. Teaching, making, gardening."

"And?"

"And none of them are mine. But that's okay. I think I'm starting to understand what is."

Elaine sets down her fork, giving you her full attention. "Tell me."

You think about how to put it into words. "The moments that felt most alive today weren't about creating something in a studio. They were about connection. When I spoke honestly in the teaching circle and Zoey thanked me. When I sat with Margaret pulling weeds in comfortable silence. When that young woman sat beside me at the fountain and said my honesty helped her feel less alone."

"What does that tell you?"

"That maybe my gift isn't about making something. Maybe it's about being present. Being real. Creating space where others feel safe to be real too."

Elaine smiles. "That sounds like a gift worth offering."

"But it feels too simple. Too intangible. How do I offer presence? How do I demonstrate that?"

"Maybe that's tomorrow's question. Tonight, just sit with what you've discovered." She pushes a bowl of fruit toward you. "You've eliminated what's not yours. You're getting clearer on what is. That's exactly where you should be on day two."

You eat together in comfortable silence, the kind you've come to appreciate. Not needing to fill every moment with words.

"The *Golden Harmony* misses you," Elaine says after a while. "She's ready for the next leg when you are."

"One more day," you say.

"Yes. Tomorrow, you offer what you have. Then the following morning, we sail for Self-Care Springs, for some well-deserved self-love and care, on the final island."

The final island. The thought sends a flutter through your chest. You've come so far from that parking lot where this all began. From the woman who didn't know who she was without her children defining her.

"I'm different now," you say quietly.

"Yes, you are."

"I still don't have all the answers."

"No one does. But you're asking better questions."

You finish eating, thank Elaine for the company, and make your way back to your cottage through paths lit by lanterns and stars.

Inside, you light the lamp, change into comfortable clothes, and sit at the small table with your gratitude journal and write:

Today I eliminated three more possibilities and learned that my gift isn't about form. It's about essence. The teaching circle taught me that speaking uncertainty creates connection. The workshop taught me that busy hands quiet anxious minds. The garden taught me I'm still pulling weeds. But the most important moment was unplanned. A young woman sat beside me at the fountain and thanked me for being honest about not having answers. That moment, when I wasn't trying to help or teach or be impressive, that's when something shifted.

Tomorrow I offer what I have. I don't know what it will be yet. But I know its essence: presence, honesty, the willingness to witness myself and others without judgment.

I'm grateful for: Patricia leaving behind her wisdom. Margaret teaching me about cultivation. Zoey speaking her truth about politeness. James still trying even when it's hard. The young woman who reminded me that uncertainty shared is better than false certainty. My body for carrying me through another day of discovery.

You close the journal and pull the **VOICE** and **EMERGENCE** cards you pulled today from your pocket, propping them beside the **TRUST** card from last night. Three cards. Three reminders. Trust the process. Use your voice. Let what wants to emerge, emerge.

After setting the question stone on the small table, beside the cards, you slip between the sheets, exhausted again but in a different way than yesterday. Yesterday, you were exhausted from searching. Tonight, you're exhausted from letting go.

Letting go of needing to be impressive. Letting go of needing the perfect answer. Letting go of needing your gift to look a certain way.

Through your window, stars begin to appear. The same stars that have watched this island for however many years it's existed. Watching people arrive uncertain and leave changed.

Tomorrow you'll discover what your offering is. Or maybe you already know and just need to trust it enough to share it. Either way, you're ready. As ready as anyone can be for the moment when they finally offer their truth to the world and see if it matters.

You close your eyes and let sleep come, carrying you toward whatever tomorrow holds.

22

Rooted In Purpose

You wake before dawn on day three, pulled from sleep by something your body knows but your mind hasn't caught up to yet.

The cottage is still dark. Through the window, the sky still holding onto its deep blue color. You dress quietly and slip outside.

Your feet know where they're going before you decide. The main garden. Your anchor point. The place where everything began two mornings ago.

The fountain greets you with its steady song, water catching the first hints of light. You settle onto the bench, pulling out the question stone from your pocket. You've carried it for three days now, feeling its weight shift with each movement.

What wants to be born through you.

You turn it over in your palm, feeling its smoothness. Yesterday you thought you knew the answer. Presence. Witnessing. Creating space for authentic connection.

But something still feels incomplete. Like you're circling the truth without quite landing on it.

You pull out your oracle deck, shuffle slowly, and draw without looking.

The card shows a circle of women, painted in soft watercolors, sitting together at tables, in what looks like a library. Their faces are turned toward each other, their hands gesturing, their bodies leaning in. Below, one word:
GATHERING

You stare at the card, something stirring in your chest.

Not just being present with one person at a time. Not just witnessing individuals. But gathering women together. Creating the container where connection happens.

"That's the one."

You look up to see Sage approaching, two cups of tea in her hands. She offers you one and settles beside you.

"The card chose you," she says, nodding toward it.

"Gathering," you say. "I think that's what wants to emerge. Not me teaching or leading or even just witnessing one-on-one. But creating spaces where women gather and witness each other."

"Tell me more."

You think about the moments over the past two days that felt most alive. "The teaching circle. When we all sat together sharing truth. That young woman at the fountain, how relieved she looked when she realized she wasn't alone. Margaret and me pulling weeds together. Even dinner with Elaine, just being together without needing to fill every moment with words."

"What do all those moments have in common?"

"Connection. Real connection. Not performing or impressing. Just... being real together."

Sage sips her tea, watching the fountain. "So if that's your essence, what's your offering? How does it take form?"

"I don't know yet," you admit. "I know it's about gathering women. Creating spaces where they can be honest. But I don't know what that looks like practically. Is it teaching? Facilitating? Hosting?"

"Maybe," Sage says, "you should stop trying to figure it out and just let it happen."

"What do you mean?"

"The studios open in an hour. People will start arriving, many coming through here on their way to work or reflect or just sit. What if you simply stayed here or showed up wherever you feel called to see what emerges naturally? Without a plan. Without trying to make something happen. Just being open to what wants to unfold."

The suggestion both excites and terrifies you. "What if nothing happens? What if no one comes, or keeps walking past me?"

"Then you'll have a peaceful morning in a beautiful garden," Sage says simply. "But I suspect something else will occur."

She stands, collecting both empty cups. "Trust what you've learned. Trust what you know. And remember, your gift isn't about you being impressive. It's about creating space for others to be real."

She leaves you alone with the fountain and the gathering card and the first birds beginning their morning songs.

You sit very still, feeling the question stone in one pocket, the oracle card in the other. Reminders of what you're here to discover.

What wants to be born through you.

Not a performance. A presence.

Not a product. A space.

Not you having all the answers. You holding space for questions.

The sky lightens gradually, color returning to the world. Gold touches the tops of trees. The fountain water catches light and scatters it like tiny stars.

You hear footsteps on gravel. A woman appears at the garden entrance, someone you haven't met yet. She's maybe forty, with tired eyes and shoulders that curve inward like she's protecting something vulnerable.

She sees you and hesitates.

"Good morning," you say gently.

She moves slowly to a bench across from you. "I'm sorry. Am I interrupting?"

"Not at all. I'm just sitting with the morning. You're welcome to do the same."

She settles onto the bench, her posture stiff at first, then gradually softening. You both sit in silence, just breathing, listening to water and birds and the garden waking up.

After several minutes, she speaks. "This is my first day. I arrived last night."

"How are you feeling?"

"Terrified." She laughs, but it comes out shaky. "Everyone here seems to know what they're doing. Like they have it all figured out. And I'm just… lost."

"I felt that way two days ago," you say honestly. "Still feel it sometimes. Like everyone else got the manual and I'm just winging it."

She looks at you with visible relief. "Really? You seem so calm. So sure of yourself."

"I'm good at appearing calm. Not always good at being calm. There's a difference."

Another woman enters the garden. Older, maybe sixty, moving with the careful slowness of someone whose body hurts. She nods at both of you and sits on a third bench, completing a rough triangle around the fountain.

More silence. Just the three of you and the water.

Then the older woman speaks. "I'm leaving today. Found my key yesterday evening."

"Congratulations," the younger woman says.

"Thank you. It's strange. I came here thinking I needed to create something impressive. Something worthy of the gallery. Spent two days trying to paint, trying to write, trying to prove I had something valuable to offer." She pauses. "And then yesterday, I realized my gift wasn't any of those things. My gift is bringing order to chaos. Creating systems that help things flow. I spent the afternoon completely reorganizing the maker's workshop. Not because anyone asked me to, but because I saw how the disorganization was preventing people from actually making anything. They kept searching for tools, getting frustrated, and giving up. So I created zones, labeled everything, built a simple system."

She smiles, remembering. "And within an hour, three people came in and actually completed projects. They thanked me, said they could finally think clearly in there, that the space felt usable for the first time. That's when I understood. My gift isn't creating things. It's creating order. Making spaces work. Helping things flow smoothly so others can do their best work."

The younger woman leans forward. "So your gift was completely different than you expected?"

"Completely. I thought I had to be creative in the traditional sense. Turns out I am creative, just differently. I see systems. I see flow. I see what's blocking people and how to clear the path. That's just as valuable as making something beautiful with your hands. Everything that serves others is a gift," the older woman says. "We just have to stop judging some as more valuable than others."

You feel something shift in the air. Something opening. Not about one specific path, but about permission to discover your own unique contribution.

The younger woman nods thoughtfully, then turns to look at you. "What about you? Have you discovered your gift yet?"

The question catches you off guard. Before you can answer, another person appears. Then another. Within minutes, five women are sitting around the fountain, drawn into this gathering place.

And you realize, this is it. This is the moment. Not planned. Not forced. Just emerging naturally.

"I think I'm discovering it right now," you begin, responding to the younger woman's question. "I spent twenty-five years creating space for my children to grow. Making sure they felt seen and heard. Holding room for their feelings. I thought when they left, that skill became useless." You pause, looking around the circle. "But maybe it's not about children specifically. Maybe I know how to create containers where people feel safe enough to be real. And maybe that's what I'm meant to offer?"

The younger woman's eyes fill with tears. "That's exactly what you're doing right now. I feel safer in this moment than I have since I arrived. Because you're not trying to fix me or teach me. You're just... here. Present."

Another woman nods. "I noticed that too. You're not performing or trying to impress anyone. You're just being real, and somehow that makes it safe for the rest of us to be real too."

The older woman smiles knowingly. "That's a rare gift. Most people can't hold space without filling it. They need to fix, advise, teach, rescue. But holding space? Just being present with someone else's experience without trying to change it? That's powerful."

A fourth woman who's been sitting quietly speaks up. "I've been to so many groups and workshops where the leader made it about them. About showing us how wise or healed they are. But this feels different. Like we're all equals here. Like our truth matters as much as anyone else's."

"Because it does," you say simply. And you realize you mean it. Not performing humility, but genuinely believing it. "I don't have more answers than anyone else. I'm figuring this out too. But maybe that's the point. Maybe we don't need someone with all the answers. Maybe we just need someone willing to gather us and hold space for whatever truth wants to emerge."

The conversation continues to flow naturally. More women gather. Each adding her voice. Someone shares about feeling invisible in her marriage. Another talks about the terror of starting over at fifty. Another admits she's been hiding behind busyness for years because stillness means facing things she doesn't want to face.

You notice you're not trying to guide the conversation, or make sure everyone gets a turn, or keep things positive. You're just holding space. Contributing when it feels natural. Staying quiet when someone else needs to speak. Gently redirecting when one person starts to dominate. Creating subtle invitations for the quieter voices.

This is it.

This is your gift.

Not facilitating in the formal sense. Not teaching or counseling or leading workshops. Just creating the conditions where authentic sharing can happen. Holding the container. Keeping it safe. Letting whatever needs to emerge, emerge.

As the sharing ebbs around the circle, a woman's eyes drift to your wrist. "I love your charm bracelet," she says, her voice threaded with genuine curiosity. "Each charm seems to tell its own story."

You glance down at the delicate reminder of Connection Cove. "They do," you reply softly. "Each one a token of friendship and belonging."

Her gaze follows your hand up to the birthstone ring on your finger. "And that ring," she adds, "it suits you. It's your birthstone, isn't it?"

You nod, feeling the warmth of that truth. Wearing these pieces from your journey feels like carrying invisible ties that both ground and uplift you, especially in moments like this one.

The sun climbs higher, warming the garden. You've lost track of time completely. You're so absorbed in the presence, the connection, the honest voices sharing truth.

Finally, one of the women glances at her watch and gasps. "We've been here almost two hours. I completely lost track."

"Me too," another says, sounding surprised but not regretful.

The younger woman who first arrived looks at you. "Thank you. I came to the garden feeling completely alone. I'm leaving feeling… less alone. Like maybe I'm not the only one struggling to figure this out."

"You're definitely not," you assure her.

The women begin to stand, stretching, some hugging, some exchanging names and promising to find each other later. The older woman approaches you last.

"You found it," she says simply. "Your gift. I saw it happen."

"I think so," you admit. "It doesn't feel like I thought it would. I thought finding my gift would feel more… dramatic. But this just felt natural. Right."

"That's how you know it's real. When it feels like coming home instead of reaching for something outside yourself."

She squeezes your hand and walks away, leaving you alone in the garden once again.

You sit back down on the bench, looking at the fountain, replaying what just happened.

You didn't plan that. You didn't create an agenda or prepare talking points or try to facilitate. You just showed up. And somehow, that was enough.

Women gathered. Truth was spoken. Connection happened.

And you held the space for all of it.

As you sit there in the quiet garden, letting it all settle, you can still feel the energy of what just happened, like the air itself holds an imprint of the connection that formed.

"That was beautiful to witness."

You turn to see Sage standing at the garden entrance. You don't know how long she's been there.

"You saw?" you ask.

"Some of it. Enough." She moves to sit beside you on the bench. "Do you understand what happened?"

"I think so. But it felt so simple. So ordinary. I didn't do anything special."

"That's exactly what made it extraordinary." Sage turns to face you fully. "You created the conditions for authentic connection without trying to control what emerged. You held space without filling it. You contributed without dominating. You noticed who needed to speak and who needed to be heard. That's not ordinary. That's skillful. That's your gift."

Your chest tightens with emotion. "But how is that something I can offer? How does honest conversation in a garden become… anything?"

"Come with me," Sage says, standing. "There's someone I want you to meet."

You follow her out of the garden, along a path you haven't taken before. It winds past the studios, past the guest cottages, to a small building tucked among trees. A simple sign by the door reads: **Legacy Planning**

Inside, a woman sits at a desk covered with papers, laptop open, phone propped on a stack of books. She's maybe fifty, with reading glasses perched on her head and the kind of focused energy that makes the air around her buzz slightly.

She looks up when you enter and smiles. "Hello there. I'm Diana."

"Diana helps women figure out how to sustain their gifts," Sage explains. "How to make purpose practical. How to build something that serves others and sustains you."

Diana gestures to chairs across from her desk. "Sit. Tell me what you've discovered."

You describe the impromptu circle around the fountain. How it emerged without planning. How the conversation flowed naturally. How it felt both simple and profound.

"And you're wondering how that becomes something real," Diana finishes for you. "How honest conversation in a garden translates to a life you can actually live."

"Yes."

Diana turns her laptop to face you. "Let me show you something."

The screen displays a website. Simple, beautiful, with an image of women sitting in a circle. The text reads: *Weekly Gatherings for Women Finding Themselves Again*

"This is Maya's site. She started gathering women in her living room three years ago. Just conversation. Honest sharing. No agenda. No credentials. She simply created space and invited women who felt lost or invisible or like they'd disappeared into their roles."

She clicks to another tab. "Here's how she sustains it. The gatherings themselves are donation-based. Suggested amount is ten to twenty dollars, but it's always pay what you can, no one turned away. Some women give more, some give less, some give nothing. And that's okay because the donations aren't her only income source."

Diana clicks through to show grant information. "Maya applied for a small community grant her first year. Five thousand dollars to pilot the program. She had to write a simple proposal explaining what she wanted to do and why it mattered. That grant covered her time for a year while she tested the model and gathered testimonials."

"Testimonials?"

"Stories from women whose lives changed because of the gatherings. Proof that the work matters. Those testimonials helped her get bigger grants. Now she's sponsored by a women's foundation and brings in about thirty thousand a year. That's not wealth, but it's enough to live on while doing meaningful work."

Your heart beats faster. "So she makes a living doing this? Just creating space for women to connect?"

"She makes enough to live simply and do work that matters." Diana clicks through several more websites. Different women, different formats, but similar essence. Weekly circles. Monthly gatherings. Some donation-based, some grant-funded, some both. All creating spaces for authentic connection.

"The infrastructure exists," Diana says. "Women's foundations. Community grants. Fiscal sponsors who handle the legal and tax complexity so you don't have to start a nonprofit. Organizations specifically looking to fund work like this. You're not inventing something new. You're joining something that's already happening."

She pulls out a folder and sets it on the desk between you. "This is yours if you want it. Contact information for fiscal sponsors who specialize in women's initiatives. Grant databases specifically for connection and empowerment work. Templates for simple proposals. Legal basics for donation-based models. Everything you need to start."

You stare at the folder, hardly believing it's real.

"But I don't have credentials," you hear yourself say. "I'm not a therapist or a counselor or a trained facilitator. Who am I to create something like this?"

Diana leans back in her chair. "Let me ask you something. This morning, in that garden, did those women feel safe? Did they share honestly? Did they leave feeling less alone?"

"I think so. Yes."

"Then you're qualified. Your credential is your willingness to show up authentically and hold space for others to do the same. The technical skills, the business knowledge, the grant writing, all of that can be learned. But the essence of what you did this morning? That's the gift. That's what can't be taught."

She taps the folder. "The women who succeed at this work aren't the ones with the most degrees or certifications. They're the ones who genuinely care about creating space for others and are willing to ask for the support they need to sustain it. Are you willing?"

Your throat feels tight. "I'm scared."

"Of course you are. You're about to step into purpose. That's terrifying." Diana's expression softens. "But you don't have to figure it all out today. Take the folder. Read through it. See what resonates. And when you're ready, there are people waiting to support work like this. You just have to be willing to reach out and ask."

Sage stands. "Come. There's one more person I want you to talk to."

You follow her back outside, the folder clutched in your hands, your mind spinning with possibilities.

"Where are we going?" you ask.

"To the dock. To talk with someone whose model might interest you. Someone who's been sustaining meaningful work for a very long time."

You realize where you're headed. The *Golden Harmony*. Elaine. When you arrive, Elaine is on deck organizing supplies, humming softly to herself. She looks up as you approach and smiles.

"Big morning?" Elaine asks, reading your face. "Come sit," she gestures.

"I'll leave you two to talk," Sage says before disappearing up the stairs.

You climb on board the *Golden Harmony,* and sit beside her, "Overwhelming morning. Clarifying morning. I don't know." You set the folder down on your lap. "I think I discovered my gift. But I feel overwhelmed. I don't know how to do something like this," you admit, pointing at the folder

"Tell me what happened."

You describe the circle in the garden. The conversation with Diana. The websites of women doing similar work.

"And you're wondering if it's actually possible," Elaine says. "How you sustain something around creating space for women to gather and be real with each other."

"Yes. It sounds beautiful but not… practical."

Elaine is quiet for a moment, looking out at the water. Then she speaks.

"Twenty years ago, I discovered my gift was guiding women through transformation. These islands, this journey, helping women remember who they are beneath all the roles and expectations, I had no idea how to sustain it. I thought I'd have to charge what transformation work usually costs, which would exclude most women who need it most."

"What changed?"

"I met someone who showed me another way. She introduced me to foundations that fund transformational work for women. She taught me how to write grant proposals, how to tell the story of why this matters. She connected me with a fiscal sponsor who handles all the legal and tax complexity so I don't have to run a nonprofit myself."

Elaine turns to face you fully. "These journeys are free to the women who take them. Completely free. Because they need to receive without obligation. They need to know what unconditional support feels like before they can offer their own gifts freely."

"But how do you survive?"

"I write grant proposals. Three or four a year. Each one takes maybe four or five hours to write once you understand the format. I'm funded by foundations that believe in women's transformation and empowerment. I receive about forty thousand dollars annually. That covers the boat's maintenance, supplies, and pays me enough to live simply. My needs are small. This boat is my home. And I get to do work that fills me in ways money never could."

She gestures around the boat. "It's not wealth. But it's sustainable. And it's meaningful. I haven't had to choose between purpose and survival. I found a way to have both."

Your chest aches with something that feels like hope. "So it's actually possible. To do this kind of work and actually live on it."

"It's not just possible. When you're clear about your gift and willing to ask for support, the resources meet you. The foundations exist. The grants exist. The fiscal sponsors exist. They're waiting for women like you to request support for exactly this kind of work."

She picks up Diana's folder. "This is your roadmap. Everything you need to know about how to start. Where to find funding. How to structure it legally. What other women have done successfully. You're not alone in this."

"But what if I fail? What if I can't write a good enough proposal, or don't get funded, or women don't come to the gatherings?"

"Then you try again. You adjust. You learn. Every woman doing this work has failed multiple times. That's part of the process." Elaine's voice gentles. "But you won't be alone. I can introduce you to my fiscal sponsor. I can review your grant proposals before you submit them. I can connect you with other women doing similar work. I can share what I've learned about sustainability."

Something shifts in your chest. "You'd do that?"

"Of course. Someone helped me get started. Now I help others. That's how this works. It's not competition. It's collaboration. We're all stronger when we support each other's gifts."

"How often do you sail through my area?" you ask.

"Every few months. I have a regular circuit, and your region is one of my stops. And besides, we can stay connected between visits. Email, phone calls, whatever you need."

You think about this. Elaine returning regularly. Ongoing mentorship. Not just sending you off to figure it out alone.

"Could we... could our work support each other somehow?" you ask hesitantly. "Like maybe women from my gatherings might eventually be ready for this journey? And maybe women returning from journeys might need community to integrate what they learned?"

Elaine's face lights up. "That's a fantastic idea."

"We'd be creating a continuum," you say, the idea expanding in your mind.

"We would. And we'd both be stronger for it. You'd have ongoing mentorship and support. I'd have a community that extends the work beyond the days on the boat. We'd be partners."

The word settles over you. Partners. Not just you alone trying to figure everything out. But collaboration. Mutual support. Shared purpose.

"I want to try," you say. "I'm terrified, but I want to try."

Elaine smiles. "That's all you need. Willingness. The courage to begin even when you're scared. Everything else unfolds as you go."

She stands. "Come on. Let's get you some lunch. Then I think you have something important to do this afternoon."

"What's that?"

"Finding your key."

After lunch at the dining pavilion, you find yourself back at the garden. Your anchor point. The place where everything shifted this morning.

The fountain continues its steady song. The sun has moved across the sky, changing the quality of light. Everything looks softer now, gentler.

You sit on the same bench where the circle gathered. Where women appeared, truth was spoken, and connection happened without you trying to make it happen.

You pull out the question stone from your pocket. You've carried it for three days, its weight becoming familiar.

What wants to be born through you.

You know the answer now. Not perfectly, not completely, but clearly enough.

Gathering women. Creating space for authentic connection. Holding containers where truth can be spoken and witnessed without judgment. Building community that sustains women as they find themselves again.

That's what wants to be born through you.

Not just an idea. An actual practice. Real gatherings. Real women. Real impact.

You turn the stone over in your palm one more time, feeling its smoothness, its solidity. This question has carried you through three days of discovery. Through studios and circles and conversations. Through doubt and clarity and everything between.

And now you have your answer.

You stand and walk to the fountain, looking into the clear water. Small coins rest on the bottom, glinting in the sunlight. Wishes from previous visitors, probably.

But you're not here to make a wish. You're here to offer gratitude.

You hold the question stone in your palm, feeling its weight one last time. Then you speak quietly to it, to yourself, to whatever force brought you to this island:

"Thank you for the question. Thank you for the patience to let me find my own answer. Thank you for showing me that my gift was already in me, just waiting to be recognized."

You bend down and gently place the stone in the fountain, letting it settle among the coins. Returning it to the water where all questions dissolve into knowing, and something catches your eye in the afternoon sun. You look closer. A golden key.

Your breath catches. You're sure it wasn't there a moment ago. But here it is, solid and real. You pick it up slowly, feeling its weight, its intricate scroll work along the shaft. And engraved on the bow: ***Treasured Wisdom***

The **Key of Treasured Wisdom**.

You sink back onto the bench, holding it with both hands, tears suddenly streaming down your face.

It's real. Your gift is real. This whole journey, everything you discovered, it's not fantasy or wishful thinking.

You found what you came for.

"There it is."

You look up to see Sage standing at the garden entrance, smiling.

"It was just here. In the fountain."

"That's how it works," Sage says, moving to sit beside you. "The question stone becomes the key when you're ready. When you've truly answered what it asked."

You stare at the key, hardly believing you're holding it. "I thought I'd have to prove myself somehow."

"You did prove yourself. By showing up authentically. By discovering your gift through honest exploration rather than performance. By being willing to claim it even when it felt too simple or not impressive enough." She pauses. "The key doesn't appear when you've created something perfect. It appears when you've recognized your truth."

You close your fingers around it. "So now what?"

"Now you open your treasure chest. Claim the gifts waiting for you. Then we climb the lighthouse."

She stands and extends her hand. You take it, letting her pull you to your feet.

Together you walk to a building you haven't entered before. It sits back among trees, smaller than the gallery but with the same sense of importance. The door is simple wood, aged and beautiful. A brass plate beside it reads:

Treasury of Treasured Wisdom

Sage opens the door and gestures you inside.

The room is circular, lit by windows set high in the walls. Sunlight streams down in golden shafts, dust motes dancing in the beams. And along the curved walls, dozens of chests. Some ornate, some simple. Each one different. Each one waiting for its owner.

"How do I know which is mine?" you ask.

"You'll know. Walk until you find it."

You move slowly along the curve, studying each chest. Some are large and elaborate, others small and plain. Dark wood, light wood, painted, carved. Each one unique.

And then you see it.

Midway around the circle, a chest of warm honey-colored wood. Not fancy, but beautiful in its simplicity. Strong joints. Careful craftsmanship. Built to last. And carved into the lid, the same word engraved on your key:

Gather

You kneel before it, your hands trembling slightly as you fit the key into the lock.

It turns with a soft click.

You lift the lid slowly, reverently.

Inside, nestled on dark blue velvet, three items wait for you.

The first is a journal. But unlike your gratitude journal from Gratitude Shores, this one is substantial. Leather-bound with thick pages. You open it and see it's divided into two sections. The front half is completely blank. Empty pages waiting for your vision, your planning, your dreams, your notes from gatherings, your reflections on what's working and what needs adjustment.

The back half is a calendar and a list of local libraries, outdoor pavilions, and community buildings that offer meeting spaces. And other local resources to explore.

A journal for both dreaming and doing.

You set it aside carefully and lift the second item.

A small wooden box, beautifully carved with an intricate pattern of interlocking circles. You open it to find it filled with business cards, each one different. You pick through them slowly, reading.

Contact information for women who facilitate similar circles with notes: *"Call me, happy to share what I've learned."* Each card is a connection. A possibility. A door that could open. A person willing to help.

Not starting from scratch. Starting from a web of support already in place.

You set the box beside the journal and reach for the third item.

A letter on thick parchment, sealed with dark blue wax. You break the seal carefully and unfold it.

The handwriting is Sage's, flowing and sure:

To the woman who discovered her gift of gathering,

This letter serves as testament that you have completed the journey of Treasure Island. Your gift is creating spaces where women find themselves through finding each other is purposeful, necessary work. The world needs containers where authentic connection can happen safely.

You are ready. You have the resources. You have the support. The infrastructure exists and awaits your engagement.

The women whose contact information fills your box are expecting to hear from you. I have made introductions on your behalf. You are not starting alone. You are stepping into a network that has been waiting for someone like you.

Go forth and gather. Build spaces of honest connection. Hold truth with tenderness. Create community that sustains and transforms.

Your gift matters. Your voice matters. Your willingness to show up authentically gives others permission to do the same.

You are no longer seeking. You are building.

With deep respect and absolute certainty in your capacity,

Sage

You read it twice, then a third time, your vision blurring with tears.

She made introductions already. They know your name. You're not reaching out cold. You're stepping into relationships already begun.

You're not alone.

You carefully fold the letter and place it back in the chest with the journal and the box of cards. Your treasury. The tools for building what you've been called to create.

You turn to look at Sage.

"Thank you," you say.

"Thank you," she replies. "This gift has always been yours to claim."

"I think I believe that. Even though I am scared, I feel what I'm about to step into is right."

"You better believe it," Sage responds joyfully.

Sage walks with you as you carry the chest back to your cottage where the other three wait. Four chests now. Four islands' worth of transformation. Four sets of gifts supporting what you're becoming.

You set this newest chest beside the others and just look at them for a moment.

From Gratitude Shores: Learning to see what you have instead of what's missing.

From Intuitive Isle: Learning to trust your inner knowing.

From Connection Cove: Learning to integrate all the fragments into wholeness.

From Treasure Island: Learning that your gift can sustain you and serve others.

Each island necessary. Each lesson building on the last. All of it leading here, to this moment of clarity about what you're meant to do.

"Ready for some dinner before the climb?" Sage asks from the doorway.

You know what she means. The lighthouse. Every island has ended there. Every climb has revealed something new.

"Yes," you say, tucking the key into your pocket. "I'm starving, actually."

You walk together toward the dining pavilion as dusk settles over the island. The air is cooling, carrying the scent of evening flowers and the meal being prepared.

Inside, the pavilion buzzes with quiet conversation. You fill a plate and scan for Elaine, spotting her at a corner table. She waves you over, and Sage excuses herself to sit with some of the staff.

"I've been waiting for you," Elaine says as you settle across from her.

"I found the key. Opened the treasury. It's all real now."

"I knew you would." She smiles. "How does it feel?"

"Terrifying and right at the same time. Like standing at the edge of something huge," you blurt out, unable to contain your excitement.

"That's exactly what purpose feels like."

You're about to respond when someone approaches your table. The younger woman from this morning's circle. She's holding a folded piece of paper.

"I'm sorry to interrupt," she says, her voice tentative. "I just wanted to give you this, to thank you for being there for me this morning."

She hands you the paper and walks away.

You unfold it and read:

Thank you for this morning. I came to the garden feeling completely alone and broken. Your willingness to be honest about your own uncertainty made me feel less ashamed of mine. You didn't try to fix me or give me answers. You just held space for my truth. That's a gift. I hope you know that. Whatever you build with this gift, I believe it will change lives. It already changed mine.

Your throat tightens. You look up to find the woman watching from across the room. You mouth "thank you" and she smiles, nodding.

Before you can fully process it, another woman approaches. One of the quiet ones from the circle. She sets a small card on the table.

"I don't usually speak up," she says softly. "But I wanted you to know what this morning meant to me."

She leaves, and you read the card:

I've been invisible for so long I forgot I had anything worth saying.

But this morning, you noticed me. When that other woman started dominating the conversation, you gently created space for my voice. You didn't make it obvious or embarrassing. You just opened a door for me to walk in. Thank you for seeing me when I couldn't see myself.

You press the card to your chest, overwhelmed.

"They see your gift," Elaine says quietly. "They're showing you what you can't see yet. The impact you have."

A third woman appears, this one you barely remember from the circle. She was there but didn't speak much. She places a folded letter beside your plate.

"Read it later," she says. "When you doubt yourself. Which you will. We all do."

After she walks away, you unfold it:

I came to this island convinced I had nothing to offer. That my years of caregiving made me obsolete. That the world doesn't need quiet women who just hold space. But watching you this morning, I realized that's exactly what the world needs. Someone who doesn't need to be the star. Someone who makes others feel safe enough to shine. You reminded me that my gift is similar. That it matters. Thank you for showing me a different kind of strength.

You can barely see through your tears now. Three women. Three testimonials. Three mirrors showing you what you couldn't see alone.

"This is your proof," Elaine says, gesturing to the notes spread on the table. "For grant applications. For when you doubt whether this matters. For when you wonder if you're qualified. Women whose lives shifted because of what you created. That's your credential."

You carefully fold each note and tuck them into your pocket with the key. Evidence. Testimony. Proof that your gift is real and necessary.

The older woman who found her key yesterday, the organizer, stops by your table on her way out.

"I saw what happened this morning," she says. "The way you held that space, the way those women opened up, that was masterful. Don't let anyone tell you that's not a skill. It absolutely is."

She squeezes your shoulder once and leaves.

You and Elaine finish eating in comfortable silence, both of you processing the weight of what those testimonials mean.

"They're waiting for you," Elaine finally says. "In your community. Women who need exactly what you discovered today. They don't know it yet, but they're waiting."

"What if I can't do it as well at home? What if it only worked here because this island is magic?"

"The island isn't magic. You are. The island just gave you space to remember." She stands, collecting both plates. "Come on. Sage is waiting to take us to the lighthouse."

"Us?"

"I'm coming with you. If that's okay. I'd like to see you complete this island's journey."

Your chest warms. "I'd really like that. But, before we do, I want to get something from my cottage."

You slip away and head to your cottage with purpose. You open the third chest and retrieve the seed. 'This is a perfect offering,' you think to yourself, before hurrying back.

You find Elaine and Sage standing together outside the pavilion, waiting in the gathering dusk.

"Your beaming," Elaine notices.

You smile and turn to Sage.

"May I plant my legacy seed in the garden surrounding the fountain?" you ask, voice steady but full of quiet hope.

A spontaneous tear appears in Sage's right eye, shimmering in the soft dusk light. She nods slowly, her smile touched with pride. "It would be an honor," she says softly.

The three of you walk toward the garden, the cool evening air wrapping around you like a gentle promise. Kneeling by the fountain's edge, you press the seed into the earth, feeling the connection deepen between what has been given and what will grow.

As you cover the seed with soil, a weight lifts from your chest. This small act, simple yet profound, pulses with the power of new beginnings. It is more than a gift to the island; it is a pledge to yourself, to nurture, to trust, to bloom.

You rise, heart light, and join the two women who now share the quiet strength of this moment. Together, you turn and walk toward the lighthouse, ready to complete the journey with open hearts and shining spirits. Its beam is already beginning its pulsing rotation against the darkening sky.

One, two, three. Pause. One, two, three.

Inside, the logbook waits. You write your entry while Sage and Elaine stand quietly behind you:

I came to this island thinking I had to create something impressive to prove my worth. I leave knowing my gift isn't about impressing anyone. It's about gathering women and holding space for authentic connection.

I discovered that twenty-five years of mothering weren't wasted. They taught me how to create containers where people feel safe. That skill is my foundation.

I learned that purpose and survival don't have to be separate. That meaningful work can be funded. That asking for support isn't a weakness, it's wisdom.

I'm leaving with resources I didn't know existed. With contacts already made. With a network ready to support this work. With testimonials from women whose lives shifted in one morning. With a partner who believes in me.

To whoever reads this: Your gift is already in you. The resources to support it already exist. You just have to be willing to claim your truth and ask for what you need to share it.

You sign your name and date it.

The climb is long but not difficult. Your body is strong now. Elaine and

Sage flank you, the three of you ascending in comfortable silence.

At each window, you pause. The gardens. The studios. The dock. The ocean beyond.

When you reach the lantern room, Sage shows you how the lamp catches and magnifies light, creating a unique gathering pulse.

"Every lighthouse has a signature," she explains. "Ships identify them by their rhythm."

You all watch in silence as the beam sweeps across the darkening sea. One, two, three. Pause. One, two, three.

"It's calling them," you whisper. "The women who need this. The ones who are waiting."

"Yes," Sage says simply.

"And tomorrow, you'll learn how to keep that light burning bright without burning yourself out," Elaine adds.

Sage places a hand gently on your shoulder. "One more thing before we leave."

She leads you to a corner of the lighthouse. There, on a small stone table, lie smooth, blank, brass plates.

"Every offering needs a plaque. she states as she hands you one along with a mallet and chisel.

"Like the ones in the gallery?" you remember.

"Yes. But, yours will be placed beside the seed in the garden," Sage says softly. "A living marker for what you've given. Not just your name, but your growth."

The blade is sharp and cool in your hand. With focused calm, you etch your first name and the year into the plate's surface. Each stroke deliberate, a permanent testament to your presence and your offering.

When finished, you breathe deeply, feeling the weight and power of this small act.

Elaine reaches out and traces her fingers over your name. "I'm so proud of you," she says quietly. "Not just for what you discovered, but for having the courage to claim it."

You hand the finished plaque to Sage, who receives it with a nod of deep respect.

"Beautiful," Sage says. "Now you're part of the legacy too."

The soft glow of the lighthouse surrounds all three of you as you start the slow descent, taking time with each step. When you reach the bottom, Sage excuses herself.

"I'll see you both at dawn for departure," she says. "Sleep well."

Elaine walks with you back to your cottage through paths lit by lanterns and the rising moon. The night air is cool and clean.

"Thank you for coming to the lighthouse," you say. "It meant a lot to have you there."

"I wouldn't have missed it." She pauses at your cottage door. "Tomorrow we sail to Spa Springs. The final island. You'll learn how to sustain all this. How to care for yourself so the well doesn't run dry."

"I'm ready."

"I know you are." She squeezes your hand. "Get some rest. Big journey tomorrow."

After she leaves, you enter your cottage and light the lamp. The four treasure chests sit in a row, waiting. You pull out your gratitude journal and write:

Today I discovered my gift and claimed it fully. I gathered women without trying. I held space without controlling. I was present without performing.

I learned that my twenty-five years of mothering gave me the exact skills I need for this work. That "wasted" time was actually preparation.

I received testimonials tonight. Three women who felt seen and heard because of the space I created. That's my proof. That's my credential.

I received resources and support I didn't know existed. My isolation was never necessary. I just didn't know where to look for help.

And I planted my legacy seed, deep in the rich, dark soil of the garden, a quiet promise of growth, resilience, and renewal.

Tomorrow I sail to the final island. But tonight, I rest in purpose. I know what I'm meant to do. And I know... and believe, I can actually do it.

I'm grateful for: The morning circle that showed me my gift in action. Diana who gave me the roadmap. Elaine who showed me it's sustainable and walked with me to the lighthouse. Sage who believed in me before I believed in myself. The three women who wrote testimonials. The treasury that proved I'm not starting alone. This journey that brought me back to myself.

You close the journal and pull out your oracle deck. You shuffle slowly and draw. The image shows a tree with deep roots spreading underground and strong branches reaching skyward, painted in rich earth tones and vibrant greens. Birds nest in its branches. The roots anchor it firmly. Below, one word: **ROOTED**

You're no longer adrift. No longer searching without anchor. You've found what you were looking for, and now you're planting it. Putting down roots. Building something that will grow and shelter others.

You place this card on your bedside table and arrange all the others you've drawn beside it. A visual story of your journey through this island: **TRUST. VOICE. EMERGENCE. GATHERING. ROOTED.**

Tomorrow you'll draw one more. But tonight, these five tell the story of how you found your gift.

Before slipping into bed, you place the testimonials safely in the treasure chest, and the key on your bedside table beside the cards.

Through the window, you can see the lighthouse beam still pulsing its gathering rhythm across the dark water.

One, two, three. Pause. One, two, three. Calling the women who are waiting. Calling you toward what comes next.

You close your eyes and sleep deeply, dreaming of circles and voices and light spreading outward like ripples on still water.

Tomorrow, the final island.

Tomorrow, you learn to sustain the flame.

23

Fair Winds and Following Seas

You wake before dawn to soft knocking on your cottage door.

"Time to sail," Elaine's voice calls gently from outside.

You dress quickly in the predawn darkness and gather your few belongings. The four treasure chests sit in a row, and you take a moment to look at them. Four islands. Four transformations. Four sets of gifts that will support everything you're building.

You carry them outside one at a time. Elaine is waiting on the path with a lantern.

"I'll help you get these to the boat," she says, lifting one.

Together you make several trips down the path to the dock, the world still quiet and dark around you. The *Golden Harmony* sits waiting, her mast silhouetted against the lightening sky.

Sage suddenly appears as if summoned. She's carrying a small basket.

"Provisions for the journey," she says, handing it to Elaine. "Bread, fruit, cheese. You'll arrive at Self-Care Springs by early afternoon if the wind holds."

"But, before you leave," Sage says, "Come, follow me." She leads you to the garden.

There, nestled beside the young sprout breaking through the earth overnight, your plaque rests firmly in the soil with your name and the year shining in the gentle dawn light.

Sage smiles warmly. "Here, your legacy will grow with the seed you planted."

You inhale the fresh morning air, feeling the profound connection between earth and spirit, past and future, all rooted in this quiet place.

"Ready for the final leg, Captain?"

"Ready," you say, accepting the cup. The warmth feels good in your hands. Sage follows you to the dock.

Once aboard, you lean over the rail. "Thank you. For everything. For believing I had a gift worth discovering."

"You did the work," Sage calls back. "I just held the space for it. That's what you'll do for others now. Hold space and trust them to do their own work."

Sage unties the dock lines and tosses them aboard. "Fair winds and following seas. And remember, the final island isn't about doing more. It's about learning to receive. To rest. To fill your own well."

Elaine uses an oar to push the *Golden Harmony* away from the dock as you slip on the mariner's compass. You take the wheel as the boat drifts into open water. Once clear, Elaine raises the mainsail and it catches the morning breeze. The boat comes alive, heeling slightly as the wind fills the canvas.

Looking back, you can see Treasure Island in the early light. The lighthouse still pulsing its gathering rhythm. The gardens where your circle formed. The studios where you eliminated what wasn't yours. The treasury where you claimed your resources.

All of it fading now as you turn toward open water.

"How do you feel?" Elaine asks, standing beside you as the island disappears behind.

"Different than I did arriving there. I came to that island still searching. I'm leaving knowing what I found."

"Scared?"

"Terrified," you admit. "But also… excited? Like I'm carrying something precious and I can't wait to share it, but I'm also afraid I'll drop it."

"That's exactly how it should feel. If you weren't scared, the work wouldn't matter enough."

The wind picks up as you clear the harbor. Elaine raises the mainsail and it fills with a satisfying snap. The boat heels slightly, cutting through the water with renewed purpose.

You settle into the rhythm of sailing, hand light on the wheel, the compass steady.

The sun breaks over the horizon, turning the water golden. You've been sailing for maybe an hour when Elaine brings up breakfast from the galley. You eat together in the cockpit, the boat steering herself for a while, sails trimmed perfectly to hold course.

"Tell me about Self-Care Springs," you say. "What should I expect?"

Elaine considers this. "It's different from the others. Quieter. The first four islands were about discovering, claiming, integrating, building. Self-Care Springs is about sustaining. About learning that self-care isn't selfish. It's essential."

"I'm not good at that. Self-care. I always feel guilty taking time for myself."

"Most women do. Especially women who've spent decades caring for others. You've been taught that your needs come last. That rest is laziness. That asking for help is weakness." She pauses. "Self-Care Springs will challenge all of that."

"How?"

"You'll see." She smiles mysteriously. "Let's just say the island has a way of forcing you to receive instead of give. To rest instead of produce. To be instead of do."

You think about this as the morning unfolds. The *Golden Harmony* cuts through calm seas, wind steady, sun warming your back. It's peaceful sailing, the kind that lets your mind wander.

You think about the gatherings you'll create. Weekly circles of women. Held in libraries or community centers. Potluck brunches where everyone contributes. Spaces where truth can be spoken without judgment.

You think about the grant proposals you'll write. The fiscal sponsor you'll contact. The network of women Diana and Sage connected you with. All the infrastructure waiting to support this work.

You think about Elaine and the partnership you're building. How your work will create community for women returning from their journeys. How her work will offer transformation for women ready to go deeper.

It's all becoming real. Not someday. Soon.

"What are you thinking about?" Elaine asks, noticing your distant expression.

"I'm thinking how much has changed."

"What changed?"

You think about this. "I stopped looking for permission outside myself. I stopped waiting to be qualified or chosen or validated by some external authority. I claimed what I knew was true and asked for support to share it."

"That's the whole journey, isn't it? Learning that you're enough as you are. That your lived experience is your credential. That your worthiness isn't contingent on achievement or approval."

"Yes." Those words feel solid. True. "But I'm also aware that I could forget this. That I could fall back into old patterns. Doubt. Comparison. Seeking external validation."

Elaine answers matter-of-factly. "That's normal. That's human. You don't complete this journey and never struggle again. You complete it knowing how to find your way back when you drift. That's the difference."

"And if I drift, how do I find my way back?"

"The gifts you've collected. The practices you've learned. The network you're joining. They're your anchors. When you drift, you return to them."

She stands and moves to adjust the jib. "But that's also what Self-Care Springs teaches. How to create practices that sustain you. How to recognize when you're depleted before you're empty. How to receive support without guilt. How to rest without shame."

You watch her work, her movements efficient and sure. Twenty years of doing this. Twenty years of sustainable purpose. She's living proof it's possible.

"Can I ask you something?" you say.

"Always."

"Do you ever burn out? Doing this work year after year? Do you ever want to quit?"

Elaine returns to the cockpit, settling back against the cushions. "I've come close a few times. Times when I forgot to rest. When I gave and gave until I had nothing left. When I said yes to every request without checking whether I had capacity."

"What happened?"

"I got sick. My body forced me to stop. And I realized I'd been treating rest as something I'd earn after I'd done enough. But enough never came. There was always another journey to plan, another woman to help, another grant to write. I was running on empty and calling it dedication."

"What changed?"

"I learned that rest isn't the reward for completing work. Rest is what makes the work sustainable. That taking a day off isn't lazy. It's strategic. That asking for help isn't weak. It's wise." She looks at you directly. "And that's what you need to learn before you start building your circles. Because the work will expand to fill every hour you give it. You have to protect your own well or you'll run dry."

The words settle over you like a weight. You know she's right. You can already feel the pull to say yes to everything, to prove your dedication, to make sure no woman is ever turned away even if it means sacrificing your own needs.

"Self-Care Springs will teach you how to set boundaries that preserve your energy. How to recognize the difference between healthy stretching and unsustainable over extension. How to receive care as gracefully as you give it."

The sun climbs higher. You're making good time. The wind holds steady from the south, pushing you north toward the final island.

Before returning to the wheel, you pull out your oracle deck and shuffle, letting your hands move without thinking to pull a card. You flip it over. The image shows hands cupped around a small flame, protecting it from wind. The flame glows golden against a dark background. Below, one word:

TEND

Not build. Not create. Not achieve. Tend.

Like tending a garden. Like tending a fire. Like tending your own heart so it can keep beating strong.

You show the card to Elaine. She smiles.

"Perfect card for this voyage. You're learning that your purpose requires tending. Not just in the world, but in yourself first."

You pocket the card. A reminder for the journey ahead.

By noon, you can see land on the horizon. At first just a dark line, then gradually taking shape. Hills covered in green. Steam rising in places, visible even from this distance.

"Hot springs," Elaine explains. "The island is volcanic. Not active, but the heat remains. That's why it's called Self-Care Springs. The whole island is built around the springs. Healing waters. Restorative practices. Everything designed to fill you back up."

As you draw closer, the island reveals itself fully. Unlike the others, which had beaches and harbors, this one is built into the hillside. Terraced gardens cascade down to the water. Stone pathways wind between buildings. And everywhere, steam rises from pools and springs cut into the rock.

"It's beautiful," you breathe.

"It is. And it's going to challenge everything you think you know about productivity and worth."

"What do you mean?"

"You'll see."

VI

SELF-CARE SPRINGS

"Almost everything will work again
if you unplug it for a few minutes, including you."
— Anne Lamott

24

New Horizons

You guide the *Golden Harmony* into a small protected bay. Unlike the other islands, this one has a simple stone quay. Natural. Unpretentious. Welcoming without fanfare.

As you tie off the lines, a figure appears on the path above. A woman, maybe sixty, with long strawberry blond hair and the kind of relaxed presence that makes you want to slow down just looking at her. She's wearing loose linen clothes and no shoes.

She waves as she approaches. "Welcome to Self-Care Springs. I'm Renee", she greets you smiling. "You must be the one Sage told me about. The gatherer."

"Word travels fast."

"The island keepers stay connected. We know who's coming, what they've learned, what they still need to discover." She looks at Elaine. "Good to see you again."

"You too, Renee. Take good care of this one?"

"Always." Renee turns back to you. "Bring what you need for a few days. The chests can stay on the boat. You won't need those here."

Something about the way she says it makes you hesitate. "Why not?"

"Because this island isn't about collecting more. It's about integrating what you have."

"I'm coming with you," Elaine says. "I could use some time in the springs

233

myself."

You feel relief flood through you. "I'm glad. I wasn't looking forward to doing this alone."

"You don't have to do anything alone anymore. That's part of what you're learning, remember?"

Renee leads you both up a stone staircase carved into the hillside. It's steep, and by the time you reach the first terrace, you're breathing hard.

"The climb is intentional," Renee says, not winded at all. "It slows you down. Makes you present. You can't rush up these stairs. You have to take them one at a time."

She's right. The urgency you've been carrying since Treasure Island starts to drain away with each step. You're forced to focus on breathing, on placement of feet, on the present moment.

When you finally reach the top, you emerge onto a broad terrace. Buildings made of stone and wood blend into the landscape. Gardens overflow with herbs and flowers. And everywhere, pools of steaming water carved into the rock, some large enough for groups, others intimate spaces for one or two.

"This is the main compound," Renee explains. "Sleeping bungalows are there." She points to small structures tucked among trees. "Dining hall is central. Treatment rooms for massage and bodywork are in that building. And the springs, well, they're everywhere. You'll find the ones that call to you."

"Why is it called Self-Care Springs?" you ask.

Renee smiles. "Because every spring, every treatment, every practice here teaches you to care for yourself with the same tenderness you give to others. The springs are healing, yes. But the real medicine is learning that caring for yourself isn't selfish, it's essential. Self-care isn't a luxury. It's survival."

"And the work?" you ask. "What's the work?"

Renee looks at you with kind eyes. "The work is learning to rest. To receive. To let others care for you the way you've learned to care for others. The work is discovering that you're worthy of tenderness, not just useful for your productivity."

Your chest tightens. "That sounds harder than the other islands."

"It is. For most women, it's the hardest work of all."

Renee turns to Elaine. "You know where your usual bungalow is. Same one as always."

Elaine nods. "I'll get settled and meet you both for lunch?"

"Perfect." Renee watches Elaine head down a side path, then turns back to you. "Your bungalow is this way."

You follow her along a stone pathway that winds through gardens. Lavender brushes against your legs. The air smells of minerals and herbs and something sweet you can't identify.

The bungalow Renee shows you is small but perfect. One room with a bed, a chair, a small table. A window overlooking a private spring that steams gently in the afternoon light. Everything is simple, clean, uncluttered.

"No distractions here," Renee says. "No screens, no clocks, no demands. Just you and what your body needs."

She sets a folded robe and towel on the bed. "Lunch is ready whenever you are at the dining hall. Take your time settling in, rest, explore, or soak. Whatever calls to you. Then join us when you're ready."

After she leaves, you stand in the center of the bungalow feeling suddenly at a loss. What do you do when there's nothing you have to do?

You move to the window and look out at the private spring. Steam rises from the surface in lazy spirals. The water looks impossibly inviting.

When was the last time you did something purely for pleasure? Not because it was productive or earned or justified by exhaustion. Just because it felt good.

You can't remember.

You undress completely, wrap the robe around you, and step outside. The stone path is warm under your bare feet. At the edge of the spring, you dip a toe in. Hot but not scalding. Perfect.

You slip into the water and immediately every muscle in your body sighs with relief. The heat penetrates deep, unknotting tension you didn't know you were carrying.

You float there, letting the water hold you, watching steam rise and dissipate into the blue sky above.

Your mind tries to spin into planning mode. The gatherings you'll create. The grants you'll write. The women you'll serve. All the work waiting.

But your body pulls you back to now. To heat. To weightlessness. To this moment of complete support.

You close your eyes and just breathe.

Time dissolves. Could be ten minutes or an hour. When you finally emerge, your skin is flushed and your limbs feel loose.

You dress in clean clothes and make your way to the dining hall, following the scent of food and the sound of quiet conversation.

The space is open-air, covered but with no walls. Long tables are set with simple food. Fresh vegetables, grains, fruit, bread still warm from the oven. Everything looks nourishing and uncomplicated.

Elaine is already there, sitting with Renee and a few other women you haven't met. She waves you over.

"Did you go in the spring?" Renee asks as you fill a plate and join them.

"Yes," you admit. "I kept trying to justify it. Like I needed a reason to be in the water besides it feeling good."

"That's what most women experience," Renee says. "We've been trained that rest is something we earn. That pleasure without productivity is selfish. That our bodies are tools for accomplishing things, not vessels deserving care."

One of the other women nods. "I've been here three days and I'm still struggling with that. Every time I get in a spring, my mind starts listing everything I should be doing instead."

"What helps?" you ask.

"Reminding myself that I can't pour from an empty cup. That caring for myself isn't taking away from others. It's ensuring I can keep showing up." She pauses. "But honestly, it's still hard. The guilt is loud."

"How long are you here?" Elaine asks her.

"Two more days. Then back to reality. Back to running a women's shelter that always needs more than I can give."

"What brought you to this island?" you ask.

"Burnout. Complete depletion. I was so focused on caring for the women in my shelter that I forgot to care for myself. Got sick. Exhausted. Resentful. My doctor basically ordered me to rest or she'd hospitalize me."

Renee touches the woman's hand gently. "And you're learning?"

"I'm trying. It's uncomfortable. But I'm starting to see that if I don't build rest into my life, my body will force me to stop anyway. Better to choose it than have it chosen for me."

You think about your plans. Weekly gatherings. Grant writing. Building a network. All important work. But also potentially consuming.

"How do you balance it?" you ask. "Meaningful work that serves others and also taking care of yourself?"

"Boundaries," Elaine says simply. "Clear ones. Protected time that's non-negotiable. I sail for nine months of the year. Three months, I rest. I anchor somewhere quiet and I do nothing. No journeys. No planning. Just being."

"Three full months?"

"Three full months. And I protect that time fiercely. Because if I don't rest for three months, I can't serve for nine. The math is simple."

Renee adds, "And it's not just long stretches of rest. It's daily practices too. Morning walks. Evening springs. Weekly massage. Regular check-ins with your body asking 'What do you need?' and actually listening to the answer."

You eat slowly, letting their words sink in. You've spent so long ignoring your body's needs, pushing through fatigue, overriding signals that said slow down. You've worn exhaustion like a badge of honor.

"What if people need me and I'm resting?" you ask quietly. "What if a woman reaches out and I'm not available because I'm taking a day off?"

The woman from the shelter speaks up. "I used to think like that. That I had to be available 24/7 or I was failing the women who needed help. But you know what I learned? When I was depleted, I wasn't helping anyone well. I was going through the motions. Present but not really there. When I started protecting rest time, I showed up better for the hours I was working.

More present. More patient. More creative. The women got a better version of me, even if they got fewer hours."

"Plus," Elaine adds, "when you model good boundaries and self-care, you teach the women in your circles to do the same. You give them permission by example."

Renee stands, collecting empty plates. "This afternoon, you're both scheduled for a massage. Body work. Releasing what's stored in your muscles and bones. Then dinner. Then evening springs. Tomorrow we'll talk about building sustainable practices."

"Scheduled?" you ask, feeling resistance rise. "I don't get to choose?"

Renee smiles. "Not today. Today you practice receiving what's offered without negotiating or trying to control it. Tomorrow you'll have more choice. But today, you let us care for you."

Your jaw clenches. Every part of you wants to say no, I'll decide what I need, I'm fine, I don't require help. But you remember the testimonials. The women who thanked you for holding space. For creating conditions where they could receive care. And you're learning, if you want to offer that to others, you have to learn to receive it yourself.

"Okay," you say, the word feeling strange in your mouth. "I'll go to the massage."

"Good," Renee says. "Elaine will show you where the treatment rooms are."

After lunch, you and Elaine walk together through the gardens toward a low building built into the hillside.

"How are you really?" Elaine asks.

"Uncomfortable," you admit. "Being told to rest feels like punishment, not care. Like I'm being benched."

"I know. I felt the same way my first time here. But Renee knows what she's doing. Receiving is a practice. A skill. You have to build the capacity for it."

"What if I'm bad at it?"

"You will be. At first. Everyone is. But that's okay. That's why you're here.

To practice in a safe place before you go home and try to build sustainability into real life."

Inside the treatment building, soft music plays. The air smells of essential oils. A woman with gentle hands and a calm presence introduces herself as Marianne.

"I'll be working with you today," she says. "Just release what you're holding. Let your body remember it's safe to soften."

You lie on the massage table, face down, and try to relax. But your muscles are tight, resistant. You keep anticipating the next touch instead of receiving the current one.

"You're bracing," Marianne observes quietly. "What are you protecting against?"

"I don't know."

"Yes you do. Your body knows."

You breathe into the question. What are you protecting?

The answer comes slowly: vulnerability. Needing help. Being seen as weak. Taking up space with your needs. Being a burden.

"I'm afraid if I fully relax, I'll fall apart," you whisper.

"And if you did? If you fell apart here, in this safe space, what would happen?"

"I don't know. I've never let myself find out."

"Maybe," Marianne says, her hands working a particularly tight knot in your shoulder, "it's time."

Something in you breaks open. Not dramatically. Just a quiet crumbling of the wall you've maintained for decades.

And you cry.

Not sad tears. Release tears. All the tension you've carried. All the times you said "I'm fine" when you weren't. All the needs you minimized. All the exhaustion you pushed through.

Marianne doesn't try to stop you or comfort you. She just keeps working, keeps creating space for whatever needs to emerge.

By the time the session ends, you feel wrung out but lighter. Like something heavy you'd been carrying was finally set down.

"Thank you," you tell her.

"Thank your body for trusting enough to release. That took courage."

You find Elaine in the waiting area. She takes one look at your face and understands.

"Hard session?"

"Necessary one."

You walk back through the gardens in comfortable silence. The afternoon light is golden now, warming everything it touches.

"I have an idea," Elaine says. "There's a spring I love. Quiet. Private. Big enough for two. Want to soak together before dinner?"

"Yes."

She leads you to a spring tucked behind a stand of bamboo. The water is deep and clear, steam rising in gentle swirls.

You both change into waiting bathing suits and slip in, the heat immediately seems to penetrate the muscles Marianne had loosened.

For a while, you just soak in silence. Two women resting. No agenda. No productivity. Just being.

"Can I tell you something?" you finally say.

"Always."

"I'm scared that when I go home, I'll forget all of this. That I'll fall back into old patterns. Saying yes to everything. Ignoring my needs. Running on empty and calling it dedication."

"You probably will," Elaine says honestly. "At least sometimes. That's normal. Old patterns have deep grooves. But now you know what it feels like to rest. To receive. To honor your needs. So when you notice yourself depleting, you'll have a choice. Keep going or pause. That choice is the difference."

"What helps you remember?"

"My three-month rest periods are non-negotiable. I schedule them a year in advance. I tell everyone who might need me that I'll be unavailable. And then I actually rest. Not half-rest where I'm still checking email or planning the next season. Real rest. Disappearing. Being unreachable."

"That sounds terrifying."

"It is at first. You're convinced everything will fall apart without you. But it doesn't. The work continues. Other people step up. And you come back renewed instead of depleted."

"What about the daily stuff? The regular practices?"

"I journal every morning, even if it's just fifteen minutes. That's my time to check in with my mind and body, to ask what I need that day. On my rest days, I take evening walks. Do my best to get a weekly massage. Once a month, I take a full day off where I do nothing work-related. Those boundaries are how I've sustained this work for twenty years."

You think about your plans. Weekly gatherings. Grant writing. Building a network. Where would rest fit?

"Help me figure it out," you say. "How to build sustainability into what I'm creating from the beginning instead of adding it later when I'm already burned out."

"That's what tomorrow is for," Elaine says. "Renee will help you create your plan. Your practices. Your boundaries. The structure that will hold you."

As you continue to soak in the warm water, you feel your body soften further. The light through the bamboo creates dancing shadows on the water's surface.

"Thank you for coming here with me," you say.

"Trust me, I needed this too. We've both been going at this journey hard. This is a good reminder that even mentors need to rest."

Eventually you both emerge, skin flushed and glowing. You dress and walk together to dinner as the sun lowers toward the horizon.

The evening meal is communal again. More women have appeared, some you recognize from earlier, some new. The energy is quiet, contemplative. Everyone moving slowly, savoring.

You fill your plate and sit with Elaine and Renee. A younger woman joins you, maybe thirty, with cheerful eyes.

"Welcome back," Renee says to her.

"I just arrived." She hugs Renee and Elaine and looks your way to introduce herself. "Hi, I'm Maya."

Your heart stutters. "Maya? You're Maya? The one who runs the circles?"

She looks surprised. "Yes. How do you know?"

"Diana showed me your website. On Treasure Island. You're part of why I'm here. You proved it's possible to do what I want to do."

Maya's face softens. "Diana sent you to me? That's how I started too. She connected me with resources, with a network. She changed my life."

"She's changing mine too." You feel tears prick your eyes. "Can I ask you something? How do you sustain it? The circles, the grant work, showing up week after week?"

"I come here," Maya says simply.

"Every three months like clockwork," Renee chimes in.

"Yes, I block out four days, come to Self-Care Springs, and completely rest. It's non-negotiable. I put it in my calendar a year in advance."

"And that's enough? Four days every three months?"

"It is when you combine it with daily practices. Morning walks. Evening baths. Weekly day off. But these intensive rest periods? They're what keep me going. I tried to skip one once, thought I was too busy. Within a month I was irritable, resentful, making mistakes. My circles suffered because I was showing up depleted."

Elaine smiles. "Maya's been coming here for three years."

"She's one of my success stories. She learned early that rest isn't optional if you want your work to last," Renee adds.

"My circles have actually grown since I started prioritizing rest," Maya admits. "I can hold more because I'm not running on empty. I'm more present, more patient, more creative. The women feel the difference when I show up resourced versus depleted."

You look at Maya with new understanding. This is what sustainability looks like. Not perfect balance, but consistent practice. Regular rest. Protected boundaries.

"So you're not here because you burned out," you clarify. "You're here because this is how you prevent burnout."

"Exactly. This is part of my business model. Rest is literally built into my operating budget. I put aside money specifically for these retreats because they're not optional. They're what make everything else possible."

After dinner, Renee leads a small group of you along a path that winds up to the highest terrace, where there's a grove of trees strung with hammocks, each one positioned to catch the evening breeze and face the ocean below.

"Pick one," Renee says. "Sometimes rest isn't about heat and water. Sometimes it's about stillness and sky."

You choose a hammock near the edge, where you can see the ocean dark and vast under the rising moon. You climb in carefully, and the fabric cradles you, swaying gently. Around you, other women settle into their own hammocks. The sound of breathing, the creak of rope, the distant rush of waves. No one talks. No one performs. Just being.

You look up at the stars beginning to appear through the canopy of leaves. Think about how far you've come. Four islands. Four transformations. And now this final lesson: learning to rest so you can sustain what you'll build for the women waiting to be gathered and the purpose you've finally claimed.

About saying no to protect your capacity to say yes.

About modeling self-care so other women learn it's not selfish.

About tending the flame so it doesn't burn out.

"Ladies," Renee says. "Before you all disperse for the evening, I want to give you something."

She hands each woman a small smooth stone from a basket. Yours is warm, as if it's been sitting in the sun.

"Tomorrow morning, we'll talk about building your sustainable practices. Tonight, hold this stone and ask your body what it needs. Not what it should need. What it actually needs to stay resourced."

You close your fingers around the stone. It fits perfectly in your palm.

After the hammock, you walk back to your bungalow through gardens lit by lanterns and moonlight. Elaine walks with you partway, then branches off toward her own bungalow.

"Sleep well," she says. "Tomorrow you'll build your plan."

Inside your bungalow, you change into sleep clothes and sit on the bed, the stone in your hand.

What does your body need?

The question feels both simple and impossible.

You close your eyes and listen.

Your body answers: Rest. Play. Movement that feels good. Connection that energizes instead of depletes. Time in nature. Creative expression. Nourishing food. Adequate sleep. Touch. Laughter. Solitude. Community. All of it. Not one thing. Many things.

You pull out your gratitude journal and write:

Today I arrived at the final island and started learning the hardest lesson: receiving. Letting others care for me. Believing I'm worthy of tenderness, not just valued for productivity.

I had my first massage where I cried releasing years of tension. I soaked with Elaine and talked about sustainability. I met Maya who's three years ahead of me on this path.

Renee handed me a stone and asked me to ask my body what it needs. My body told me: everything I've been denying it. Rest and play and movement and connection and solitude. Not one thing. Balance.

Tomorrow I build my plan. The structure that will hold me so I can hold others.

I'm grateful for: Renee who sees what I need before I do. Elaine who came here with me. Marianne whose hands created space for release. Maya who proved I'm not alone in this. My body for still trusting enough to tell me what it needs after years of being ignored.

You close the journal and reach for your oracle deck. You shuffle and pull without looking. The image shows a woman sleeping peacefully, moon visible through a window, stars scattered across a dark sky. Below, one word: **REST**

The permission you need. The practice you're learning. The foundation of everything else.

You place the card beside **TEND** on your bedside table. Both guiding you toward the same truth: you cannot sustain what you don't tend. You cannot tend what you don't rest.

You slip into bed, the stone from Renee still in your hand, and fall asleep almost immediately.

Deep, dreamless sleep. The kind that only comes when your body finally feels safe enough to fully let go.

25

Filling Your Own Cup

You wake to soft light filtering through your window. For the first moment in what feels like forever, you don't immediately think about what you need to do. You just lie there, noticing the comfort of the bed, the warmth of sunlight on your face, the ease in your body.

The **REST** card sits on your bedside table beside **TEND**. Two reminders of what you're learning.

You slip your robe on and step outside. The morning air is cool and clean, carrying the scent of jasmine and mineral-rich water. Your private spring steams gently, inviting.

Without overthinking it, you disrobe and slip into the water. Just fifteen minutes, you tell yourself. Just to start the day with something nourishing.

But as the heat soaks into your muscles, you realize there's no rush. No schedule demanding you hurry. Nothing you have to accomplish right now.

So you stay. Twenty minutes. Thirty. However long your body wants.

When you finally emerge, you feel clear. Present. Ready.

You find your way to the dining hall where breakfast is already laid out. Fresh fruit, warm bread, yogurt with honey, tea steaming in clay pots.

Elaine and Maya are sitting together, deep in conversation. They wave you over.

"Morning," Elaine says. "How did you sleep?"

"So good. That hammock, the stars, something about it all just… let me

246

let go."

"That's what this place does," Maya says. "It gives you permission to stop holding everything so tight."

You fill a plate and join them. "I did something this morning without planning it. I soaked in my spring just because it felt good. Not because I earned it or needed to justify it. Just because."

Maya smiles. "That's the practice. Doing things for your body without needing a reason beyond 'this feels nourishing.' It sounds simple but it's revolutionary for women like us."

"Women like us?"

"Women who were taught our needs come last. That rest is selfish. That we're only valuable when we're productive." She takes a bite of bread. "Unlearning that is the work of a lifetime. But it starts with moments like your morning spring. I did the same thing this morning."

Renee appears with her usual unhurried grace. "Good morning, ladies. After breakfast, I'd like to work with all of you on building your sustainability plans."

"All of us?" you ask.

"Yes, it's good to revisit your practices. Make sure they still serve. And you're building yours from scratch. Please bring your stone," Renee pours herself tea.

"I'd love that," Maya says.

After breakfast, the four of you gather in a quiet room overlooking the terraced gardens. Cushions are scattered on the floor around a low table. Renee brings paper, pens, and a basket of smooth stones.

"Let's start with honesty," Renee begins, settling onto a cushion. "What does your body actually need to stay resourced? Not what you think it should need. Not what sounds reasonable or manageable. What does it truly need?"

She places a stone in the center of the table. "Each of you, hold your stone and ask your body the question. What does my body need? And listen without editing. Your body knows."

You take your smooth stone from your pocket, hold it gently in the palm of your hand, close your eyes, and ask the question.

Your body answers immediately: Sleep. Real sleep, not the exhausted collapse kind. Morning movement. Time outside every day. Creative expression. Connection with people who energize you, not drain you. Silence. Space. Permission to say no. Food that nourishes. Water. Sunlight. Touch that isn't sexual or demanded. Laughter. Beauty. Music. All of it.

"It's a long list," you say when Renee asks you to share.

"Good. Long lists mean you've been ignoring a lot. Write it all down."

You write while Elaine and Maya share their own lists. Elaine's includes sailing, morning springs, monthly complete days off, her three-month rest periods. Maya's includes daily walks, weekly therapy, monthly full moon circles just for her own renewal, quarterly trips here.

"Now," Renee says, "let's talk about the gap between what your body needs and what your life currently provides."

You look at your list and feel overwhelmed. "My life provides almost none of this. I've been running on fumes for years."

"Then that's what we're here to change. Not all at once. But starting with the foundation." Renee slides paper toward you. "Let's build your daily practice first. What's non-negotiable? What has to happen every day or you start depleting?"

You think about this. "Morning check-in with my body. Some kind of movement. Time outside. Adequate sleep."

"Good. Let's make those concrete." Renee helps you create a structure:
Morning:

- Wake naturally when possible (no alarm unless necessary)
- 15 minutes in silence with tea, asking body what it needs today
- 20-30 minutes movement (walk, yoga, dance, whatever feels good)

Throughout day:

- At least 20 minutes outside
- Drink water

- Eat nourishing food without distraction
- Notice when energy dips and pause

Evening:

- Disconnect from screens 1 hour before bed
- Some kind of release practice (journaling, bath, gentle stretching)
- In bed by 10pm to allow 8 hours sleep

"This seems like a lot," you say, looking at the list.

"It's about 90 minutes total spread across your day," Renee points out. "That's not a lot. That's bare minimum for staying resourced. And it will make everything else you do more effective."

Maya nods. "When I first started my daily practice, I thought I couldn't afford the time. But I actually became more productive. I show up clearer, more focused, more creative. The time I 'lose' to self-care is more than made up for in quality of presence."

"Now," Renee continues, "weekly practices. What needs to happen weekly?"

You think about this. "A full day off? One day where I'm not working or producing or being available?"

"Yes. Non-negotiable. Which day?"

"Sunday?"

"Good. Write it: Sunday, completely offline. No circles, no emails, no planning. Just rest and restoration."

"What if women need me?"

"They'll need you more if you show up depleted than if you take one day to rest," Elaine says firmly. "And you model healthy boundaries by having them. You teach women it's okay to protect their energy by protecting yours."

Renee adds to your plan: Weekly:

- Full day off (Sunday)

- At least one meal with someone who energizes you
- Something creative just for pleasure (no productive purpose)
- One thing in nature (hike, beach, garden, park)

"Monthly?" Renee prompts.

You're starting to see the pattern. "Maybe a full day of deeper rest? Like a personal retreat day?"

"Perfect. And quarterly?"

"Could I come here?" you ask tentatively. "Like Maya does? Four days every three months?"

"You could. Or you could create your own version. The point is intensive rest periods where you fully unplug and restore. These aren't optional extras. They're essential maintenance."

Your plan is taking shape: Quarterly:

- 4 days complete rest (Self-Care Springs or personal retreat)
- Review what's working and what needs adjustment
- Reconnect with why this work matters

"And annually?" Renee asks.

You look at Elaine. "Could I do what you do? Take a full season off?"

Elaine nods. "You could. Maybe start smaller, two weeks or a month. But yes, building toward a full season of rest annually. That's how you sustain decades of meaningful work."

"But how can I afford to take that much time off?"

"How can you afford not to?" Maya counters. "I built rest into my business model from the beginning. I factor it into grant requests. I tell the women in my circles that I take quarterly breaks. I'm transparent about my boundaries. And you know what? No one's ever said I'm unreliable. They respect the boundaries. Some even thank me for modeling what they need to do."

Renee pulls out a new sheet of paper. "Now let's talk about boundaries in your work. The gatherings you're planning. How will you structure them to be sustainable?"

You haven't thought about this deeply. "Weekly circles. Maybe two hours?"

"How many circles per week?"

"I don't know. As many as needed?"

"No." Renee's voice is gentle but firm. "Not 'as many as needed.' How many can you sustain while maintaining your daily, weekly, and quarterly rest practices?"

You do the math. If you need Sunday off, and you need your morning and evening practices, and you need quarterly rest periods… "Maybe two circles per week?"

"Start with one," Elaine suggests. "You can always add a second once you see how it feels. But starting with one means you're building sustainability from the foundation, not adding it later when you're already overextended."

"One feels like not enough."

"One circle serving twelve women is 12 women per week, 48 per month, nearly 600 per year," Maya points out. "That's significant impact. And you'll show up better for those 12 women than you would for 24 if you're depleted."

Renee adds to your plan: Work boundaries:

- One gathering per week (start with Wednesday)
- Maximum 12 women per circle
- 2-hour gathering (arrival, circle, potluck)
- No gatherings during quarterly rest periods
- Email response time: within 3 days (not immediate)

"What about the women who need more?" you ask. "What if 12 isn't enough? What if women need me between gatherings?"

"Then you refer them to other resources," Renee says. "Therapists, other circles, support groups. You're not meant to be everything to everyone. You're meant to hold one space consistently well."

"And as your circles grow," Maya adds, "you might train other women to facilitate. You could have multiple circles led by different women, all following the model you create. That's sustainable expansion. Not you doing more, but you empowering others to do it with you."

The idea blooms in your mind. Not you holding everything alone, but creating a model others can replicate. A network of circles, each one led by a woman who's discovered her gift of gathering.

"That's legacy," Elaine says, seeing your face. "Not you working yourself to death, but you creating something that multiplies beyond you."

Renee stands and moves to the window. "Let's talk about the hardest part. Saying no. Disappointing people. Being unavailable when someone wants your time."

Your stomach clenches. "I'm terrible at that."

"Most women are. We've been taught that saying no makes us selfish or unkind or unreliable." Renee turns back to face you. "But every yes to something that depletes you is a no to your own well-being. Every time you override your boundaries, you teach people your boundaries don't matter."

"How do I get better at it?"

"Practice. With support. Let's role play." Renee sits across from you. "I'm a woman from your circle. I email you on Sunday, your day off, asking if we can meet. I'm struggling and I need your support. What do you say?"

Your instinct is to immediately say yes, of course, I'll make time. But you breathe and think about what you've learned.

"Okay, I'm not if I can actually do this yet, but what I'd like to be able to say is: Thank you for reaching out. I'm glad you trust me enough to share what you're struggling with. I'm offline on Sundays to rest so I can show up better for our circles. I'll respond on Monday, and we can figure out how to support you. In the meantime, if you need immediate help, here are some crisis resources."

Renee smiles. "Perfect. You acknowledged her need, maintained your boundary, offered help within your capacity, and provided backup resources. That's how it's done."

"It feels harsh."

"It feels unfamiliar," Renee corrects. "Harsh would be ignoring her completely. This is boundaried care. You're still caring, you're just caring in a way that's sustainable."

Maya jumps in. "I had to learn this the hard way. A woman from my circle started calling me late at night when she was anxious. At first I always answered because I wanted to help. But after a few weeks, I was exhausted, resentful, and not helping her well. So I had to say: I care about you, and I can't be your crisis support. Here's a crisis line. Here's a therapist. I'll see you at circle. It felt terrible. But it was necessary. And she actually got better help than I was providing."

"Boundaries aren't mean," Elaine adds. "They're honest. And they model for other women that it's okay to protect their own energy too."

Renee brings the conversation back. "Let's talk about your support system. You can't do this alone. Who's in your circle of support?"

You think about this. "Elaine. Maya now, maybe?"

"Yes, of course," Maya chimes in.

"Thank you," you smile. "Probably a fiscal sponsor. The women in the network Sage introduced me to."

"Good. Write their names down. These are the people you reach out to when you're struggling, when you need advice, when you're doubting yourself." Renee pauses. "And add one more thing: monthly check-ins with one person who knows your boundaries and will call you on it when you start overextending."

"Like an accountability partner?"

"Exactly. Someone you're honest with about your capacity. Who asks the hard questions like 'are you resting?' and 'is this sustainable?' and who you trust to tell you the truth."

Elaine speaks up. "I'll be that person if you want. We'll talk regularly anyway because of our partnership. And I will hold you accountable once a month to your boundaries."

Your throat tightens with gratitude. "I'd really like that."

By the time the session ends, you have a complete plan:

Daily: Morning practice, movement, time outside, evening wind-down

Weekly: Full day off, creative time, nature, nourishing connection

Monthly: Personal retreat day
Quarterly: 4-day intensive rest at Self-Care Springs
Annually: Building toward 2-4 week complete break

Work structure:

- One weekly circle (12 women max)
- Wednesday
- No gatherings during rest periods
- Email boundaries (3-day response time)
- Clear referral resources for needs beyond your capacity

Support system:

- Weekly check-ins with Elaine
- Network of other facilitators
- Fiscal sponsor for business support
- Quarterly meet-ups with other circle leaders

"This feels doable," you say, looking at the paper. "Still scary, but doable."

"It is doable," Renee confirms. "But only if you actually follow it. The plan means nothing if you override it every time something feels urgent."

"How do I remember? How do I not fall back into old patterns?"

Renee walks to a cabinet and pulls out a small wooden box. She hands it to you.

Inside are seven smooth stones, each one with a word carved into it:
REST
BOUNDARIES
NO
ENOUGH
RECEIVE
PLAY
TRUST

"Keep these visible," Renee says. "One for each day of the week. Let them remind you what you're practicing. This isn't about perfection. It's about returning. When you notice yourself overriding boundaries, you return. When you catch yourself depleting, you return. These stones are your anchors."

You hold the box, feeling their weight, reach in and touch their smoothness. Seven reminders that rest is not optional.

"There's one more thing," Renee says, standing. "Follow me."

She leads you outside, through the gardens, up another terrace to a grove of trees you haven't seen before. In the center, surrounded by flowering bushes, is a small fountain. Not grand or ornate. Simple stone, water flowing gently from center to edge and back again. A perfect circle of continuous flow.

"This is where people find their final keys," Renee says. "Not by searching. By receiving."

You feel your heart beat faster. "The **Key of Self-Love and Care**?"

"It appears when you've truly understood the lesson. When you know in your bones that caring for yourself isn't selfish. It's necessary. When you're ready to protect your own well-being with the same fierceness you protect others.'"

She gestures to a bench near the fountain. "Sit. Ask yourself honestly: Am I ready to honor my needs without guilt? Am I ready to say no without over-explaining? Am I ready to rest without earning it? Am I ready to receive care as gracefully as I give it?"

You sit, the questions settling into your chest like stones dropping into still water.

Are you ready?

Your instinct is to say yes immediately, to prove you've learned, to graduate from this final lesson.

But Renee said honesty. So you sit with the truth.

Part of you is ready. The part that's tired of running on empty. The part that felt relief in Marianne's massage when you finally released. The part that floated in the hammock under stars and thought yes, this, more of this.

But part of you is still scared. Scared that if you rest, everything will fall apart. Scared that if you say no, you'll disappoint people. Scared that if you prioritize your needs, you're selfish. Scared that without productivity, you have no value.

Both parts are true.

"I'm ready and I'm scared," you say out loud. "I want to honor my needs but I'm terrified of what that means. I want to rest but I don't know if I trust that it won't all fall apart without me holding it together."

"That," Renee says softly, "is the most honest answer you could give. You don't have to have it all figured out. You just have to be willing to practice. To return when you forget. To choose yourself again and again even when it feels uncomfortable."

She stands. "Look in the fountain. Tell me what you see."

You move to the edge and look down into the clear water. Coins rest on the bottom, glinting in the sunlight. Wishes from others who came before you.

But there, among the coins, something else catches light. Golden. Substantial.

A key.

Your breath catches.

"Go ahead," Renee says. "It's yours. You earned it by being honest. By admitting you're still learning. By choosing to practice even when you're scared."

You reach into the cool water and close your fingers around the key. It's warm despite the water, solid and real in your palm.

The **Key of Self-Love and Care**.

You hold it up to the light, tears streaming down your face.

Engraved on the bow: *Self-Love and Care*

"I found them all," you whisper. "All five keys."

"You did. And now you hold the complete set. Everything you need to build and sustain your life's work."

Elaine steps forward, smiling. "Five keys that spell out the greatest treasure: **G.I.F.T.S.**"

You look at her, curious.

"Five islands, five keys," Elaine says. "Each island taught you something, and each key you found represents a gifts. Together, they spell GIFTS. Everything you need to live your purpose."

"The Key of Gratitude from Gratitude Shores. Where you learned to see what you have. The Key of Intuitive Intention from Intuition Isle. Where you learned to trust your inner knowing and choose to act on it. The Key of Family and Friends from Connection Cove. Where you learned to heal old wounds and create new belonging. The Key of Treasured Wisdom from Treasure Island. Where you discovered your unique gift to share. And the Key of Self-love and Care from Self-Care Springs. Where you learned to tend to yourself first so you can sustain your purpose."

"**G.I.F.T.S.**," you repeat softly, feeling how each key fits together.

Renee gently adds, "And each island helped you remember the gifts you already carried. You didn't collect them. You unlocked them by discovering the five keys."

"I'm so happy for you," Elaine says warmly. "The woman with all five keys. Ready to build something sustainable and beautiful."

Maya hugs you. "I'm so glad I got to witness this. Welcome to the practice. Welcome to the lifelong work of choosing yourself."

The afternoon unfolds gently. You soak in springs. You rest in a hammock, reading. You walk through gardens with Elaine and Maya, talking about the work you're each building, the partnerships forming, the ways you can support each other.

At dinner, Renee announces to the gathered women that you found your key. Everyone applauds, understanding the significance without needing explanation.

After the meal, Renee brings out a special tea. "This is tradition here. When someone finds their key, we drink blessing tea together. Each woman offers a blessing for the journey ahead."

You sit in a circle with a dozen women, the tea warming your hands.

One by one, they offer blessings:

"May you remember that rest is productive."

"May you say no without guilt."

"May you receive help with grace."

"May you honor your body as sacred."

"May you know you're enough, always enough."

"May you build work that sustains instead of depletes."

"May you teach other women by your example."

When it comes to Elaine, she looks at you with so much warmth. "May you trust that the work will hold without you having to hold it all. May you discover that partnership is stronger than martyrdom. May you sail home knowing you're not alone."

Maya adds, "May you remember on the hard days that rest is not the enemy of productivity. It's the foundation. May you protect your boundaries fiercely and forgive yourself when you slip. May you find your way back, always back, to the truth that you matter."

Renee speaks last. "May you carry these lessons into your life like seeds into soil. May you plant them, tend them, trust them to grow. May you return here whenever you need to remember. This place, these practices, this community, they're yours now. Forever."

You drink the tea together, the warmth spreading through your chest. Not just from the liquid, but from the blessing, the belonging, the knowledge that you're part of something larger than yourself.

After the blessing circle disperses, Renee approaches you and Elaine. "Ready to open your treasure chest?"

"I'd love too," you answer.

"It's waiting for you in the lighthouse. The lighthouse is most beautiful at sunset. We'll open the chest, then climb together."

The three of you walk through the gardens as the light begins to turn golden. The path leads upward, past the terraced springs, toward the lighthouse. It's smaller than the others, built of pale stone that seems to glow in the late afternoon sun.

At its base, a simple door stands open. Inside, the circular room is quiet and cool. And there, on a stone pedestal, sits a chest.

It's different from the others. Made of bamboo. Carved into the lid is a single symbol: a cup overflowing with water.

"The symbol of receiving," Renee says softly. "Of being filled, of having enough to overflow to others."

You fit the **Key of Self-Love and Care** into the lock. It turns with a soft click.

Inside, nestled in silk the color of morning sky, are three items.

The first is a cup. But not just any cup. It's hand-thrown pottery, the glaze a deep, rich blue that seems to shift in the light. The shape fits perfectly in two hands, substantial and grounding. And carved around the rim in delicate script: *Fill your own cup first*

You lift it carefully, feeling its weight, its solidity. "It's beautiful."

"For your morning practice," Renee explains. "Your tea, your moment of checking in with your body, asking what you need. This cup represents the daily commitment to fill yourself before you pour out for others. The blue is intentional. It's the color of the throat chakra, of speaking your truth, of expressing your needs."

You trace the words with your finger. Fill your own cup first. The permission you need, carved in permanent script.

The second item is a white gift box, small and smooth. You open it to find four small amber bottles, each labeled: *Lavender* for calming, *Eucalyptus* for clarity, *Rose* for heart-opening, *Sandalwood* for grounding.

"Essential oils," Renee says. "For your evening practice. A few drops in your bath, on your pulse points, in a diffuser. Whatever helps you transition from doing to being. The scent becomes an anchor, signaling to your body: it's time to rest now."

You open the lavender bottle and breathe in. Immediately your shoulders drop, your jaw unclenches. The scent reaches something deep in your nervous system that understands: safe. Rest. Let go.

The third item makes you smile. An hourglass, about six inches tall, the glass hand-blown, the sand inside a soft rose gold color. You turn it over and watch the sand begin its steady flow.

"Sixty minutes," Renee says. "Your protected hour each day. When you turn this over, that time is yours. Not for emails, not for planning, not for anyone else's needs. Just yours. When the sand runs out, you can return to the world. But while it flows, you're unavailable."

"It's perfect," you whisper, watching the sand fall. "All of it is perfect."

Elaine steps closer, looking at the three items. "These aren't just symbols. These are tools. Things you'll use every single day."

"That's the point," Renee says. "Self-care isn't an idea. It's a practice. These gifts support that practice. Make it tangible. Make it real."

You carefully place each item back in the chest. Your chest now. The fifth and final one.

"Ready to climb?" Renee asks.

The three of you begin the ascent. The spiral staircase is narrow, the steps worn smooth by countless feet before yours. Windows at intervals show the island falling away below, the gardens and springs and bungalows getting smaller with each turn.

When you reach the lantern room, the sun is touching the horizon. The whole sky is painted in shades of rose and gold and deepening purple.

"This is my favorite lighthouse," Elaine says, moving to the windows. "I've climbed all five over the years. This one always feels like coming home."

You understand what she means. The other lighthouses taught lessons, showed you perspectives, marked achievements. This one feels different. Gentler. More intimate.

"Look at the lamp," Renee says.

The lens in the center isn't rotating like the others. It's still, steady, capturing the sunset light and holding it. Not sending it out in sweeping arcs but radiating in all directions simultaneously. A constant glow rather than a pulsing beam.

"The other lighthouses guide ships," Renee explains. "This one welcomes them home. It says: here is rest. Here is safety. Here is where you anchor and restore."

You watch the light fill the room, warm and constant. This is what you need to become for yourself. Not just the lighthouse that guides others.

But the one that welcomes yourself home. That says: rest here. You're safe. You're enough.

Elaine puts her arm around your shoulders. "I'm proud of you. Not just for finding all five keys, but for being willing to do the hardest work. Learning to receive."

You stand together watching the sun sink lower, the light in the lantern room growing richer, deeper.

"Can I tell you something?" you say to both of them. "When I started this journey, I thought the hardest part would be discovering my purpose. What my gift was. But it wasn't. The hardest part was believing I'm worthy of care while I do that work. That I can serve others and still honor my own needs."

"That's what most women discover," Renee says. "We can learn to give endlessly. Learning to receive? That's revolutionary."

"What happens now?" you ask. "I have all five keys. I've opened all five treasure chests. I've learned the lessons. What comes next?"

"Life," Elaine says simply. "Real life. You go home and you practice. Some days you'll remember everything you learned. Some days you'll forget and fall back into old patterns. But now you know what it feels like to be whole, to be resourced, to be sustained. So when you drift, you'll recognize it. And you'll find your way back."

"How do I find my way back?"

"The gifts," Renee gestures to the chest waiting below. "The practices. The network. The boundaries you've established. They're your map home. Anytime you're lost, you return to them."

The sun drops below the horizon, and for a moment the whole sky blazes with color. Then slowly, gently, it fades to dusk.

"There's one more tradition," Renee says. "The logbook."

She leads you to a small table where a leather-bound book rests. You open it and see entries from women before you. Brief reflections on what this island taught them.

You pick up the pen and write:

I came to this island exhausted from discovering my purpose. I leave knowing that purpose without self-care is unsustainable. I learned that filling my own cup first isn't selfish. It's essential. That rest is productive. That boundaries are love. That I am worthy of the same tenderness I offer others.

To whoever reads this, you cannot pour from an empty cup. You cannot sustain meaningful work while running on empty. Rest is not optional. It is the foundation. Care for yourself with the same fierceness you care for others. You are worth it.

You sign your name and date it.

The final entry in the final logbook.

"Perfect," Renee says, reading over your shoulder. "Now you're complete."

The three of you descend together as night settles over the island. At the bottom, you retrieve your chest and carry it back to your bungalow.

Inside, you light the lamp, pull out your gratitude journal, and write:

Tonight I climbed the final lighthouse.

I have everything I need. Five chests of gifts. A sustainability plan. A network of support. A partner in Elaine. A model in Maya. A practice in these stones and oils and this beautiful cup.

Tomorrow I sail home. Not to the old life. To a new one. Built on everything I've discovered and claimed.

I'm grateful for: Renee who taught me the hardest lesson with such gentleness. Elaine who witnessed my entire journey. And these five islands that gave me back to myself, whole.

You pull out your oracle deck and shuffle slowly, feeling the weight of completion, and draw. The image shows a woman walking forward on a path that glows with golden light. Behind her, five islands fade into mist. Ahead, the path is clear and bright. She carries nothing visible, but light radiates from within her. Below, one word: **HOME**

Not the place you left. The person you've become.

You're going home. But home is no longer a location. Home is this wholeness. This integration. This knowledge that you are enough, you have enough, you've learned enough.

Tomorrow you sail back to your life. But you're not the same woman who left. You're whole now. Ready. Resourced.

You slip into bed and sleep deeply, dreaming of circles and springs and the life you're about to build.

VII

HOMEWARD

"The ache for home lives in all of us,
the safe place where we can go as we are and not be questioned."
— Maya Angelou

26

The Crossing

As the *Golden Harmony* pulls away from Self-Care Springs, you stand at the rail watching the island fade.

"Come take the wheel," Elaine calls. "Let's get you home."

You settle into position, hands finding the familiar spokes. Five of them, just like the bronze coin in Heritage Heights on Connection Cove. The wheel that required both sides, both aspects of yourself integrated and whole.

The morning unfolds in comfortable silence. Just the sound of water against the hull, wind in the sails, seabirds calling. You're not the same woman who stood at this wheel a couple weeks ago, terrified of the storm. You know how to hold steady now. How to adjust without over correcting. How to trust.

"Tell me what you're thinking," Elaine says after a while.

"I'm thinking about going home. About whether I can actually do this."

"Build the gatherings?"

"All of it. It felt possible on the islands. But out here, heading back to real life, I'm starting to wonder if I just got caught up in something that won't translate."

Elaine is quiet for a moment. "That doubt? That's normal. Every woman feels it on the crossing home. The islands gave you space to discover and practice. Now you're returning to the place where old patterns live. Where people expect you to be who you were."

"What if I can't hold onto what I learned?"

"You will lose pieces of it. That's inevitable. Some days you'll forget. Some days you'll slide back into old habits. But now you know what wholeness feels like. So when you drift, you'll recognize it. And the gifts will help you find your way back."

You think about the chests below. The gratitude glasses that help you see what's present instead of what's missing. The journal for processing. The compass that points toward your true north. The stones that remind you what you're practicing. The cup that says fill yourself first.

"Use them," Elaine says, reading your thoughts. "That's what they're for. Not to sit in a chest looking precious. To be lived with. Worked with. Integrated into your daily practice."

You adjust the wheel slightly, feeling the boat respond. A comfortable silence settles between you, just the sound of water and wind. Then something surfaces. A question that's been sitting in the back of your mind since Connection Cove.

"Can I ask you about something?" you say. "The bronze coin at Heritage Heights. The one with the wheel and the compass."

"What about it?"

"I've been thinking about it. About what it meant. You said I'd understand the five spokes later, and I do now. Five islands, and five keys. But there was something else about it. The two sides. The wheel on one side, the compass on the other."

Elaine's expression shifts, becomes more intent.

"Tell me what you think it means."

You consider this, letting the pieces come together.

"The wheel was about steering. Taking control. Actively navigating. Making choices."

"And the compass?"

"The compass was about direction. True north. Knowing where you're going. Your internal guidance."

"Keep going."

"And they were on opposite sides of the same coin."

You pause, the insight crystallizing.

"You need both. You can't just have a compass pointing to your true north without taking the wheel and steering toward it. And you can't just take the wheel and try to force your way forward without knowing your true direction first."

Elaine smiles.

"Exactly. What else?"

You think back to that moment, standing with the child version of yourself.

"The coin was also about integration. Two sides, one coin. I was fragmented: the child in the basement, the adult trying to move forward. I couldn't steer my life effectively because I wasn't whole. The coin showed me that both sides had to come together. The past and the present. The hurt child and the capable adult. Both sides of me, integrated into one whole person."

"Yes. And?"

"And..." You grip the wheel more firmly, feeling its five spokes beneath your palms. "The wheel had five spokes. Five points of contact. Five ways to hold on and steer. Just like the five keys: Gratitude, Intuitive Intention, Family and Friends, Treasured Wisdom, Self-Love and Care. I need all five to steer my life. If I'm only holding onto one or two, I can't navigate well. I need all five in balance."

Elaine leans back, satisfied. "Now you understand. The coin wasn't just showing you that you needed to integrate. It was showing you the whole journey ahead. That wholeness requires all five keys working together. That you need both your compass, your inner knowing of what's true for you, and your willingness to take the wheel and actually steer toward it."

"I couldn't see it all then. I was still in the middle of the journey."

"You saw what you needed to see in that moment. The integration. The two sides becoming one coin. But now, with all five keys collected, you can see the fuller picture. The coin showed you that transformation isn't just about finding your true north. It's about having the courage to steer toward it. And you can't steer effectively unless you're whole: past and present, both integrated. You can't reach your destination using only your compass or only your will. You need both. Interior knowing and exterior action."

You sail in silence for a while, letting this settle. The coin makes sense now in a way it couldn't before. You had to complete the journey to understand what it was showing you from the beginning.

"The coin also showed me something else," you say slowly. "About worth."

"Tell me."

"Coins have value. They're currency. They're worth something. But their worth doesn't change based on which side is showing. Heads or tails, it's still worth the same amount. The two sides of me. The wounded child and the capable adult both have worth. The integration didn't make me valuable. I was always valuable. The coin was already whole. I just couldn't see it yet."

Elaine's eyes shine. "Now you truly understand. The coin at Heritage Heights was your whole journey in one symbol. Integration, navigation, value, wholeness. All of it, right there. Waiting for you to be ready to see it."

You look down at your hands on the wheel.

"Thank you," you say quietly. "For holding that wisdom until I was ready to receive it."

"That's what the journey does. It gives you pieces when you need them and trusts you'll understand the whole picture when you're ready."

The wind shifts and you adjust course slightly, feeling the boat respond. This is what the journey taught you. Small corrections. Constant adjustments. Trusting the process instead of forcing the outcome.

By midday, you're making good time. The sea is calm, the wind steady. You and Elaine eat lunch in the cockpit, the boat steering herself for a while.

"I've been thinking about the first gathering," you say. "When I get home. How to even begin."

"What does your gut say?"

You think about this. "Start small. Simple. Maybe at the library. Wednesday. I think a mid-morning brunch. Just see who shows up."

"How will you invite people?"

"I don't know. Post something online? Fliers at the library?"

"Both. Keep it simple. Women seeking authentic connection. Weekly circle. Potluck style. Come as you are. That's all you need to say."

You picture it. A room at the library. Folding chairs in a circle. Women arriving with covered dishes and curious faces. No agenda. No performance. Just space for truth.

"What if no one comes?"

"Then you sit in the space you created and you practice holding it. But women will come. They're waiting for exactly this. They just don't know it yet."

The afternoon passes in that easy rhythm. You trade off at the wheel, giving each other breaks. You go below and pull out your gratitude journal, writing about the crossing, about the doubt and the determination living side by side.

When you come back on deck, Elaine is smiling.

"What?" you ask.

"I was just thinking about the first time you took this wheel. You were so uncertain. Asking permission for every adjustment. Now look at you. You just navigate."

"I had a good teacher."

"You had willingness. That's what made the difference. You kept showing up even when you were scared. That's what you'll do at home too. Show up. Practice. Adjust as you go."

As the sun lowers toward the horizon, you see it. The coastline. Familiar shapes. The marina where this all began.

Your stomach flutters. This is it. The return.

"How do you feel?" Elaine asks.

"Nervous. Excited. Scared I'll disappoint myself."

"You won't. Want to know why?"

"Why?"

"Because you're not the same person anymore. You can't unsee what you've seen. You can't unknow what you know. The transformation isn't something you have to maintain. It's something you've become."

The words settle over you like a blanket. Warm. True.

You guide the *Golden Harmony* into the marina as dusk falls, the same dock where you left. But nothing looks the same. Or maybe you're just seeing it differently.

You tie off the lines with practiced efficiency. Elaine helps you carry the five chests onto the dock, stacking them carefully into a wagon.

"These go home with you," she says. "Everything you need."

"When will I see you again?"

"I'll be back through in three months. We'll check in before then. Email, calls, whatever you need. And you have the network now. Diana, Maya, Sage, Renee. You're not alone in this."

You hug her, feeling tears prick your eyes. "Thank you. For everything. For believing I could do this before I believed it myself."

"You did the work. I just held the space." She pulls back, looking at you directly. "Now go build something beautiful. And remember, fill your own cup first. That's not optional."

"I know."

"I mean it. The gatherings matter. But you matter more. Don't forget that."

"I won't."

You wheel the chests to your car, fitting them carefully in the trunk. Everything you discovered, everything you claimed, coming home with you.

When you slide into the driver's seat, exhaustion hits. Good exhaustion. The kind that comes from completing something real.

You sit for a moment before starting the engine, just breathing. The same parking lot where this began. The same car. But you're different. Fundamentally, irreversibly different.

You pull out your phone and see messages waiting. Your husband. Your daughter. Your mother. All the people who didn't know where you went or what you were doing.

But before you respond to any of them, you text Elaine: *Made it to the car. Thank you again. Talk soon.*

Her response comes immediately: *Proud of you, Captain. Now go home and rest.*

Rest. Yes. That's what you need before anything else.

You drive through familiar streets, noticing everything. The coffee shop you used to meet friends at. The grocery store where you stood crying in the frozen food aisle. The elementary school where your kids learned to read. All of it, part of your old life.

When you pull into your driveway, the house looks smaller than you remember. Ordinary. The lawn needs mowing. The paint on the shutters is peeling.

But it's home.

You sit in the car for a moment, gathering yourself. Then you text your husband: *I'm home. In the driveway.*

"*I'll be home in 20 minutes. Just grabbing a bite to eat. Want anything? I'm at Sal's drive-through,*" he texts back.

I'm all set, thanks.

You grab one chest, the one from Self-Care Springs. Leave the others for later. You need to establish this first. The cup, the oils, the hourglass. The tools that will protect your capacity to show up.

Inside, the house smells the same. Feels the same. But you're not the same, and that changes everything.

You carry the chest upstairs to your bedroom and set it on the dresser. Open it carefully. The blue cup catches the evening light streaming through the window. You lift it out, feeling its weight, reading the words carved around the rim.

Fill your own cup first.

You carry it to the kitchen and place it beside the sink where you'll see it every morning. A daily reminder. A daily practice. A daily choice.

The essential oils go on your nightstand. The hourglass beside them. These aren't decorations. They're tools for the work of staying whole.

You hear footsteps on the stairs. Your husband appears in the doorway, looking uncertain.

"Hey," he says. "You're back."

"I am."

"How was it? Your trip?"

Trip. The word feels too small for what you experienced, but you let it be. "Life changing. Really."

He looks at the open chest, at you standing there with your birthstone ring and charm bracelet, and the rose quartz pendant he's never seen before.

"You look different," he says.

"I am different."

"Good different?"

"Yes. Really good." You pause. "I have a lot to tell you. But not tonight. Tonight I just need to rest. Is that okay?"

He nods slowly. "Sure. There's an apple pie if you'd like some.

"Not tonight, thanks."

He hesitates at the door. "I'm glad you're home. I missed you."

Something in his voice makes you look at him fully. He looks older somehow. Tired. Like maybe the past 10 days were harder for him than he let on.

"I missed you too," you say, and mean it.

After he goes downstairs, you change into comfortable clothes. Your pajamas feel foreign after three weeks of simple linen and bare feet. But they're familiar. Yours.

You pull out your gratitude journal and write:

I'm home. The crossing was smooth, the goodbye to Elaine harder than I expected. I carried one chest inside, established the morning cup and evening oils. Small acts that will hold me.

Tomorrow I'll bring in the other chests. Tomorrow I'll start figuring out how to integrate everything I learned into this life. But tonight, I'm just here. Home. Different. Whole.

Grateful for: The safe crossing. Elaine's belief in me. This bed, this room, this familiar space that gets to hold the new me. The journey that brought me back to myself.

You close the journal and slip under the covers. Through your window, you can see stars. The same stars that shone over all five islands. The same stars that watched you become who you are now.

You sleep deeply, dreamlessly, held by your own bed in your own home. Tomorrow the real work begins. But tonight, you rest.

27

First Steps

You wake naturally, no alarm. Sunlight streams through your bedroom window. For a moment you're disoriented, expecting to see the *Golden Harmony* cabin or a cottage on one of the islands.

Then you remember. You're home.

You reach for your phone out of habit, then stop. That's old pattern. That's what you used to do, dive immediately into everyone else's needs and demands.

Instead, you get up, go to the kitchen, and heat water for a cup of tea. The blue cup sits beside the sink, exactly where you placed it last night. You fill it, carry it back to bed, and sit against the pillows.

What does my body need today?

The question from Self-Care Springs. The practice Renee taught you. You close your eyes and listen.

Rest. More rest. Gentle movement. Time outside. Simple food. No rushing.

You pick up your phone again, scroll through messages, dozens of them accumulated. Ones from your daughter checking in, your mother wondering where you are, friends asking if you're okay, and your husband's periodic updates about the house and his day.

You don't respond yet. That's old pattern too. The immediate reply, the need to reassure everyone, to make yourself available to every request.

Instead, you open your notes app and write:

Daily practice:

Morning: Tea in blue cup, asking what I need

Movement: 20-30 minutes (walk? yoga? dance?)

Outside time: At least 20 minutes

Evening: Bath with oils, journal

Bed by 10pm

Weekly:

Sunday: Complete day off

Creative time: Something just for pleasure

Nature: One longer experience

Connection: Meal with someone who energizes me

You save it. This is your anchor. When you start to drift, you vow to return here.

Downstairs, you hear your husband coming back from walking the dog, moving around. The coffee maker beeps. Normal morning sounds.

You dress in comfortable clothes and bring the blue cup with you.

In the kitchen, he looks up when you enter.

"Morning. Coffee?"

"Tea, actually." You refill the blue cup from the kettle.

He eyes the cup curiously. "New?"

"From my trip. It's part of a morning practice I'm starting."

"What kind of practice?"

You settle at the table across from him. "Checking in with myself. Asking what I need. Before I dive into the day's demands."

He nods slowly, processing. "That sounds… healthy."

"It is. It's necessary, actually." You wrap your hands around the warm cup. "I have things to tell you. About where I was. What I learned. But I need to ease back in. Is that okay?"

"Sure. Yeah. Whenever you're ready."

You both sit in silence for a moment. Not uncomfortable, just unfamiliar. You're used to filling every silence, managing the emotional temperature, making sure everyone's okay. But right now you're just sitting. Drinking tea. Being.

"I'm going for a walk this morning," you say. "Just around the neighborhood. Clear my head. Want to come?"

He looks surprised. "Really?"

"Really."

"Okay. Yeah. I've got time. My first meeting isn't until 11:00 today."

After breakfast, you both set out. It's warm already, summer establishing itself. You walk at an easy pace, not rushing, just moving.

"So this trip," he says after a few blocks. "What was it exactly? You were pretty vague when you left."

"I won a spot on a transformational journey. Five islands. Each one teaching something different."

"That sounds intense."

"It was. But good intense. Necessary intense." You pause at a corner, letting a car pass. "I learned some things about myself. About who I became after the kids left. About what I want to build now."

"Like what?"

"I want to create gathering spaces for women. Weekly circles where we can be real with each other. No performance. No pretense. Just honest connection."

He's quiet for a moment. "Like a support group?"

"Sort of. But less formal. More organic. Just women gathering and witnessing each other."

"And you think people will come to something like that?"

The question lands wrong. Not because he means it negatively, but because it reveals how he sees the world. Practical. Skeptical. Needing proof before belief.

"Yes," you say simply. "I know they will. Because I've experienced it. I've seen what happens when women feel safe enough to be real. It's powerful."

"Okay." He's trying, you can tell. Trying to understand something outside his experience. "So you're going to do this? Start these groups?"

"Gatherings. And yes. I'm going to contact the library this week about space. Start small. See what unfolds."

You walk another block in silence. Then he says, "You do seem different. More sure of yourself or something."

"I am. I discovered some things that matter. And I'm not going to apologize for taking up space with them."

He glances at you, something shifting in his expression. "I never asked you to apologize."

"I know. I was apologizing anyway. Without anyone asking. That's what I'm working on."

When you return home, he heads to the den to watch TV before leaving for work. You go outside to your car and retrieve the other four chests, carrying them to the spare bedroom one at a time. You've never claimed this room before. It was storage, overflow, the place things went to be forgotten.

Now it becomes yours.

You spend the morning arranging the chests, unpacking the gifts from each island, creating a space that holds everything you've learned. The gratitude glasses go on a small shelf near the window. The mirror propped where morning light will find it. The conch shell on the dresser. The compass. The stones. The resource journal and business cards from Treasure Island. All of it visible, accessible, ready to support what comes next.

When you're finished, the room feels like a sanctuary. A place you can return to when the world gets loud. When doubt creeps in. When old patterns try to reassert themselves.

You stand in the doorway looking at what you've created. Your space. Your tools. Your practice made visible.

Your phone buzzes. A text from your daughter: *Mom, are you okay? Are you back yet? Call me when you can.*

You respond: *I'm good, sweetheart. Really good. I'll call you tomorrow. Just settling back in. I love you.*

Another buzz. Your mother: *Where have you been? I've been worried.*

You type: *I took a trip. I'm home now. I'll fill you in soon. Thanks for checking on me.*

One more. A friend: *Haven't heard from you in weeks. Everything alright?*

You start to type an explanation, then delete it. Instead: *Yes. Really well actually. Let's have coffee next week?*

You're not avoiding them. You're just protecting your capacity. Easing back in on your terms, not theirs.

The rest of the day unfolds gently. You make lunch. Take another walk. Spend an hour in your sanctuary room, just sitting with the gifts, remembering what each island taught you.

You make a simple dinner, and set a plate aside for your husband to reheat when he returns from work.

In the evening, you draw a bath and add three drops of lavender oil. The scent fills the bathroom immediately, signaling to your body: time to rest. Time to release.

You soak for twenty minutes, feeling the day's slight tension dissolve. This is the practice. Not waiting until you're depleted. Filling your cup daily. Small deposits that prevent withdrawal.

After, wrapped in your robe, you sit on your bed with the gratitude journal and write:

Day one home. I practiced the morning cup ritual. Walked with my husband. Created my sanctuary space. Set boundaries with responses. Drew an evening bath with oils. Small acts that will build the sustainable life I'm claiming.

Tomorrow I'll call the library about space. Start making the gatherings real. But tonight, I'm proud of myself for these small beginnings. For not rushing. For choosing myself first.

Grateful for: Morning tea. Walking without rushing. This sanctuary room. The gifts that guide me. My body that held me through the transition home. The practices that feel good instead of like obligations.

Before bed, you turn over the hourglass. Sixty minutes of protected time. You pick up a book you've been meaning to read, just for pleasure, not for improvement or productivity. When the sand runs out, you're ready for sleep.

You hear your husband moving around downstairs, the microwave dings, followed by the sound of the TV.

You set the book aside, turn off the light, and lie in the darkness feeling accomplished. Not because you did anything impressive. Because you honored yourself. Because you practiced what you learned. Because you chose differently.

And tomorrow, you'll choose again.

28

The Library

The following day, you walk into the public library with your resource journal tucked under your arm. At the information desk, a woman with kind eyes looks up. "Can I help you?"

"I'm hoping to inquire about meeting room space. For a weekly gathering. Wednesday mid-morning."

"Let me get you Sarah. She handles room bookings."

A few minutes later, Sarah appears. She's maybe fifty, with short blond hair and the practical energy of someone who makes things happen.

"You're looking for Wednesday?" she asks, leading you to a quieter corner. "How many people?"

"Twelve maximum. But I'm just starting, so probably fewer at first."

"What kind of gathering?"

This is the moment. The first time you'll explain it to someone outside the island network. You feel the rose quartz pendant warm against your chest, grounding you.

"A circle for women seeking authentic connection. No agenda. No program. Just space to be real with each other. Potluck style, so everyone contributes what they can. No one turned away."

Sarah's expression shifts. Softens. "How long have you been facilitating groups?"

Here's where you could embellish. Make yourself sound more qualified.

But the lessons from the islands sit solid inside you.

"I'm not a facilitator in the traditional sense. I don't have credentials or training. But I know how to hold space. How to create containers where truth can be spoken safely. That's my gift."

Sarah studies you for a moment. Then she nods. "We have a room. Wednesdays from 10:00 am to 12:00 noon. It's free for community programming. All I need is insurance."

Your stomach drops. "Insurance?"

"For liability. Most community organizations have it. But if you're just starting…" She pauses, thinking. "Do you have a fiscal sponsor? Someone who could hold the programming under their umbrella?"

You pull out your resource journal, flipping to where you wrote Diana's contact information. "I was connected with a fiscal sponsor who specializes in women's programming. I haven't reached out yet."

"Do that. Explain what you're doing. Most fiscal sponsors will cover community gatherings like this as part of their umbrella. Then you're good to go."

"That's it? That's all I need?"

"That's all I need from you. The rest is up to you." Sarah smiles. "When do you want to start?"

You think about your sustainability plan. The boundaries you set. Wednesday brunch. Starting simple. Building slowly.

"Three weeks from now. That gives me time to get the insurance sorted and spread the word."

"Perfect. I'll block the room for you. Wednesdays, 10:00 am to 12:00 noon, starting…" she checks her calendar. "July eighteenth. The room holds twenty, so twelve is a good size. Kitchen access included for your potluck."

She hands you a form. "Fill this out. Return it with your certificate of insurance. You're all set."

Walking out of the library twenty minutes later, you feel breathless. It's real. It's actually happening. In three weeks, you'll hold your first gathering.

You sit in your car and pull out your phone. Time to make the next call.

Diana answers on the third ring. "Hello?"

"Hi Diana. This is… we met on Treasure Island. You gave me resources. Contact information for fiscal sponsors."

"Of course I remember you. The gatherer. How are you?"

"I'm good. I'm home. And I'm ready to start, but I need help with fiscal sponsorship. The library needs insurance and I don't know how to…"

"Slow down," Diana says gently. "Take a breath. This is normal. This is exactly what I help with."

You breathe. "Okay."

"Tell me specifically what you need."

You explain the Wednesday gatherings. The library space. Potluck model. Donation based but no one turned away. Starting with one circle, maybe expanding later if it grows.

"That's perfect for a fiscal sponsorship arrangement," Diana says. "You don't need to start your own nonprofit. That's expensive and complicated. Instead, you work under an established organization's umbrella. They handle legal, insurance, tax stuff. You just do the programming."

"How does it work financially?"

"The fiscal sponsor becomes the legal entity. Donations and grants come to them, they hold the funds, and they pay them out to you. Usually they take a small percentage, five to ten percent, to cover their administrative costs. But you don't have to deal with any of the paperwork or compliance."

"That sounds perfect. Which one do you suggest I call first?"

"Which ones did I give you in your folder?"

You give her the names.

"Perfect," she says. "All of them specialize in women's community programming. I suggest calling Betty first. She's a doll, always looking for projects like yours. You'll apply, explain what you're doing, and if accepted, she'll send a certificate of insurance you can give the library."

"How long does that take?"

"Usually a week or two. But tell Betty you need it quickly for a start date."

Relief floods through you. "Thank you. This is exactly what I needed."

"One more thing," Diana says. "Once you're established with a fiscal sponsor, you can start applying for grants. Small community grants at first, usually a few thousand dollars. They'll help you with proposals. That's how you build sustainability."

"I remember. Elaine told me about her grants."

"Elaine's a great model. She's been doing this twenty years. Sustainable, meaningful work. That's possible for you too."

After hanging up, you sit in the parking lot processing. It's not as complicated as you feared. There's infrastructure. Support. People who want to help.

You open your resource journal and write:

Meeting room: Secured. Wednesdays 10:00 am to 1200 noon starting July 18.

Next steps: Apply to fiscal sponsor. Get insurance certificate. Create simple flier/post. Let it be organic.

Remember: Start small. One gathering. Twelve women max. Let it unfold naturally.

That evening, you sit with your laptop at the kitchen table. Your husband is watching TV in the den. The house feels different at night now. Quieter. More yours.

You open a blank document and start writing. Not a formal announcement. Not something polished. Just truth.

Women's Circle: Wednesday Mornings
Seeking authentic connection?
Tired of surface conversations?
Join us Wednesday mornings at the public library for
honest conversation, shared food, and genuine community.
Just women gathering and holding space for each other.
Potluck style. Bring something to share if you can.
Starting July 18, 10:00 am to 12:00 noon.
Meeting room B.
All women welcome.

You read it three times. It's simple. Maybe too simple. But it's honest. And that's what matters.

You save it, planning to print copies tomorrow and post them at the library, coffee shop, community center. Maybe create a simple social media post. Nothing fancy. Just putting it out there and seeing who responds.

"What are you working on?" your husband asks, appearing in the doorway.

"flier for the gatherings. I secured space at the library."

He moves closer, reading over your shoulder. "This is really happening."

"It is."

"Are you nervous?"

"Terrified," you admit. "But excited too. I know this is what I'm meant to do.

He's quiet for a moment. Then, "I'm proud of you. For figuring out what you want and just doing it. That's brave."

The words surprise you. Warm you. "Thank you. That means a lot."

Later, lying in bed, you reach inside your nightstand and pull out your oracle card deck. You haven't pulled a card since returning home. It feels like time.

You shuffle slowly, asking the question: *What do I need to know right now?*

And draw a card. You turn it over. The image is of a woman standing at a doorway, light streaming from the open door, her hand on the handle. Behind her, darkness. Ahead, golden warmth. One word below: **BEGIN**

You prop the card on your nightstand and look through the stack of cards you've drawn so far. **TRUST. VOICE. EMERGENCE. GATHERING. ROOTED. TEND. REST. WHOLE. HOME. BEGIN.**

Ten cards. Ten reminders. The full journey mapped and this new chapter starting.

You turn off the light and lie in the darkness feeling ready. Not perfectly prepared. Not without doubt. But ready to begin anyway.

Because that's what the islands taught you. You don't wait until you're certain. You don't wait until you're impressive. You just begin. Imperfect, authentic, whole. And you trust the process to meet you.

29

The Gathering

The days between securing the library, and the first gathering pass in a rhythm of preparation and practice. You print fliers and post them at the library, coffee shop, yoga studio, community bulletin boards. You create a simple social media post with the gathering details.

And then you wait.

The fiscal sponsor application takes a week. Diana's contact, Betty, runs an organization called Women's Bridges Foundation, accepts you immediately. The certificate of insurance arrives by email three days later.

"That's it?" You call Betty to confirm your next steps on the phone. "I just give this to the library?"

"That's it. You're official now. You can accept donations, though I recommend keeping it simple at first. Suggested amount of ten to twenty dollars, but emphasize that no one is turned away for lack of funds."

"And when I'm ready for grants?"

"Just a simple proposal. Nothing fancy. Just explaining what you're doing and why it matters. Small community grants are usually a few thousand dollars. That's enough to sustain this work for a year while you're establishing."

"Thank you. For all of this."

"Thank me by doing good work. That's all I ask."

The practices from Self-Care Springs become your anchor. Every morning, tea in the blue cup. The question: *What does my body need today?* Movement, at least twenty minutes walking or gentle yoga. Evening bath with lavender oil. Journaling before bed.

Sundays, you claim completely. Your husband adjusts, slowly. At first he's confused. Then he starts respecting that Sunday is yours.

"I'm walking to the farmers market," you tell him on the second Sunday home. "Then I'm sitting in the park. Reading. Just being. I'll be back when I'm back."

He nods. "Okay. I'll probably watch the game."

"Perfect."

The freedom of it still surprises you. The permission to just be. To have a day with no productivity, no obligation, no one needing you for anything.

Your daughter calls. "Mom, we need to talk about Thanksgiving. I know it's months away but we're trying to plan."

"Can we talk about it tomorrow? I'm holding Sundays completely free."

She's quiet. Then, "Okay. Sure. I can call back tomorrow. But are you okay? You seem different."

"I am different. Better different. I'll explain when we talk."

Monday morning, after speaking with your daughter, you reach out to Maya through the contact information Diana provided.

I'd love to connect!

She texts you back enthusiastically. *Sure. Let's do a video call. I have Wednesday morning at 9:00 am free. I can share what's worked for me and answer questions.*

The call happens two weeks before your first gathering. Maya's face fills your screen, warm and familiar even though you've only met once.

"How are you feeling?" she asks. "Nervous?"

"Terrified. What if no one comes? What if I don't know what to do? What if I'm not good enough at this?"

Maya laughs, but it's kind. "I had all those same thoughts before my first circle. And you know what happened? Three women showed up. We sat awkwardly for the first twenty minutes. Then someone got brave and shared something real, and everything opened up."

"That's it? That's the secret?"

"That's it. You don't have to be perfect. You don't have to have all the answers. You just have to create space and trust women to fill it. The wisdom is in the circle, not in you."

"What do you do? Like, practically? How do you start?"

"I introduce myself briefly. Just my name and what brought me to this work. Then I invite everyone else to share their name and what drew them to come. That's it. No pressure, no performance. Then I ask if anyone has something they'd like to share or process. And we go from there."

"What if the silence gets uncomfortable?"

"Let it. Silence is okay. Sometimes that's when the deepest stuff surfaces. Don't rush to fill it. Trust the process."

You write this down. Simple opening. Let silence be. Trust the circle.

"And boundaries?" you ask. "How do you handle women who need more than the circle can give?"

"Did Diana give you a resource list of therapists, crisis lines, and support groups?"

"Yes, I have it."

"Great. If someone shares something that's clearly beyond the circle's capacity, acknowledge it, validate their courage in sharing, and after the gathering, what I do is give them the resource list privately."

"Do people get upset? That you can't fix them?"

"Sometimes. But I'm clear from the beginning that I'm not a therapist. I'm just holding space. Most women respect that. The ones who don't usually don't come back, and that's okay. This isn't for everyone."

The call lasts an hour. By the end, you feel steadier. Less like you're making it up as you go and more like you're joining something that already exists. A network of women holding space for each other in small, authentic ways.

"One more thing," Maya says before ending the call. "After your first gathering, call me. Tell me how it went. I'll be thinking about you."

"Thank you. Really."

"We're in this together. That's how it works."

The weekend before the first gathering, you print copies of the resource list. Therapists who specialize in women's issues. Crisis helplines. Online support groups. You do some research, adding a few support groups located in the area.

You also prepare a small basket for donations with a handwritten sign: *Suggested contribution $10-20, but all are welcome regardless of ability to pay.*

Your husband watches you prepare on Tuesday evening, the night before the first gathering.

"You're really doing this," he says. It's not a question.

"I am."

"What if it doesn't work out?"

You pause, considering. A month ago that question would have sent you spiraling. Now it just is.

"Then I'll learn something and try again differently. But it will work. I know it will."

"How?"

You touch the rose quartz pendant at your chest. "Because I've lived it. I've experienced what happens when women feel safe enough to be real. The need is there. I'm just creating space for it."

He nods slowly. "Well, good luck tomorrow."

"Thanks."

That night you barely sleep. Not from anxiety exactly. More like anticipation humming through your body. You keep running through Maya's advice. Simple opening. Trust the silence. Hold space without fixing.

At 4am you give up on sleep and go downstairs. Make tea in your blue cup. Sit in the darkness asking your body what it needs.

Calm. Grounding. Trust.

You pull out the gratitude journal and write:

> *Today is the day. My first gathering. I'm terrified and ready at the
> same time. I keep reminding myself that I don't have to be perfect. I*

just have to show up authentically and trust the circle.

Everything I learned on the islands prepared me for this. The gratitude to see what's present. The intuition to trust my knowing. The integration that made me whole. The resources that proved I'm not alone. The rest that keeps me resourced.

Whatever happens today, I've already succeeded. Because I'm showing up. Because I'm offering my gift. Because I'm not waiting for permission or certainty or perfect conditions. I'm just beginning.

Grateful for: This morning's quiet. My body that's carried me here. The women who will show up. The network supporting me. The courage to try.

You shower, dress in comfortable clothes. Nothing fancy. Just you.

At breakfast your husband says, "I'll pick up dinner. You shouldn't have to cook on top of everything else."

The gesture touches you. "Thank you. That's thoughtful."

"What time do you leave?"

"Around 9:00. It starts at 10:00 but I want to be there early. Set up."

"You'll do great."

At 8:45 you load your car. The donation basket. Resource lists. A folding chair in case there aren't enough. Your purse with the gratitude journal tucked inside. You wear the birthstone ring, the charm bracelet, the rose quartz pendant. Armor and reminder both.

The drive to the library takes ten minutes. You arrive at 9:00. The meeting room is unlocked, empty, waiting.

It's smaller than you remembered. Maybe twelve folding chairs arranged in a circle. A table against one wall with coffee supplies. A door that leads to the small kitchen area.

You set the donation basket on a table near the entrance with the handwritten sign. Place resource lists nearby. Arrange your chair in the circle and sit, feeling the space.

It's just a room. Beige walls, fluorescent lights, vinyl tile floor. Nothing special.

But you're about to make it sacred.

At 9:45 you hear voices in the hallway. Your heart pounds. You stand, smoothing your shirt, touching the pendant once for courage.

The door opens.

A woman enters, maybe thirty, with nervous eyes and a covered dish in her hands. "Is this the women's gathering?"

"Yes. Welcome. I'm so glad you came."

She exhales visibly. "I almost didn't. I sat in the parking lot for ten minutes trying to decide."

"I'm glad you chose to come in. I'm nervous too. This is my first time facilitating."

"Really? That makes me feel better." She sets her dish on the kitchen counter. "I'm Rachel."

"Thank you for being brave enough to be first."

Another woman appears. Then another. By ten o'clock, eight women are arranged in the circle. Not twelve. Not two. Eight.

Perfect.

You look around at their faces. Young and old. Different races. Different expressions. But all of them carrying the same thing. Hope mixed with fear. The vulnerability of showing up to something unknown.

Your hands are shaking slightly. You fold them in your lap, feeling the smooth metal of the birthstone ring.

"Thank you all for coming," you begin. Your voice is steadier than you feel. "I'm not a therapist or trained facilitator. I'm just someone who discovered the power of authentic connection and wanted to create space for it. So this is new for me too."

Heads nod. Someone smiles.

"I thought we could start by sharing our names and what brought you here tonight. I'll go first." You take a breath. "I'm here because I spent twenty five years being a mother and when my kids left, I didn't know who I was. I felt invisible. Like I'd disappeared into roles and forgotten there was a person underneath. So I went on a journey to find myself. And what I discovered is that I'm not alone. That lots of women feel this way. And that we need spaces where we can be real about it. So, that's what I'm hoping to create here."

You look to your left. "Would you like to share?"

Rachel shifts in her seat. "I'm Rachel. I saw your flier at the library and something about it just, I don't know, called to me. I've been feeling really lost lately. Like I'm going through the motions but not actually living. And I don't have anyone I can talk to about that. So I'm here."

The woman next to her is older, maybe sixty. "I'm Elizabeth. I'm recently widowed. Everyone keeps telling me I'm so strong, so brave. But I'm not. I'm lonely and scared and I don't know how to be just me after forty years of being a wife. I need people who understand that strength and falling apart can happen at the same time."

One by one, they share. A young woman struggling with new motherhood and the loss of identity that came with it. A woman in her fifties whose marriage is ending. Another navigating a career transition that's shaking her sense of self. A woman who simply said, "I'm tired of pretending I have it all together."

By the time the circle completes, something has shifted in the room. The air feels thicker. More present. These eight women don't know each other, but they've already witnessed something real in each other.

"Thank you," you say softly. "For trusting this space enough to be honest. Let's take a short break. There are plates by the food table, and the library provided tea and prepared coffee for us. Help yourself. We'll continue in about 15 mins."

Once the women see you sitting down to start again, they follow your lead. "Does anyone have something they'd like to explore or process together?"

Silence. The kind Maya warned you about. You resist the urge to fill it. Let it be.

Then the young mother speaks. "Can I say something?"

"Of course."

"I feel so guilty all the time. Guilty that I'm not enjoying motherhood the way I'm supposed to. Guilty that I miss my old life. Guilty that I look at my baby sometimes and feel trapped instead of blessed. Everyone tells me to savor every moment, that it goes so fast. And I just want to scream because it doesn't feel fast. It feels endless."

Her voice breaks. She's crying now. "I love my baby. I do. But I also hate how much of myself I've lost."

The silence that follows is different. Heavy with recognition.

Then Elizabeth speaks. "I remember that. The guilt. The feeling like you're supposed to be grateful every second and if you're not, you're a bad mother."

Rachel adds, "I don't have kids but I felt that same thing in my marriage. Like I was supposed to be grateful for a good man and a stable life. And I was grateful. But I was also dying inside. And the guilt of that was crushing."

The conversation opens. Women sharing their experiences with guilt, with the gap between how they're supposed to feel and how they actually feel. You mostly listen, occasionally asking gentle questions. Holding the space without trying to fix or teach.

Another hour passes. At 11:50am, you glance at the clock.

"We should probably wrap up."

Groans of disappointment. "Already?"

"Can we do this every week?" someone asks.

"That's the plan. Same time, same place. Wednesdays at 10:00 am."

As women gather their dishes and bags, several approach you.

"Thank you for creating this," Rachel says. "I feel lighter than I have in months."

Elizabeth hugs you. "I'll be here next week. And I'm bringing my friend."

The young mother is last to leave. "I was terrified to come. But I'm so glad I did. Just knowing other women feel this way, it makes such a difference."

After they've all left, you sit alone in the circle for a moment.

The room looks ordinary again.

Folding chairs, beige walls, fluorescent lights.

But something happened here.

Something real.

You pull out your phone and text Maya:

First gathering done. Eight women. It was perfect.

Her response comes immediately:

I knew it would be. Proud of you. Call me tomorrow and tell me everything.

You text Elaine:

First circle complete. It worked. Everything you said it would be, it was. Thank you for believing.

Her reply:

You did the work. I just held the space. Now keep going. This is only the beginning.

You pack up slowly, checking the donation basket. Sixty dollars. Three twenties. Not much, but something. Proof that people value this enough to contribute.

Driving home, you feel wrung out but full. The good kind of tired. The kind that comes from doing something that matters.

At 6:00pm your husband walks in the door holding a big dinner bag. Ribs from Lucille's BBQ. "How was it?"

You grab plates and help him unpack the bags. Everything is still hot. "Sprite or Orange soda?" you ask him.

"Sprite, thanks."

"Thank you for bringing dinner home." At the dining room table you sit in the chair across from him. His getting ribs from Lucille's feels like a celebration.

"One of your favorites, right?"

"You know me well," you chuckle. "I'm starving."

"So tell me, how was it?" he repeats.

"Eight women came. We talked for two hours. It was exactly what I hoped it would be. Maybe better."

"That's great. Really." He seems to mean it. "Are you going to do it again?"

"Every Wednesday. As long as women keep showing up."

He nods. "Well, congratulations. I know this was important to you."

"It is. But it's not just important. It's necessary. For them and for me." You pause. "I've been thinking about us. About our marriage. How we've been coexisting more than actually connecting."

His expression shifts. Guarded. "Okay."

"I'm not saying this to blame you. Or to start a fight. I just..." You pause. "After feeling what real connection looks like, I want more of it. Including with you."

"What does that mean?"

"I don't know exactly. But maybe we could try. To actually talk to each other instead of just reporting logistics. To be curious about each other's inner lives. To show up for each other the way I showed up for those women today."

He's quiet for a long moment. Then, "I'd like that. I don't really know how to do all that, but I'd like to try."

"We'll figure it out together. That's all we can do."

Later, before bed, you write in your gratitude journal:

Today, eight women showed up and shared their truth. The space held exactly the way I hoped. I didn't have to be perfect or have all the answers. I just had to be present and trust the process.

One woman said she felt lighter. Another said she's bringing a friend next week. They valued it enough to contribute sixty dollars. Small beginnings that feel enormous.

And tonight I had the most honest conversation with my husband that we've had in years. Not fixing everything. Just opening a door. Starting.

This is what the islands gave me. Not just the work. The wholeness that makes the work possible. The capacity to show up authentically everywhere, not just in the gatherings.

Grateful for: The eight women who were brave enough to come. Maya's guidance. The practices that kept me grounded. The blue cup and evening oils and all the small tools that help me stay resourced. This beginning. This perfect, imperfect beginning.

You close the journal and turn out the light. Through your window, stars shine. The same stars that watched over five islands. The same stars that witnessed your transformation.

You're home now. Building what you discovered. Living what you learned.

And it's only just beginning.

30

This is Home

Three months have passed since you returned home.

The Wednesday gathering has grown. Not dramatically. Organically. Some weeks eight women. Some weeks twelve, the maximum you set. A few regulars who come every time. Others who appear when they need it and disappear when they don't.

You've learned to trust the ebb and flow.

In early September, you applied for your first grant. A small community foundation offering three thousand dollars for women's programming. Maya helped you write the proposal. Simple, honest, just two pages explaining what you do and why it matters.

You included testimonials from the gatherings. Women who wrote about feeling less alone, more seen, able to be real for the first time in years. Their words carried more weight than anything you could say.

The grant came through in late October. Three thousand dollars deposited into your fiscal sponsor account. Not enough to live on, but enough to cover your quarterly Self-Care Springs visits, some supplies, and prove this work has value.

"You did it," Betty said on the phone when she called with the news. "This is the first step. Next year you can apply for larger grants. Build from here."

The morning after getting the grant, you sat with your blue cup and cried. Not sad tears. Recognition tears. You're actually doing this. Building sustainable work around your gift. It's real.

The practices from Self-Care Springs have become non-negotiable. Morning tea and check-in. Movement. Evening oils and bath. Sunday completely offline. Once a month, a personal retreat day where you do nothing productive.

And every three months, four days at Self-Care Springs. You just returned from your first visit back last week. Renee greeted you like an old friend.

"Welcome back. How's the work?"

"Hard. Good. Sustainable because I'm following the plan we built."

"Any boundary violations?"

"A few. A woman called me late one night in crisis. I almost answered. But I remembered the practice. I let it go to voicemail, texted her crisis resources, and told her I'd see her at the next gathering. She got help. She's okay. And I didn't deplete myself trying to be everything."

Renee smiled. "That's the work. Choosing yourself without guilt."

Your relationship with your husband has shifted too. Slowly. Imperfectly. But shifted.

You have a standing Friday date night. Nothing fancy. Just dinner out and conversation. Learning to be curious about each other again. He asks about the gatherings and actually listens when you answer.

And you've learned to share what you need instead of expecting him to guess. Things like:

I need you to just listen right now, not fix it.

I need physical affection that isn't a prelude to sex.

I need you to take on this household task because I'm at capacity.

Sometimes he gets it right. Sometimes he doesn't. But the asking itself has changed things. Made you visible to each other again.

Your son video-called last week to say he'll be home for Thanksgiving break. He looked different. More grown-up. More thoughtful. Out of nowhere, he asked, "So what was that trip you took, Mom? Grandma said you went somewhere and came back... different."

"I went on a journey to figure out who I am beyond being a mom," you said. "And it changed everything."

He nodded slowly. "That makes sense. You do seem… I don't know, more like yourself or something."

There was a pause, then: "That's cool, Mom. Like, actually cool."

He shifted on his dorm bed, a little awkward but sincere. "Anyway, I gotta go. I'll text you when I book my flight home."

Before ending the call, he added quickly, "Love you."

Simple words, but something in his tone was different. Genuine. Like he was seeing you as a person, not just Mom.

Your daughter visited last month with the baby. You held your grandson and felt joy without the old urgency to fix, help, or take over. You offered what was asked for. Held back what wasn't.

"You're different, Mom," she said. "Calmer. More present."

"I did some work on myself. Figured some things out."

"It shows. In a good way." She paused. "I want whatever you found. That peace. That certainty."

You almost offered to connect her with Elaine. But something stopped you. She has to find her own journey. You can't hand her yours.

"When you're ready," you said instead, "there are resources. Ways to figure out who you are underneath the roles. I can point you toward them if you want."

"I want. Not now. But someday."

"Whenever you're ready."

Your mother calls less often now. Not because you've pushed her away, but because you've stopped being endlessly available. You call her once a week, Saturday afternoons, and keep the conversation to thirty minutes.

She complained at first, "You're too busy for your own mother now?"

But you hold the boundary gently.

"I love you, Mom. I'll call you again next week."

She's adjusting. The relationship isn't perfect, but it's honest. And sometimes, in brief moments, you catch glimpses of the mother you always wanted, asking about your week, actually listening, even saying she's proud of you. The wounds are still there. But you're not waiting for her to heal them anymore. You've done that work yourself.

The gatherings have taught you things Maya's advice couldn't. How to hold space when women are angry at each other. How to redirect someone who dominates without shaming them. How to know when silence is generative versus when someone needs gentle encouragement.

You've made mistakes. Interrupted when you should have stayed quiet. Let someone monopolize when you should have intervened. Tried to fix when you should have just witnessed. But you're learning. Each week, you learn.

Last month, a woman shared that she'd been in an abusive marriage. Still was. The women in the gathering held her story with such tender fierceness. Women offering resources, validation, solidarity. No one told her what to do. But everyone made clear she wasn't alone.

She didn't come back the next week. Or the week after. You worried you'd handled it wrong. Then she emailed: *I needed time to think. To plan. I'm leaving him. The gathering gave me courage to see it clearly. Thank you.*

That's when you understood. You're not fixing anyone. You're creating conditions where people can find their own clarity. Their own courage. Their own next right step.

It's enough. More than enough. It's everything.

This Wednesday morning, you arrive at the library early as always. Set up the circle. Place the donation basket. Light a candle you've started bringing, small ritual that marks the space as different from ordinary.

The room fills. Nine women today. Four regulars, five newer faces. You begin the same way you always do.

"Welcome. I'm grateful you're here. Let's go around and share names and what's present for you in this moment."

As they share, you notice your own body. Relaxed. Open. Confident in a quiet way. This is your work. Your gift. You don't have to prove anything. Just show up and hold space.

Halfway through the circle, a woman starts crying. Not dramatic, just tears streaming while she talks. "I'm sorry," she says. "I don't usually do this."

"Don't apologize," Rachel says gently. She's been coming since that first night. "This is the place for it. Cry all you need."

"I just," the woman's voice breaks, "I just feel so seen here. Like I can finally stop pretending."

The circle holds her. No one rushes to comfort or fix. They just let her cry. Let her be real. Let her take up space with her grief.

This is it. This is the gift you discovered on Treasure Island. Not teaching. Not healing. Not fixing. Just gathering women and creating space where truth can be spoken and witnessed. Where pretending falls away, and realness can breathe.

After the gathering, as women linger over conversation and food, Elizabeth approaches. She's been coming every week, growing steadier each time.

"I wanted to tell you something," she says. "I'm starting a circle in my community. Different focus, grief and loss specifically. But the model you created here, the way you hold space, that's what inspired me. I wanted you to know."

Your chest tightens with something bigger than pride. This is legacy. Not you doing more. You are empowering others to create their own spaces. Exactly what Maya said. Exactly what the islands taught.

"That's incredible. Do you need help getting started? I have resources."

"I'd love that. Can we talk after the gathering next week?"

"Absolutely."

Driving home, you text Maya:

A woman from my gathering is starting her own. The model is replicating.

Her response:

That's how it works. You create something authentic and others feel empowered to do the same. You're not just facilitating. You're teaching by example. That's leadership.

At home, you run an evening bath. Add three drops of rose oil tonight. The scent fills the bathroom, sweet and opening. You sink into the water and let the day settle.

Three months. Twelve gatherings. Roughly one hundred women have come through that library room. Some once. Some every week. All of them changed by the experience of being real together.

And you're changed too. Not depleted. Filled. Because you built sustainability into the foundation. Because you tend yourself as carefully as you tend the gatherings. Because you learned to receive as gracefully as you give.

You dry off, slip into comfortable clothes, and open your gratitude journal. The pages are full now. Three months of entries tracking the journey from returning home to building something real. You write:

Three months since the first gathering. The work is sustaining me instead of depleting me because I honor the boundaries I set. Morning practice, evening ritual, Sunday rest, quarterly Self-Care Springs visit. Not optional. Essential.

Tonight Elizabeth told me she's starting her own circle. The model is spreading. Not because I'm pushing it, but because it's authentic. Because it meets a real need. Because women are starving for spaces where they can be real.

I'm not the same person who stood in that parking lot nearly four months ago, crying in the frozen food aisle, feeling invisible and purposeless. I'm whole now. Clear. Certain of my place in the world.

The islands gave me everything I needed. The gifts guide me daily. The practices sustain me. The network supports me. And the work, oh the work fills me in ways I didn't know were possible.

Tomorrow I'll email the woman crying tonight. Check in without fixing. Friday is date night with my husband, our weekly practice of actually connecting. Sunday I rest. Next Wednesday, the gathering will gather again.

This is my life now. Not perfect. Not impressive. Just real.

Sustainable. Mine.

Grateful for: The women who keep showing up. Elizabeth replicating the model. Maya's ongoing mentorship. Elaine checking in monthly. The practices that hold me. This body that carries me. This gift that chose me. This wholeness that makes everything possible.

You close the journal and check your phone one last time. An email from Elaine:

Sailing through your area next week. Dinner Thursday? Would love to hear how everything's going.

You respond immediately:

Yes! I'll make reservations. So much to tell you.

The Wednesday gathering has grown. Not dramatically. Organically. Some weeks eight women. Some weeks twelve, the maximum you set. A few regulars who come every time. Others who appear when they need it and disappear when they don't.

You've learned to trust the ebb and flow.

In early September, you applied for your first grant. A small community foundation offering three thousand dollars for women's programming. Maya helped you write the proposal. Simple, honest, just two pages explaining what you do and why it matters.

You included testimonials from the gatherings. Women who wrote about feeling less alone, more seen, and able to be real for the first time in years. Their words carried more weight than anything you could say.

The grant came through in late October. Three thousand dollars deposited into your fiscal sponsor account. Not enough to live on, but enough to cover your quarterly Self-Care Springs visits, some supplies, and prove this work has value.

"You did it," Betty said on the phone when she called with the news. "This is the first step. Next year, you can apply for larger grants. Build from here."

The morning after getting the grant, you sat with your blue cup and cried. Not sad tears. Recognition tears. You're actually doing this. Building sustainable work around your gift. It's real.

The practices from Self-Care Springs have become non-negotiable. Morning tea and check-in. Movement. Evening oils and bath. Sunday completely offline. Once a month, a personal retreat day where you do nothing productive.

And every three months, you plan to continue to spend four days at Self-Care Springs. Your first one back last week was fabulous. You recall how Renee greeted you like an old friend.

"Welcome back," she said.

When she asked about your work, you were honest. "Hard. Good. Sustainable because I'm following the plan we built."

"Any boundary violations?"

"A few. A woman called me late one night in crisis. I almost answered. But I remembered the practice. I let it go to voicemail, texted her crisis resources, and told her I'd see her at the next gathering. She got help. She's okay. And I didn't deplete myself trying to be everything."

She smiled. "That's the work. Choosing yourself without guilt."

Your relationship with your husband has been shifting. Slowly. Imperfectly. But you feel like it's shifting in the right direction. You have a standing Friday date night. Nothing fancy. Just dinner out and conversation. Learning to be curious about each other again.

He asks about the gatherings and actually listens when you answer. And you've learned to share what you need instead of expecting him to guess. Things like:

I need you to just listen right now, not fix it.

I need physical affection that isn't a prelude to sex.

I need you to take on this household task because I'm at capacity.

Sometimes he gets it right. Sometimes he doesn't. But the asking itself has changed things. Made you visible to each other again.

Your son video called to say he's be home for Thanksgiving break. He looked different. More grown-up. More thoughtful. Out of nowhere, he asked, "So what was that trip you took, Mom? Dad said you went somewhere and came back… different."

You glanced at your husband, who just shrugged. Your son, watching both of you, actually curious.

"I went on a journey to figure out who I am beyond being a mom," you said. "And it changed everything."

He nodded slowly. "That makes sense. You do seem… I don't know, more like yourself or something."

The conversation moved on to other things, but later that night he hugged you goodnight. Something he hadn't done in years. A real hug, not just a quick squeeze. Like he was seeing you as a person, not just his Mom.

Your daughter also came with the baby. You held your grandson and felt joy without the old urgency to fix, help, take over. You offered what was asked for. Held back what wasn't.

"You're different, Mom," she said. "Calmer. More present."

"I did some work on myself. Figured some things out."

"It shows. In a good way." She paused. "I want whatever you found. That peace. That certainty."

You almost offered to connect her with Elaine. But something stopped you. She has to find her own journey. You can't hand her yours.

"When you're ready," you said instead, "there are resources. Ways to figure out who you are underneath the roles. I can point you toward them if you want."

"Not now. But maybe someday."

"Whenever you're ready."

Your mother calls less often now. You answer with a text. Not because you've pushed her away, but because you've stopped being endlessly available. And you make it a point to call her once a week. She complained at first, "You're too busy for your own mother now?" But you held the boundary gently.

"I love you, Mom," you say. No further explanation needed. Confident that she'll eventually adjust. The relationship isn't perfect, but it's honest.

Sometimes, in brief moments, you catch glimpses of the mother you always wanted, asking about your week, actually listening, even saying she's proud of you. The wounds are still there. But you're not waiting for her to heal them anymore. You've done that work yourself.

The gatherings have taught you things Maya's advice couldn't. How to hold space when women are angry at each other. How to redirect someone who dominates without shaming them. How to know when silence is generative versus when someone needs gentle encouragement.

You've made mistakes. Interrupted when you should have stayed quiet. Let someone monopolize when you should have intervened. Tried to fix when you should have just witnessed. But you're learning. Each week, you learn.

Last month, a woman shared that she'd been in an abusive marriage. Still was. The women gathering held her story with such tender fierceness. Women offering resources, validation, solidarity. No one told her what to do. But everyone made clear she wasn't alone.

She didn't come back the next week. Or the week after. You worried you'd handled it wrong. Then she emailed: *I needed time to think. To plan. I'm leaving him. The gathering gave me courage to see it clearly. Thank you.*

That's when you understood. You're not fixing anyone. You're creating conditions where people can find their own clarity. Their own courage. Their own next right step.

It's enough. More than enough. It's everything.

This Wednesday morning, you arrive at the library early as always. Set up the circle. Place the donation basket. Light a candle you've started bringing, small ritual that marks the space as different from ordinary.

The room fills. Nine women tonight. Four regulars, five newer faces. You begin the same way you always do.

"Welcome. I'm grateful you're here. Let's go around and share names and what's present for you in this moment."

As they share, you notice your own body. Relaxed. Open. Confident in a quiet way. This is your work. Your gift. You don't have to prove anything. Just show up and hold space.

Halfway through the circle, a woman starts crying. Not dramatic, just tears streaming while she talks. "I'm sorry," she says. "I don't usually do this."

"Don't apologize," Rachel says gently. She's been coming since that first night. "This is the place for it. Cry all you need."

"I just," the woman's voice breaks, "I just feel so seen here. Like I can finally stop pretending."

The circle holds her. No one rushes to comfort or fix. They just let her cry. Let her be real. Let her take up space with her grief.

This is it. This is the gift you discovered on Treasure Island. Not teaching. Not healing. Not fixing. Just gathering women and creating space where truth can be spoken and witnessed. Where pretending falls away and realness can breathe.

After the gathering, as women linger over conversation and food, Elizabeth approaches. She's been coming every week, growing steadier each time.

"I wanted to tell you something," she says. "I'm starting a circle in my community. Different focus, grief and loss specifically. But the model you created here, the way you hold space, that's what inspired me. I wanted you to know."

Your chest tightens with something bigger than pride. This is legacy. Not you doing more. You empowering others to create their own spaces. Exactly what Maya said. Exactly what the islands taught.

"That's incredible. Do you need help getting started? I have resources."

"I'd love that. Can we talk after the gathering next week?"

"Absolutely."

Driving home, you text Maya:

A woman from my gathering is starting her own. The model is replicating.

Her response:

That's how it works. You create something authentic and others feel empowered to do the same. You're not just facilitating. You're teaching by example. That's leadership.

At home, you run an evening bath. Add three drops of rose oil tonight. The scent fills the bathroom, sweet and opening. You sink into the water and let the day settle.

Three months. Twelve gatherings. Roughly one hundred women have come through that library room. Some once. Some every week. All of them changed by the experience of being real together.

And you're changed too. Not depleted. Filled. Because you built sustainability into the foundation. Because you tend yourself as carefully as you tend the gatherings. Because you learned to receive as gracefully as you give.

You dry off, slip into comfortable clothes, and open your gratitude journal. The pages are full now. Three months of entries tracking the journey from returning home to building something real. You write:

Three months since the first gathering. The work is sustaining me instead of depleting me because I honor the boundaries I set. Morning practice, evening ritual, Sunday rest, quarterly Self-Care Springs visit. Not optional. Essential.

Tonight Elizabeth told me she's starting her own circle. The model is spreading. Not because I'm pushing it, but because it's authentic. Because it meets a real need. Because women are starving for spaces where they can be real.

I'm no longer the person feeling invisible and purposeless. I'm whole now. Clear. Certain of my place in the world.

The islands gave me everything I needed. The gifts guide me daily. The practices sustain me. The network supports me. And the work, oh the work fills me in ways I didn't know were possible.

Tomorrow I'll email the woman crying tonight. Check in without fixing. Friday is date night with my husband, our weekly practice of actually connecting. Sunday I rest. Next Wednesday, the gathering will gather again.

This is my life now. Not perfect. Not impressive. Just real. Sustainable. Mine.

Grateful for: The women who keep showing up. Elizabeth replicating the model. Maya's ongoing mentorship. Elaine checking in every month. The practices that hold me. This body that carries me. This gift that chose me. This wholeness that makes everything possible.

You close the journal and check your phone one last time. An email from Elaine: *Sailing through your area next week. Dinner Thursday? Would love to hear how everything's going.*

You respond immediately: *Yes! I'll make reservations. So much to tell you.*

Setting the phone aside, you realize you're smiling. Not because everything is perfect. Because it's real. Because you're living what you discovered instead of just remembering it.

You reach for your oracle cards and pull from the deck, asking: *What do I need to know right now?*

You turn the card over. The image shows a tree in full bloom, roots deep, branches wide, birds nesting, fruit hanging heavy. Below, one word: **FLOURISHING**

You place it with the others. Eleven cards now. The journey plus this moment. Proof that what you planted is growing. That the work you're doing is bearing fruit. That tending yourself and others can coexist. That purpose and rest are partners, not enemies.

You slip into bed, turn out the light, and lie in the darkness feeling complete. Not finished. Complete. Whole. Integrated. Living from the truth of who you are instead of the story of who you should be.

Tomorrow you'll wake to tea in the blue cup. Ask your body what it needs. Move, work, rest, connect. Small acts that build the sustainable life you claimed.

But tonight, you simply rest. Held by your own bed, your own home, your own hard-won wholeness. The same stars shine through your window that watched over five islands. But you don't need islands anymore.

You carry them with you. In the gifts. In the practices. In the knowing that lives in your bones now, solid and unshakable.

You are enough.

You have enough.

You've learned enough.

And from that wholeness, you give. Not until empty. From overflow. From the cup you fill first every morning. From the well you tend carefully, daily, without apology.

This is the life the islands gave back to you. Not a new life. Your life. The one that was always yours, waiting beneath the roles and expectations and stories that weren't true.

You found it. Claimed it. Built it. And now you're living it.

One morning practice. One gathering. One boundary. One choice at a time.

Sustainable. Authentic. Whole.

This is home.

EPILOGUE: FULL CIRCLE

Two years later

The library meeting room holds twenty folding chairs arranged in a circle now instead of twelve. You've learned that your capacity can grow when it's properly tended. Not because you push yourself, but because you've built the practices that support expansion.

Every morning, you spend twenty minutes in your sanctuary room. Touching the gifts. Remembering the islands. Grounding yourself in what you've learned. The room isn't a museum. It's a practice space. A place to return when you drift.

Wednesday mornings, 9:45 am. You arrive, but now you're not alone. Two other women are already setting up. Mindy, who started coming eight months ago and asked to co-facilitate. And Jennifer, who's training to lead her own circle in the next town over.

"I brought tea candles tonight," Mindy says, placing small glass holders around the circle's center. "To mark the two-year anniversary."

"Perfect," you say, touching the rose quartz pendant that still hangs against your chest every single day.

The gatherings have evolved. Not in structure, but in depth. Some women have been coming weekly for two years. Others flow in and out as they need. You've witnessed marriages ending and beginning. Jobs lost and found. Children leaving and returning. Deaths, births, diagnoses, healings.

And through it all, the gathering holds.

You now facilitate three circles weekly. One here. One at a community center in the next town. One specifically for young mothers, meeting Saturday mornings. Eighteen women total capacity. Perfectly manageable with your sustainability plan intact.

The grants have grown too. Last year you received twelve thousand dollars between three different foundations: a women's empowerment grant from the Community Foundation, a small grassroots organizing grant, and a capacity-building grant for your second year of programming

This year you're on track for twenty thousand. Not wealth. But enough to cover your needs, and fund quarterly trips to Self-Care Springs where Renee still greets you like coming home.

Your husband joins you sometimes now. Not to the women's circles, but to couples gatherings Sarah, from the library, started hosting monthly. Learning to be real together. Learning that vulnerability isn't weakness.

He's different too. Softer. More present. Your marriage isn't perfect, but it's authentic. You both show up now. Actually show up. Some days that's enough. Some days it's everything.

At 10am exactly, women begin arriving. You recognize most faces. Elizabeth, still coming every week, her grief about her husband mellowed into something she carries instead of something that carries her. Rachel, who found a new career path and shares that journey with fierce honesty. The young mother from that first night, now pregnant with her second child and more at peace with motherhood's complexity.

New faces too. Always new faces. Women finding their way to this space through word of mouth, through fliers, through some internal compass pointing them toward what they need.

Tonight there are seventeen women. The circle feels full without being crowded. Just right.

You light the tea candles one by one, small ritual that's become tradition.

"Welcome," you begin, the words familiar but never stale. "Thank you for being here. Tonight marks two years since the first gathering. We've held space for each other through so much. I'm grateful for every one of you."

You pause, looking around the circle. "Let's share names and something you're celebrating. Big or small. Doesn't matter. What feels like a win right now?"

They go around. Promotions and divorces both celebrated. A woman who finally set a boundary with her mother. Another who took a painting class just for joy. Small victories and large ones. All of them honored equally.

When it comes to you, you're surprised by what emerges. "I'm celebrating that I know how to rest. That I don't feel guilty about taking my Sundays completely offline or spend four days at Self-Care Springs every quarter. I'm celebrating that I've learned my worth isn't tied to my productivity. That I matter just because I exist."

Heads nod around the circle. These women have witnessed your journey too. The times you overstretched and had to recommit to boundaries. The moments you forgot and remembered again. The ongoing practice of choosing yourself.

The evening unfolds like always. Someone shares something hard. The gathering holds it. Someone shares something joyful. The gathering celebrates it. Laughter and tears both welcome. No topic off limits as long as it's spoken with honesty and received with compassion.

At 11:45, you begin closing. "Before we end, I want to share something. Jennifer here has been training to start her own circle in Riverside. She's ready. Her first gathering is next Tuesday evening at the Riverside Community Center."

Jennifer stands, nervous but excited. "I've learned so much here. About holding space. About trusting women to do their own work. About sustainability and boundaries. I'm not trying to replicate what we have here. I'm creating my own version. But I wanted you all to know it's happening because of what I experienced in this circle."

The room erupts in applause. Women hugging Jennifer. Offering encouragement. Elizabeth hands her a piece of paper. "My phone number. Call me if you need support."

This is what two years built. Not just one gathering, but a model that spreads. Not because you're pushing it, but because it's needed. Because women are creating spaces for each other all over, learning from each other, supporting each other's gifts.

After everyone leaves, you stay to clean up. Blow out the candles. Stack the chairs. Elizabeth and Jennifer help.

"Thank you," Jennifer says. "For teaching me that holding space is enough.

That I don't have to be perfect or have all the answers."

"You taught yourself," you reply. "I just held the space for you to discover it."

In the parking lot, you sit in your car for a moment before starting the engine. Through the window you can see the library, ordinary building holding extraordinary moments.

Your phone buzzes. A text from Elaine: *Thinking of you today. Two year anniversary right? Proud of you, Captain.*

You respond: *Seventeen women. Jennifer starting her own circle. The work is spreading. Thank you for believing when I couldn't.*

Her reply comes quickly: *You did the work. I just held the space. Sound familiar?*

You smile. The phone buzzes again. Maya: *Happy two year anniversary! Celebrate yourself today. You earned it.*

And Diana: *Two years! That's remarkable. Let's talk next week about the three-year sustainability plan.*

The network that held you while you built this, still holding you. Still celebrating you. Still reminding you that you're not alone.

At home, you run your evening bath. Rose and lavender tonight, both oils together. You sink into the water and let the day settle.

Two years. Over a thousand women. Three circles now. Grants and sustainability and a model that works.

But more than that. Wholeness. The integration that lets you show up authentically everywhere. The practices that keep you resourced. The boundaries that protect your capacity. The network that supports your work. The marriage that's real now instead of just routine. The relationship with your adult children that's evolved into mutual respect. The life that's yours, fully yours, instead of borrowed or performed.

You dry off and slip into the robe, the same one from Self-Care Springs that's traveled home with you. Soft. Worn. Beloved.

In your sanctuary room, the five treasure chests still sit. You open them sometimes. Touch the gifts. Remember what each island taught.

And you write:

Two year anniversary. The work is thriving because I built it on the foundation of tending myself first. The gatherings are full because I show up whole. The model is spreading because it's authentic.

I'm not the woman who started this journey in that parking lot. That woman was invisible to herself. Lost. Certain she had nothing to offer.

I'm not even the woman who returned home, terrified she couldn't hold onto what she learned. That woman still doubted. Still questioned whether she was enough.

I'm someone different now. Someone who knows her gifts and shares them without apology. Someone who fills her own cup first without guilt. Someone who sets boundaries and keeps them. Someone who rests without earning it. Someone who receives as gracefully as she gives.

Sometimes I wonder about the seed I planted at Treasure Island's fountain. How much it's grown. If someday another woman will sit in its shade, grateful for the shelter.

The islands gave me back to myself. But I did the daily work of staying found. The morning practice. The evening ritual. The weekly rest. The quarterly restoration. The ongoing choice to honor myself as much as I honor others.

That's the real lesson. Transformation isn't something you achieve and keep. It's something you practice. Daily. Imperfectly. Consistently.

I'm still learning. Still growing. Still making mistakes and course-correcting. But I know how to find my way back. The gifts guide me. The practices hold me. The network supports me. The work sustains me.

And from that wholeness, I give. Not until empty. From overflow.

This is what the islands taught. This is what I'm living. This is what I'm teaching by example, not instruction.

Grateful for: Two years of showing up. The women who keep coming. Jennifer replicating the model. Elizabeth co-facilitating. The grants that prove this work has value. My husband's willingness to grow with me. My body that carries me. My voice that speaks. My intuition that guides. My connections that sustain. My rest that resources.

Grateful for five islands that gave me five keys to unlock my own wholeness. For Elaine who held space. For Sage, Renee, Diana, Maya, and all the women whose names I've forgotten but whose impact remains. For the treasure chests still guiding me. For the practices that became my foundation.

Most of all, grateful for the courage to begin. To say yes to an unknown journey. To trust the process. To let transformation unfold instead of forcing it. To return home and build something real.

This is the life I claimed. Authentic. Sustainable. Mine.

You close the journal and pull from your oracle deck. Not for guidance now, but for acknowledgment.

You shuffle and draw. The image shows a woman standing on a shore. Behind her, five islands fade into mist. Before her, the ocean stretches infinite and sparkling. She's not looking back. She's facing forward, arms open, light radiating from her center. Below, one word: **EMBODIED**

You place the card with all the others. Trust through Embodied. The transformation from lost to found, from seeking to claiming, from doubting to knowing.

The journey doesn't end. It evolves. The islands aren't behind you. They're inside you. Integrated. Lived. Made real through daily practice and consistent choice.

This is what it means to embody transformation. Not to remember it fondly. To live it fully. To be it completely.

You turn off the light and slip into bed. Your husband is already asleep, breathing deeply. You listen to that rhythm for a moment, grateful for his presence, for the life you're building together, imperfect and real.

Through the window, stars shine. The same stars. But you see them differently now. Not as distant lights offering vague hope, but as witnesses to your becoming. Constant. Present. True.

Tomorrow you'll wake to tea in the blue cup. You'll ask your body what it needs. You'll move, work, rest, connect. Small acts building the sustainable life you've claimed.

Friday you'll have dinner with Elaine, who's sailing through town again. You'll share everything that's unfolded since you last connected. She'll tell you about the women she's currently guiding through their own five-island journeys. The ripple effect of transformation, ever expanding.

Sunday you'll rest completely. Maybe walk to the farmers market. Sit in the park with a book. Do absolutely nothing productive and feel no guilt about it.

Next week you'll meet with Diana to plan for another year's sustainability strategy. Discuss larger grants. Talk about the possibility of training other facilitators in your model. Building something that extends beyond you while still protecting your capacity.

And next Wednesday, women will gather again. Some familiar faces. Some new. All of them seeking what you sought two years ago. A place to be real. To be seen. To remember who they are beneath the roles and expectations.

You'll hold space for them. Not because you're special or enlightened or have it all figured out. But because you know what it's like to be lost and then found. To feel invisible and then seen. To believe you have nothing to offer and then discover your gift.

And you'll do it without depleting yourself. Without sacrificing your well-being. Without martyring yourself to the work.

Because the islands taught you the most important lesson of all: you cannot give what you don't have. You cannot hold others without first being held yourself. You cannot pour from an empty cup.

So you fill yours first. Every single day. Without guilt. Without apology. Without exception.

That's not selfish. That's sustainable. That's the only way meaningful work lasts.

You close your eyes, feeling sleep pull you under. But before you surrender completely, one more thought rises.

Thank you.

Not to anyone in particular. To everything. The journey. The islands.

The teachers. The gifts. The practices. The women. The work. The life.

Your own wholeness made visible and shared.

This is what you were always meant to become. Not perfect. Not impressive. Not extraordinary in the ways the world measures value.

Just whole. Just real. Just yourself, fully claimed and fully expressed.

The woman who stood in that parking lot two years ago couldn't have imagined this. She was too buried under doubt and comparison and the belief that her best years were behind her.

But she was wrong.

Her best years weren't behind her. They were inside her. Waiting to be discovered. Waiting to be claimed. Waiting for her to say yes to an invitation she didn't fully understand but couldn't refuse.

The phone call that started everything. The woman's voice asking if she was tired enough to stop pretending. If she was ready to remember who she was beneath the noise.

She said yes.

And everything changed.

Not overnight. Not magically. But gradually, through consistent practice and courageous choice, the transformation became real. Became lived. Became her.

Now she's the woman making the calls. The woman holding space. The woman creating conditions for other women to discover what she discovered.

Not by teaching. By being. By showing up whole and inviting others to do the same.

This is the gift. This is the work. This is the legacy.

Not something you build once and walk away from. Something you tend daily. Something you practice imperfectly. Something you return to again and again when you drift.

The islands aren't a destination you reached and left behind. They're a map you carry. A set of practices you live. A wholeness you embody.

Five keys. G.I.F.T.S. that built the life you're living now.

The Key of Gratitude. Learning to see what you have instead of what's missing. To recognize your strengths, honor your journey, and appreciate the present moment. The foundation that shifts everything.

The Key of Intuitive Intention. Trusting the wisdom that lives in your body. Setting intentions that guide your choices. Following your inner compass even when the path isn't clear. Believing you are trustworthy.

The Key of Family and Friends. Forgiving what was and embracing what is. Releasing guilt, honoring both the thorns and roses in your relationships. Claiming your birthright to belong, exactly as you are.

The Key of Treasured Wisdom. Discovering that your lived experience is your credential. That endurance through storms gives you something valuable to offer. That creating space for others to be real is a gift worth sharing.

The Key of Self-love and Care. Learning that rest isn't earned, it's essential. That filling your own cup first isn't selfish, it's sustainable. That receiving care is as important as giving it.

And tomorrow, you'll live it again. Imperfectly. Authentically. Wholly. Because that's what transformation looks like in real life. Not a finish line you cross. A practice you commit to. A choice you make again and again.

To fill your own cup first.
To honor your needs without guilt.
To set boundaries and keep them.
To rest without earning it.
To give from overflow instead of depletion.
To be yourself, fully and without apology.
This is what the islands gave you.
This is what you give yourself now.
This is the gift you offer others.

Not perfection. Not arrival. Not having it all figured out.

Just the courage to keep choosing yourself. To keep practicing wholeness. To keep showing up real.

One morning cup of tea. One evening bath. One gathering. One boundary. One rest day at a time.

Sustainable. Authentic. Yours.

You drift fully into sleep now, held by your own bed, your own choices, your own hard-won peace.

The stars keep watch. The ocean keeps breathing. The islands keep holding space for the next woman ready to say yes.

And you keep living the answer you found.

Whole. Resourced. Home.

The End

About the Author

Elaine Lombardi, CHHC, AADP, is a Certified Holistic Health Coach and Belief Coding® facilitator dedicated to helping women navigate life transitions with compassion, clarity, and purpose. She is the author of several self-help and wellness titles, including Hurricane Lucy: A Caregiver's Guide and The G.I.F.T.S. Method: The Five Keys System to Lasting Change.

With extensive experience as a teacher and director of education, Elaine brings a wealth of understanding about growth, change, and nurturing transformation. She graduated from the Institute for Integrative Nutrition in New York City and holds board certification from the American Academy of Drugless Practitioners.

Married for over fifty years, Elaine is a mother of four, a grandmother of ten, and a great-grandmother of two. When she isn't writing, she enjoys traveling and painting. Her passion is supporting women on their journeys to reclaim their authentic selves.

Connect with Elaine at ElaineLombardi.com to learn more about her work and upcoming projects.